APPROACHES TO LITERATURE THROUGH AUTHORS

APPROACHES TO LITERATURE THROUGH AUTHORS

THE ORYX READING MOTIVATION SERIES

BY MARY ELIZABETH WILDBERGER

ORYX PRESS
1993

The rare Arabian Oryx is believed to have inspired the myth of the unicorn. This desert antelope became virtually extinct in the early 1960s. At that time several groups of international conservationists arranged to have 9 animals sent to the Phoenix Zoo to be the nucleus of a captive breeding herd. Today the Oryx population is nearly 800, and over 400 have been returned to reserves in the Middle East.

Copyright © 1993 by Mary Elizabeth Wildberger
Published by The Oryx Press
4041 North Central at Indian School Road
Phoenix, Arizona 85012-3397

Published simultaneously in Canada

Printed and Bound in the United States of America

∞ The paper used in this publication meets the minimum requirements of American National Standard for Information Science—Permanence of Paper for Printed Library Materials, ANSI Z39.48, 1984.

Library of Congress Cataloging-in-Publication Data
Wildberger, Mary Elizabeth.
  Approaches to literature through authors / by Mary Elizabeth Wildberger.
    p. cm. — (The Oryx reading motivation series)
  Includes bibliographical references and index.
  ISBN 0-89774-776-3
  1. Literature—Study and teaching (Elementary) 2. Children—Books and reading. 3. Reading (Elementary) I. Title. II. Series.
  LB1575.W55   1993
  372.64'044—dc20
                                           92-42266
                                           CIP

For my husband, Marty:
colleague, partner, friend

Contents

Series Statement

What makes an individual want to turn the page and read more? That question has puzzled many in the field of education. The answer is not always forthcoming. And, the answer is not the same for every individual. However, that is the question that prompted this series of books about getting students to read. The Oryx Reading Motivation Series focuses on the materials and approaches that seem to be prominent for grouping literature. The prime purpose for the investigation is to identify promising methods, techniques, and strategies that might motivate students or get students in grades five through nine to "turn the pages."

Each book in the series examines a particular approach to grouping literature: thematic, subject, genre, literary form, chronological, author, and comprehension skills. In each case, the literature is grouped for presentation in a different way to meet a specific purpose. For example, the comprehension-skills approach groups literature useful for teaching the same skill. That skill might be comparison: literature of all types that might be grouped together to exemplify the pattern of comparison. Literary form examines the structure of the literary work, such as the diary, novel, short story, and so forth, with an emphasis on the elements of those structures, including plot, characterization, etc. An author approach provides a study of the works of one author that might allow students to examine style, growth, and changes a writer has undergone. Works written over a given period of time or at the same time might be grouped for a chronological approach. Such an approach allows the reader to examine interrelationships between writers and their society. The interest of students in a particular subject makes the subject approach useful for grouping different literary formats and forms about the same subject. The genre approach capitalizes on particular student interests or skills, such as problem solving or history, and combines this with works of similar literary form and subject patterns. And finally, the thematic approach groups materials around a common theme that may be investigated in depth by students.

Each book in the series is written for the classroom teacher and library media specialist. This partnership offers rich possibilities for combining the knowledge of teaching and literary content with the multiple resources of two professions that have long addressed literature and have searched for ways to make students want to turn the pages. Although the approaches, methods, strategies, and techniques may be used at any level, the materials have been selected for use by students in grades five through nine and are so noted in interest and reading levels. The titles may, in fact, be appropriate for older readers as well. Grades five through nine represent a period of development during which many students become lost and begin to lose faith in reading as a way of finding answers and gaining satisfaction.

Each book in the series is meant to provide one method for beginning an exploration with students. One would not expect every approach to work with every individual. Nor would one expect every teacher and library media specialist to enjoy or feel comfortable with every approach. Each approach is an option.

Finally, the sources and materials suggested in the series were selected given a number of criteria:

- General literary quality and accuracy;
- Availability;
- Readability and interest levels;
- Ethnic, racial, and sex-role representation;
- Availability of media support materials; and
- Recommendations in selected journals and guides.

It is the hope of the author that the suggested books and materials will serve as stimuli for grouping literature in attractive packages. Perhaps each package will tempt some reader to open the book and turn the page.

Paula Kay Montgomery

Preface

"I want to share books with the students that I liked reading myself," a colleague says. "But by the time I deal with skills and the Criterion Referenced Tests, there's not time to simply enjoy a book with them."

"I need some program that will get my students working together as a team—having an identity, and enjoying each other as active learners."

These are common complaints among classroom teachers. Current trends in education make accountability the primary concern and test results the basis for evaluation. With a maximum of seven hours, and a list of curriculum needs to address, it is no wonder that today's classroom teachers are harried, frustrated, and filled with self-doubts about their effectiveness.

The library media specialist, part of the planning team charged with designing a workable program of reading and literature, empathizes with the dilemma of the classroom teacher: How to encourage reading as a lifetime habit when reading for pleasure has to be set aside in favor of drill-and-practice for standardized tests?

Creativity, enthusiasm, and innovative ideas need to be part of each day's activities in the classroom, but finding time to develop these hard-to-measure qualities is becoming more and more difficult. One way of addressing the reading/literature paradigm is through a systematic design of literary arts. In this model, reading skills are integrated into a literature-based, modified whole-language approach. The basal reader is used in conjunction with paperback popular fiction, and the partnership is invigorating for both the students and their teachers.

This book describes the course of action taken in two schools to promote reading as a lifetime activity for students.

Initially, the project developed at Phyllis E. Williams Elementary School, a comprehensive, kindergarten through sixth-grade school in Prince George's County, Maryland, represented a team effort by classroom teachers, reading specialist, and library media specialist. In an effort to provide meaningful literary experiences for students, the team designed a course of study that was based on reading "trade" books by popular authors. Coincidentally, a new basal reading series was introduced systemwide, and provided a framework for extending reading skills to an immersion in literature. For example, in the first grade, basal readers included a"Frog and Toad" story by Arnold Lobel. The library media specialist used this student experience to continue the adventures of these two characters through the many books written by this talented and versatile author/illustrator. Activities ranging from a Toad Mailbox, into which students could place a letter and expect to receive a response in the classroom mailbox the next day, to the composition of lyrics for a Frog and Toad Musical Review, gave first-grade students an introduction to the literature-based classroom. Each grade level selected authors appropriate to the age and abilities of the readers. Time frames ranged from six to twelve weeks, but the intensity of effort was proportionate to the time alloted for the course of study.

The second approach to a program of literary arts grew out of a project designed for a K-8 magnet school for creative and performing arts. In this model, students from first through eighth grade read and studied the work of a single author daily for six weeks, immersing themselves in the literary output of each author, and developing the habit of daily reading for recreation rather than for reckoning.

The effectiveness of these projects has led to the adoption of the course of studies as a countywide option for schools interested in combining skill-based reading instruction with literature appreciation. But the true success of the program is demonstrated by students who read for enjoyment, practice higher level thinking skills in analyzing and evaluating fiction, and who carry these skills with them into real-world settings.

Mary Elizabeth Wildberger

Introduction

This book offers suggestions for a developmental approach to both reading skills and the skills intrinsic to a modified whole-language approach to literary arts. Chapter 1 offers a rationale for selecting an author approach to literature and discusses whole-language strategies. Chapters 2 through 7 offer models for incorporating and integrating the work of various authors or illustrators into long-term units of literature-based instruction. The authors selected for study in this book have made a particular contribution to literature for young people through a variety of literary and artistic styles.

Chapter 2 describes how a literary arts program may be integrated with the reading instructional program through a study of authors and illustrators who have been awarded the Caldecott Medal for the most distinguished American picture book for children for each year. Students study the text in relation to the illustrations, identifying style, vocabulary development, and the illustrator's ability to integrate picture with story. Units are based on the work of Marcia Brown, Robert McCloskey, Barbara Cooney, Diane and Leo Dillon, and Chris Van Allsburg, who have won the Caldecott Medal more than once. When students study the criteria used by the judges to award the Caldecott Medal, they begin to see the specific literary and artistic elements that weigh heavily in the choice of a winning picture book.

Chapter 3 describes a model based on the realistic fiction of Beverly Cleary; students can use the model to explore the chapter book and gradually develop skills of literary criticism through the sequential introduction of books with increasing complexity of plot and characterization. Rebecca Lukens in *A Critical Handbook of Children's Literature* points out that "literature for children can and should do the same things for young readers as literature does for adults." Teachers and library media specialists can become partners with their students in a lifelong enjoyment of reading by selecting works that have excellence of form and expression, that express ideas of interest to all children at a certain level of experience and maturation, and that provide the same satisfaction and enjoyment for children as for adults.

An author approach to contemporary realistic fiction, one of the most frequently encountered literary types in trade books, is discussed in Chapter 4. Authors who know and understand the deep concerns and problems that children have with a world over which they have little control convey a sense of reassurance to their readers. "Death, divorce, and overweight" issues were once the most frequently encountered themes in contemporary realistic fiction, but today's troubled society sees violence, physical and emotional abuse, and the subsequent problems that arise in both urban and suburban localities reflected in fiction for children. Many authors are compassionate observers of the human condition and are able to invent characters who may be victims initially, but who grow into strong figures coping with the problems they face.

Betsy Byars and Walter Dean Myers are selected for in-depth study of contemporary realistic fiction. Both authors address current concerns directly, and their books describe characters very much like the actual people that children deal with in daily life—extended families, day care providers, foster parents, dysfunctional families, and "significant others." Both write books on many levels of reading ability and emotional maturity and both provide a broad spectrum of plots, characters, and settings that appeal to readers at a variety of developmental levels.

Chapter 5 is devoted to the study of high fantasy through two imaginative and creative authors. Lloyd Alexander, author of the *Chronicles of Prydain,* is chosen for study because of his humorous and delightful way of interpreting high fantasy. In reading about the mishaps, adventures, and quests of Alexander's fictional inventions, we observe the foibles and quirks of our own reality. Laurence Yep introduces readers to the wealth of Chinese fantasy in his novels. Real-world and fantasy world intertwine throughout his novels, and the legends and mythology of China are beautifully integrated in the books of this gifted Chinese-American writer.

Discovering the multilevels of fantasy is an important consideration in this chapter, and graphic organizers allow the reader to sort out the many layers of symbolism that exist in a well-written fiction piece. Readers are given the opportunity to use computers to participate in an individualized, one-to-one dialogue between instructor and student reader.

Chapter 6 is devoted to an exploration of authors who regularly write in series or who use the same characters in different books to achieve an ongoing knowledge of character development and maturation. Ursula LeGuin, Cynthia Voigt, and John Christopher are authors who have written powerful and exciting books in which basic characters are engaged in various conflicts through several plots within similar settings.

Authors of series books are studied with major emphasis on style and characterization, while interpretation is the focus for plot study. An appreciation for the polished style used by authors who are able to define and refine characters is the goal of this chapter.

Chapter 7 is devoted to an author who is generally considered (in the current vernacular) "the mother of all writers"; although the gender is incorrect, the admiration is not. William Shakespeare and his works are the foundation for a modified whole-language approach to using classical literature across grades in a schoolwide immersion program.

1

An Author Approach to Literature

Children selecting books for independent recreational reading offer a wonderful lesson in human nature and the dynamics of thinking. Observe the fifth-grade student assiduously compiling a file of books written by a favorite author. There is no deterring this child from a single-minded search of the shelves for a Katherine Paterson book that might have been overlooked. This reader is going for the world record for total reading of an author's body of work.

There is the seventh-grade reader, the "trekkie" who knows every imaginary galaxy, and who is determined to read everything that Madeleine L'Engle and John Christopher have ever written—in order.

The recently liberated sixth-grade humanitarian, who has discovered a multicultural world of fiction in Walter Dean Myers, and who intends to read Myers with as much thoroughness as was formerly devoted to the books of Cynthia Voigt, is another example of the reader who finds excitement in the plots of a specific author.

The artist-in-residence who can tell friends all about the changing styles of writing and illustrating in books by Marcia Brown, or the surrealistic approach of Chris Van Allsburg, also contributes to the dynamics of book selection.

The *nouveau* chapter book enthusiast reveling in freedom from the "easy" collection expresses this new maturity by announcing an intention to read everything that Beverly Cleary has ever written.

Readers of all ages enjoy the comfortable relationship that exists between them and a favorite author. Mildred Laughlin (1986) points out that authors and illustrators of children's books have an especially intimate connection with their young readers because these writers communicate so vividly that the reader can share the emotions, experiences, and ideas depicted.

Trying to instill a love of reading with any one approach is very difficult, but using an author approach to literature is one strategy that conveys a depth of understanding far beyond the basic skills. Recalling that an author's books begin in the mind of a creative person allows children, as readers, to both appreciate and evaluate books critically. By studying, comparing, and contrasting a writer's contributions students are able to establish emotional connections with the characters and ideas in their favorite books.

RATIONALE FOR SELECTING AN AUTHOR APPROACH

When an author writes a book, it is for one or more of the following reasons: to entertain, to inform, to express opinions, to persuade. Fiction gives authors latitude in exploring the experiences that shape lives, using real-life events and experiences or imagination and creativity as catalysts.

Approaching literature through writers brings a certain intimacy to the learning and enjoyment process. It is a sophisticated way to develop thinking skills that transcend the cognitive knowledge area. To grow as readers, we must grow as thinkers. Judging and evaluating literary efforts by assessing an author's ability to involve the reader emotionally and intellectually requires specific skills that emerge from both living and reading.

Readers evaluate how well an author meets their standards or expectations by examining both the details and elements of a work of fiction at the cognitive or comprehension level. These details are then open for comparison with other books by the same (or similar) writer, or with the reader's own experiences in life. This is the analysis and synthesis level. Readers may next decide how well an author has achieved his or her purpose in writing the book by determining how well all its details and elements work together as a whole.

In an author approach to literature, readers are encouraged to expand their thinking to form independent and individual opinions. A recent "For Better or Worse" comic strip (January 9, 1992) portrays a student asking the teacher why heads don't expand with all the knowledge that needs to be crammed in. The student asks how the teacher evaluates students, since their heads are all about the same size. The teacher responds, "By the questions they ask." Readers who formulate questions while examining character, setting, plot, and theme of a novel are using a helpful strategy for evaluation. Criteria for judging fiction works are given in later chapters, but the individual questions that arise from reading a book are often the most gratifying and insightful ones.

An author has the power to develop characters for good or evil, to imply attitudes through a narrator voice or a first-person chronicle, to create a mood and sustain or shatter it, and to use language to enhance enjoyment of the story. These abilities bring intimacy to an exploration of an author's fiction. Other ways to classify an examination of fiction include a thematic approach, a genre approach, or a subject approach. All are equally valid in promoting an enjoyment of reading as a lifelong goal. But there are quantifiable differences in the various approaches.

There can be little argument in classifying fiction by *genre*. For example, a mystery story is one that meets the criteria established for it—suspense, a swiftly moving plot, an action that must be addressed, and a satisfying solution to the dilemma. A mystery is a mystery, but the genre embraces the works of many writers, from series that use formula plots like Encyclopedia Brown, to the unique story lines of *The Westing Game* (Ellen Raskin) or *From the Mixed-Up Files of Mrs. Basil E. Frankweiler* (E.L. Konigsberg). Readers quickly judge their own maturing tastes when they begin to look for more sophisticated plots and characters within the genre of mystery books.

When fiction is approached through *theme,* the selection process is determined by reading levels of students, their higher-order thinking skills, and their general knowledge of universal philosophical concepts. Friendship, death, divorce, ambition, and other concepts acknowledged by students to be important themes in their own lives may be evaluated by addressing works that treat those themes.

A theme approach to literature is a convenient and practical way to motivate readers by stressing their own major concerns and life experiences. Yet evaluation of the many books that come under the umbrella of a particular theme is still based on the author's talent in moving the reader to identify with the characters and their problems.

A *subject* approach to literature is a practical one when integration with curricular studies is indicated. Fiction pieces that emphasize settings (such as the United States during the Revolutionary War) are frequently used as an enhancement to the social studies units. Drug awareness is a subject of intense interest, and novels that address this subject are popular and tremendous inducements to reading. Readers, however, quickly learn to evaluate trendy subject matter in fiction, and books by an author who uses a subject such as drug abuse as a wraparound for examining social ills are usually put aside, firmly and irrevocably. But the author who uses the complex aspects of a character's personality in defining the parameters of drug abuse becomes a favorite.

Specific ways in which to approach the appreciation of literature are important because readers come to literature with different levels of skills and knowledge. Many children entering kindergarten bring with them a rich preschool experience in enjoying books, or a background of public library story hours happily enjoyed with parents who encourage reading. However, there are growing numbers of children entering school who have had little or no experience with reading (or being read to). Teachers and library media specialists are continually challenged to devise new methods and strategies for introducing literature to the latter group of students without boring the former.

The common factor for any work of literature is that it has been composed by a person. To be a work of fiction, there must be an author, someone who has conceived an idea and written it down with style, originality and creativity. Teachers and library media specialists can use this fact as a basis for developing a literature-based curriculum, and design literary activities that offer a broad spectrum of choice for students of varying abilities. To invite participation and to include *all* students in the exploration of a particular author's works is the true goal of an approach to literature through authors.

BASAL READER AND LIBRARY BOOK: THE PARTNERSHIP

Ira Aaron (1989) reiterates the major aim of reading instruction programs: to develop readers who not only *can* read, but *do* read. And the way to ensure that, he maintains, is to combine systematic instruction in the skills of reading with ample opportunities for children to read good literature.

The current emphasis on using a whole-language approach in which literature is used across the curriculum, not only to enrich learning and understanding, but also to teach needed skills, is a dynamic force in education. However, the importance of a basal reading textbook as a functional tool in teaching the skills of reading cannot be underestimated. Both teachers and students benefit when they discover the impact of combining the two in a partnership for lifetime enjoyment of reading.

A casual introduction to an author through an abridged chapter from a popular trade book may lead to a longtime affection for the works of that author. An adaptation of a writer's novel, used in a basal reading text to demonstrate the effective use of metaphorical language, may stimulate a talented and gifted student to explore that author's trilogies for pure pleasure.

The combination of basal reading text and whole-language approaches to literature is a highly effective strategy. The basal reading series, used as core instructional materials, offer opportunities to motivate students to read more. Aaron (1989) points out that some of this extended reading may be done in the classroom, through guided instruction, oral reading, and discussion that involves students and teacher in a lively dialogue. But much of the extended reading will occur at home outside the formal instructional arena, and it is this outreach to reading enjoyment that provides a climate for a lifetime enjoyment of reading literature.

By selecting authors whose works fit comfortably into the series of reading skills necessary at different developmental levels, teachers provide an appropriate environment in which students can learn a specific comprehension skill and savor the author's talent for plot development.

WHOLE-LANGUAGE STRATEGIES

Whole language has an impressive lineage in the language arts curriculum: language experience, individualized reading, literature-based reading, and writing process programs. Its current definition emphasizes the concept of integration, through which productive (speaking, writing) and receptive (listening, reading) activities are merged, given equal importance, and infused into the entire curriculum.

This approach to reading is learner-centered and offers an opportunity to reemphasize the importance of the student's engagement with ideas, and the educational reassurance that effective learning requires an integration of stimuli received by all our senses.

The term whole language first appeared in the literature in 1977 in an article by Jerome Harste and Carolyn Burke (*Yearbook of the National Reading Conference*, 1977). Jeannette Veatch (1988) defines whole language in a dual context: as an approach that helps children improve their reading, speaking, listening, and writing through an integratred language arts curriculum, and an educational philosophy that supports teaching and learning processes used in whole-language classrooms.

The student chooses what is to be learned, and the teacher sets up the situation. This is a philosophy known and practiced by successful library media specialists. Self-selection, reader choice, and a wide range of resources from which to choose have been the program and process. The synergism of teacher, library media specialist, and students working together to incorporate whole-language techniques can benefit all participants.

The National Council of Teachers of English, in a document titled "The English Coalition Conference: Assumptions, Aims, and Recommendations of the Elementary Strand," recognized this partnership and defined the process of empowerment. NCTE emphasizes that the aims and goals of whole language include empowering students as "lifelong learners whose command of language is exemplary and who gain pleasure and fulfillment from reading, writing, speaking, and listening."

The NCTE also addresses the role of teachers in the whole language process: "to empower teachers as active learners who serve as coaches, mentors, and collaborative creators of learning experiences rather than as dispensers of information." The working papers developed by NCTE, 1988-89 ("NCTE's Position on the Teaching of English: Assumptions and Practices") speak positively and decisively to the issue of whole language and clearly emphasize each participant's role in the "community of learners."

Veatch suggests that whole-language approaches provide moderate, attainable goals, structured through a combination of student control and teacher input, which is the essence of a learner-centered educational program. "In this center," writes Veatch, "is direct teaching in response to [student]-chosen content, as well as learning experiences that take place without any direct teacher input."

The model of a literary arts curriculum described in the ensuing chapters is based on the understanding of the term direct teaching coupled with a conviction that a classroom teacher and a library media specialist can change roles smoothly and knowledgeably.

Direct teaching is any immediate action a teacher or library media specialist takes to show a child how to do anything. Examples of practical applications in a whole-language setting are embedded in the study of the literary output of an individual author of children's fiction.

Many of the activities are extensions of those already being implemented in library media centers and classrooms. These activities involve students in speaking and writing, as well as listening and reading, and are, in fact, whole language in content and philosophy.

Ken Haycock (1988) challenges Veatch's definition of whole-language approaches by claiming that "whole language" has much broader applications than a single emphasis as a language arts component.

> Whole language is not a change in a few procedures but a complete change in attitude, strategies, resources and management. It involves the implementation of many changes: from one text to multiple resources, from teaching "reading" to integrated language develop-

ment within different curricular areas, from individual and competitive classrooms to cooperative learning, and from a single teacher to cooperative program planning and team teaching with the school's library media specialist.

Haycock maintains that whole language is an attitude—a philosophy of how children learn—in addition to a teaching strategy. The range of resources must extend well beyond fiction books.

By including activities that extend into the science, social studies, and history curricula, the units described in the following chapters support Haycock's theories.

In 1985, the California State Department of Education launched a language, literacy, and literature campaign for California's nearly five million students. This ambitious project is known as The California Reading Initiative. The stated goal of the project is to develop in students a lifelong positive attitude toward reading and writing. In Phase I of CRI, schools are asked to examine their existing programs in order to identify strengths and needs in both instructional and curricular resources. Phase II is the planning component, and Phase III is the implementation module, a schoolwide program for improving English-language arts instruction. The California Reading Initiative, with the motto "Open Books = Open Doors," was hailed as a dynamic and powerful statement about the importance of whole-language practices in schools.

But the funding problems affecting California are now mirrored in most school districts, where resources are severely limited. Lillian Biermann Wehmeyer (1984) addressed this issue when she wrote: "The California Reading Initiative is a challenging and provocative statement. It calls forth true professionalism: the courage to build a liberating, literature-based reading curriculum and the wisdom to retain valuable insights from the past." Wehmeyer points out the need for creating programs that address and balance genre, style, authors, and other literary considerations, but argues that developing these areas requires time, expertise, and money.

A common thread running through the research of professionals on whole language is the conviction that library media centers and specialists are currently practicing whole-language approaches and have been for some time. Researchers agree that successful library media specialists regard themselves as partners in teaching. They not only provide resources, but actively publicize and promote literature and learning. They not only create exciting and student-centered activities in the library media center, but also cooperate with teachers to design, teach, and evaluate resource-based classroom units at the heart of the curriculum.

In designing the literary arts curriculum described in this book, curriculum writers found that basing a study of literature on the authors was the most satisfying and effective format. David M. Brown (1988) had suggested that a compromise program of whole-language instruction might be effected through a combination of reading skills development using basal texts and a designer program using children's literature available in library media centers, public libraries, and book stores. Building on Brown's recommendations, a literary arts program was developed that gave equal time to both teachers and student participants. Brown named his model a "whole reader approach," but in this book the literary arts program is referred to as a "modified whole-language approach." Student groups spend one-half of the reading time block (42 minutes) in teacher-directed, basal reader activities. This is a time of intense interaction; because the reading group—typically about 15 students—has the full attention of the instructor, learning can take place with minimum distraction.

While one group of students participates in directed reading activities in the classroom, the second group meets with the literary arts teacher (or library media specialist) for daily independent or guided reading activities based on the works of a selected author. Journal writing is an integral part of the literary arts program, as are research skills as they apply to the content of the fiction. In this way, teachers and students have benefits provided by each approach to the teaching and appreciation of reading: the structure and sequence of basal readers and the self-selected variety of the whole-language approach.

After five weeks of this segment of the program, students move to a different "modified whole-language" study—computer arts, media production, or a comparable program.

The curriculum is based on a team approach, in which teachers in the various disciplines cooperatively plan and implement student-centered experiences with children's literature. "It is another opportunity for us to move from a one-dimensional, impersonal process to one that addresses all the language arts in an integrated, student-centered fashion" (Brown, 1988).

The caveat exists: This is a costly system, both in personnel and resources. But within the parameters of budget reductions, there is still an opportunity for teachers and library media specialists to be responsible leaders for the educational needs of the population. Perhaps it is time to become more assertive and aggressive in support of alternative reading programs or library media programs that reflect a belief that all members of an educational community may take responsibility for their learning.

PROFESSIONAL RESOURCES

Aaron, Ira. 1989. *Preface to Scott-Foresman Reading Series.* Dallas, Texas: Scott Foresman.

Brown, David M. 1988. "A Half-Time Compromise to the Whole Language Approach," in *School Library Media Annual, 1988, Volume 6.* Jane Bandy Smith, ed. Englewood, CO: Libraries Unlimited.

California State Department of Education. 1986. *Recommended Readings in Literature: Kindergarten through Grade 8.* Sacramento, CA: California State Department of Education.

Goodman, Kenneth. 1986. *What's Whole About Whole language?* Portsmouth, NH: Heinemann.

Harste, Jerome and Carolyn Burke. 1977. "A New Hypothesis for Reading Teacher Research," in *Reading: Theory, Research and Practice, 26th Yearbook of the National Reading Conference,* P. David Pearson, ed. St. Paul, MN: Mason, pp.32-40.

Haycock, Kenneth. 1988."Whole Language Issues and Applications," in *School Library Media Annual, 1988, Volume 6.* Jane Bandy Smith, ed. Englewood, CO: Libraries Unlimited.

Laughlin, Mildred Knight and Letty S. Watt. 1986. *Developing Learning Skills Through Children's Literature: An Idea Book for K-5 Classrooms and Libraries.* Phoenix, AZ: Oryx Press.

Kulleseid, Eleanor R. "1988. The Whole-language Approach: Readings in Theory and Practice," in *School Library Media Annual, 1988, Volume 6.* Jane Bandy Smith, ed. Englewood, CO: Libraries Unlimited, pp. 56-69.

Ravitch, Diane and Chester Finn, Jr., 1987. *What Do Our 17-Year-Olds Know?* New York: Harper & Row.

Smith, Charlene. 1988. "A Principal View of Whole language," in *School Library Media Annual, 1988, Volume 6.* Jane Bandy Smith, ed. Englewood, CO: Libraries Unlimited.

Vandergrift, Kay E. 1988. "Whole-language, Literacy, and the School Library Media Center," in *School Library Media Annual, 1988, Volume 6.* Jane Bandy Smith, ed. Englewood, CO: Libraries Unlimited.

Veatch, Jeannette. 1988. "En Garde, Whole-language," in *School Library Media Annual, 1988, Volume 6.* Jane Bandy Smith, ed. Englewood, CO: Libraries Unlimited.

Wehmeyer, Lillian Biermann. 1984. *The School Librarian as Educator, 2d ed.* Littleton, CO: Libraries Unlimited.

2

The Caldecott Club

INTRODUCTION

The library media center can be many things for the user. This chapter introduces the library as art museum, and the "old masters" that every art literate child should recognize are the illustrators and artists who have been awarded the highest honor in children's book illustration: the Caldecott Medal.

Named for Randolph Caldecott, an English illustrator of the nineteenth century, the award is given annually by the Association for Library Service to Children, a division of the American Library Association, to the artist of the most distinguished American picture book for children. Since the award was established by Frederick Melcher, 55 books have been honored. When one considers the enormous output of picture books yearly, and the sophisticated processes that now exist in the publishing field, it is an incredible statement about the abilities of artists who have earned the Caldecott Medal.

In this chapter, students are guided through the literature and art of the picture book. They learn to consider the artist as an inspirer, working with the author in spirit to create a picture book. In oral discussions, students consider how an artist approaches the illustration of a book, and learn to recognize that an artist is a stylist, illuminating a text from a personal point of view.

Through guided activities, students are led to a definition of illustration as the creation and development of characters and the portrayal of the scenes necessary in mood or action to bring a story to completion. They become aware that artists achieve this intense relationship with the story as each drawing, each painting contributes another image and adds another dimension to the character, setting, or story.

By selecting books that have been judged outstanding by professional evaluators, students gain a knowledge, not only of what makes a picture book memorable, but also of the artists who contribute to excellence in children's book illustration.

In this chapter, emphasis is placed on those illustrators who have won the Caldecott Medal more than one time. Picture books awarded Honor Book status are also integrated into the unit. Books were selected for study because:

- The illustrator has won the Caldecott Medal.
- The literary merit of the book is comparable to the art.
- The books are representative of a style of art used by contemporary illustrators.
- The books can be integrated into a literary arts curriculum through concept development and reading skills development.
- The books represent a multicultural heritage.
- The books can be read and enjoyed by children.

An appreciation for art and an ability to appreciate line, form, color, pattern, and emotion are anticipated student outcomes. To encourage children to explore the storytelling qualities of picture book illustrations, comparisons are made with similar art work in museums. Students are asked to consider the difference between a single painting or art piece and the series of beautiful pictures that are arranged to tell a story in a bound picture book.

The rationale for this approach is twofold: Children have an innate aesthetic sensitivity, responding freely to balance, order, rhythm, and originality, and art is communication, whether in a museum, in a book, or on the television screen. Patricia Cianciola (1981a) comments on the integrity and variety of childrens' book illustrations:

> There is a proliferation of picture books illustrated in art styles strongly suggestive of expressionism, impressionism, pointellism, native art, folk art, surrealism, and even punk art. . . One hopes teachers and librarians will choose the picture books that reflect artistic and literary excellence, for these are the books that will help children grow aesthetically.

A beginning awareness of art criticism is encouraged and nurtured in this unit, and criteria for evaluating childrens' book illustrations are established through cooperative learning strategies.

Barbara Elleman (1986), editor of *Booklist,* offers some practical advice for teachers, library media specialists, and reviewers. She writes that reviewing picture books has been "an evolutionary process, made up of reading a variety of books about art and illustration, visiting galleries and museums, listening to knowledgeable colleagues, and looking—hard and long—at picture books themselves." These guidelines work well in encouraging children to an appreciation for quality and artistic integrity, while instilling a thoughtful approach to a whole-language reading program in a literature-based curriculum.

Just as students study the art work of creative geniuses such as Jean Miro, Henri Matisse, or Rembrandt and identify similar elements of design in Caldecott-winning picture books, they also learn imitative art techniques based on the art media used by book illustrators. Projects that reflect the type of art work in Caldecott-winning books are designed so that students have their own art portfolio at the end of the unit.

A "Caldecott Art Gallery" is set aside as an environment for the display of student art work, a Caldecott Fashion Show is presented, a video in the style of a news magazine program is conceptualized and produced, and a "Calde-quilt" is designed, sewn, and hung.

Emphasis in this chapter is on books that are significant as artistic works that can also be used as educational tools. To look, like Elleman, "with the eye of an artist, the needs of a librarian [teacher], and the appetite of a child," is the theme of this chapter.

CREATIVE THINKING

Most educators view the development of imaginative thinking as a major goal. "Just as we can throttle our imagination, we can likewise accelerate it. As in any other art, individual creativity can be enhanced through the use of certain techniques," writes Sidney Parnes (1990).

David Perkins (1988) defined creative thinking as an ability to get "original and otherwise appropriate results by the criteria of the domain in question." Techniques described in this chapter include the process of creative thinking, defined here as the ability to form new combinations of ideas to fulfill a need. In the units described below, students must evaluate illustrations and text in a Caldecott Medal book.

The domain under consideration here is the literary and artistic integrity of those picture books that have been selected as the finest examples of the union of art and text. Criteria used throughout the chapter in sample units of instruction are an adaptation of the criteria used by members of the Caldecott Selection Committee, and reflect the generally accepted criteria for judging picture books. These criteria include:

- the unity of the picture with the text
- the appropriate style of the art (realistic, abstract, stylized)

- the harmony between text and illustration conveyed through the media used (acrylics, crayon, water color)
- the use of color
- the format used to create total impact
- accurate and authentic cultural settings

THE INCLUSION PROCESS

Teaching strategies used as examples in this chapter include a model for teaching thinking skills developed by Antoinette M. Worsham and Anita J. Stockton (1986) that is currently in use in at least four Maryland counties. Known as the inclusion process, this model is one of direct instruction that first considers the objectives of a curriculum and the needs of the learner and then identifies the cognitive skills necessary to attain those objectives. It is a structured procedure for learning the skills and using them to achieve mastery of the curriculum.

Lower-order thinking levels of knowledge, comprehension, and simple application are traditionally considered appropriate for emphasis in the primary grades. However, primary level students are also capable of engaging in more complex creative reasoning skills if the content is suitable for their level of understanding. For example, in examining the illustrations in a picture book, younger students are able to make valid predictions within their realm of experience, even though prediction is generally considered a higher-order thinking skill.

The inclusion process provides a way for teachers to begin and to continue to teach students how to think more effectively and creatively.

Both *convergent* (interpretive, analysis) and *divergent* (developing creative ideas, creative problem-solving) questioning styles are used in considering the artistic merit and story line of books that have been awarded the Caldecott Medal.

UNIT OBJECTIVES

The six units in this chapter will enable the student to:

- describe the Caldecott Medal and explain its significance.
- use artistic criteria in evaluating illustrations in Caldecott Medal picture books.
- recognize the art work of selected illustrators.
- define line, color, balance, and shape as elements of an illustration.

- recognize how pictures convey the story in picture books.
- practice creative thinking skills in analyzing picture books.
- design, complete, and share projects related to Caldecott-winning books.
- compile a bibliography of books by a specific illustrator.

Teaching Strategies

1. The teacher:	The students:
introduces a display of many picture books and asks what the students can recognize as a symbol common to all of the covers of the books. (The gold Caldecott Medal).	identify the symbol, and what the the symbol represents, if they know.
explains that the Caldecott Medal is given to only one book each year, and that is why the book is special.	follow the instruction.
shows an enlargement of the Caldecott Medal on an overhead, and identifies the figures on the medal.	view medal and its figures.
distributes folders that have a gold seal on the cover.	receive the folders and view the seal.
asks students to imitate the Caldecott Medal, using the transparency as a model.	use a sharp pencil to imitate medal figures.
invites students to select a title for their portfolio that is individual to their tastes in art and stories.	decide on a title and write it on the cover of their portfolios.

2. The teacher:	The students:
shows the Weston Woods filmstrip or video on the life of Randolph Caldecott.	view sound filmstrip or video.
leads a discussion about the history of the Caldecott Medal and the artist for whom it was named.	participate in discussion.

2. The teacher:	**The students:** *(cont.)*
asks students to write a brief paragraph to introduce their student portfolios. The introduction may begin with a writing prompt: "The Caldecott Medal is a very special award for books."	compose and write a brief paragraph on the Caldecott Medal and its meaning.
assists students with composing task.	complete the assignment.
invites students to select a book from the classroom or library media center that is a Caldecott Medal winner.	select a book.
provides ample time for browsing and reading.	read a book of their choice.

3. The teacher:	**The students:**
explains that during class meetings, Caldecott books will be examined and evaluated for artistic style and literary content.	
distributes hand-outs giving the criteria* used for evaluating picture books.	listen, receive hand-outs, review criteria.
lists those artists who have won the Caldecott Medal more than once, and asks students to copy the information in their journals.	write information in their journals or portfolios.

*These criteria are given in the "Creative Thinking" section of this chapter, above. Teachers may wish to modify the vocabulary for younger students.

UNIT 1: NONNY HOGROGIAN

Biographical Information

After graduating from Hunter College in New York, Nonny Hogrogian began her career in art by becoming a designer and art buyer for a prestigious New York publishing firm. Using an artist's eye to select illustrations and paintings done by others, she developed a fine sense of composition, color, line, and form that led comfortably and directly to her own illustrating style for children's books. Nonny Hogrogian has worked as an illustrator for most of the major publishing houses. Her own work, flavored with an Eastern European warmth and sturdy fresh-baked-bread quality, enhances the folk tales that have won the Caldecott Medal.

Nonny Hogrogian has an artistic sense of humor, and her wonderful babushka-hooded women and mischievous children let readers know that she truly enjoys her art. Her love of classical music, particularly the works of Vivaldi and Bach, round out a personality reminiscent of a true Renaissance woman.

Always Room for One More (Caldecott Medal, 1966)

Art Notes

Always Room for One More is a good example of the difference between drawn line and color line effects. The "wee house in the heather" and the characters in this old Scottish rhyme are outlined by pen-and-ink lines for faces and silhouetted by a most dramatic use of hatching and cross-hatching. "Hatching" is achieved by drawing short, parallel lines, and cross-hatching is done by drawing one set of horizontal lines intersecting another set of vertical lines, usually at different angles. By varying the thicknesses of the lines, a very textural effect is achieved, and a sense of contour is conveyed. All of the hatching and cross-hatching in this book is done with black pen-and-ink.

Purples, greens, and grays are used as a background to suggest a heathery landscape, storm clouds, and the safety and warmth of the little cottage. Nonny Hogrogian achieved this tonal background by using colored chalk and a wash dabbed on with paper napkins. A great deal of research went into the preparation of the pictures in this book. Scottish people, traditional costumes, and cottages of Scotland emerged in illustrative accuracy while the artist played Scottish music in the background to establish a mind set and a mood.

Visually innovative and original in concept, Nonny Hogrogian's work is a delight for producers of media. Her characters, clarity of composition, and integrity of setting allow her books to be easily extended.

The Story

Every child who has ever had an uproarious birthday party—and the parents of the birthday child—will empathize with the story line of *Always Room for One More.* In this retelling of an old Scottish tale, a hospitable and generous man offers shelter to "every stranger who stopped by his door," and is so fond of company and fun, that he urges his guests to enjoy his hospitality in food and drink. Eventually the small cottage literally explodes with merriment, but the guests help rebuild the cottage with good-natured willingness. The words and music for the song are printed at the end of the story, and when children learn the melody, they can sing the story in a rollicking, joyous interpretation of a warm and funny folk tale from Scotland.

Discussion Questions and Student Art Activities

The discussion questions relate to both the story (S) and the pictures (P) to emphasize that unity must exist between the two elements in a picture book.

1. (S) Why do you think all the people want to come into the old man's cottage?
2. (S) Where do you think the story is happening? What do we call it when people speak with a certain accent? (dialect). Do you have friends or family who speak with a "dialect"?
3. (S) The old man repeats: "Always room for one more," to all the people who ask to come into his cottage. Why do you think he tells them this? Could his cottage possibly hold all the people, animals, and other things that come in? What do we call it when the author has the characters do impossible things? (exaggeration, fantasy).
4. (P) How does the author solve the problem when the cottage falls down?
5. (P) The illustrator of this story uses pen-and-ink lines to add details to each page. If you have access to a computer with a drawing program, you can imitate the style of artist Nonny Hogrogian. Using the drawing program, add lines of hatching and cross-hatching to a picture you design. Print the picture and add it to your portfolio.
6. (P) This book is a good way to illustrate the process of animation in film-making. If you have a single-frame capability on your video camera, you can work with a partner to create an animated sequence based on the book. First draw a picture in the style of the artist very lightly on paper. Then draw over the outline with short pencil strokes (about 1/4 inch in length). After each stroke, have the camera person take three frames of video, then add another stroke. When the picture is completed, the video will appear to draw itself when it is replayed.
7. (P) Read about animation techniques and "persistence of vision," in books from the library media center. They are found in the 700s—the fine arts section. Two good books are: Yvonne Andersen, *Teaching Film*

Animation to Children. New York: Van Nostrand Reinhold Co., 1970; and William Kuhns and Robert Stanley, *Exploring the Film.* Dayton, OH: Pflaum-Standard, 1968.

8. (P) Nonny Hogrogian used pastels (colored chalk) and damp paper towels to achieve a special effect in her pictures. Practice using the same technique and produce a picture that suggests the place where you live.

One Fine Day (Caldecott Medal, 1972)

Art Notes

Lyn Ellen Lacy's notes (1986) on the artistic values in *One Fine Day* offer a fine analysis of Nonny Hogrogian's choice of media.

> *One Fine Day* was illustrated by oil painting...the fox who lost his tail seems presented deliberately as artistic cliche of the fox motif in folk literature, stylistically simple and idealized in vivid red-orange. Other figures, though, are individualized with humorous smug, nagging, or flirtatious facial expressions. The fox begins his journey unobtrusively through the forest in the book's front matter itself; this early entrance prepares the audiences for the humor of his exit in the last illustration.

The Story

A cumulative tale in the tradition of *The Gingerbread Man* and other folk tales known and cherished by children, *One Fine Day* is the retelling of an old Armenian folk tale in which a fox has to pay for drinking an old woman's jug of milk with the loss of his tail. Afraid that all of his friends will laugh at him because he has no tail, he begs the old woman to sew his tail back on. There ensues a series of tasks that must be performed before the happy ending arrives. The fox, ordered to return the milk, enlists the help of a cow, who in turn, needs some grass. When the field is approached for grass, it requires water; the stream must have a jug in which to put the water; a young lady wants a blue bead, the peddler who *has* a blue bead bargains for an egg. The fox, now looking very subdued and tired, goes to a hen, who in turn, makes him promise to get grain. Finally, an old miller feels sorry for the fox, gives him the grain, and the journey is reversed. At each level of request, the original problem is repeated, and the additional tasks are added, so that by the climax of the story, children are able to join in and repeat the events that lead to a satisfying conclusion as the fox, happily reunited with his tail, trots back to the forest and his friends.

Questioning Framework for Developing Critical Thinking Skills

Four techniques of questioning are appropriate to introduce at this point. These include cognitive memory, convergent, divergent, and evaluative questions. The simple plot and story line of *One Fine Day* offers a nonthreatening base for developing critical thinking skills in very young children. Sample questions are:

- *Cognitive memory:* Who was_____? What did_____say? _____do? Where was_____?
- *Convergent (interpret, analyze and integrate ideas):* Can you retell the story in your own words? Can you act out the story as the author told it? Can you compare the story to_____?
- *Divergent (develop creative ideas, elicit the unexpected, help students solve a problem):* Can you retell the story with a change? For example: If the old woman had been friendly? If the miller had not felt sorry for the fox? From the point of view of the old woman (trying to get some more milk)? What do you suppose would have happened if? How do you think_____ looked after_____?
- *Evaluative (develop judgment, establish standards for story and for art):* Do you feel sorry for_____? Why or why not? Do you think it was all right for _____ to _____ ? Why or why not? Would you have acted as _____ did? Why or why not? Do you think the pictures help tell the story? Why or why not? Could you tell the story just by looking at the pictures? Why or why not?

As a cumulative tale with rising and falling action, punctuated by a dramatic climax and turn of the plot, *One Fine Day* is an excellent model for teaching the story mountain to develop the skill of recognizing story structure. By introducing the elements of fiction through this delightful picture book, teachers can lead students to an appreciation of chapter books and books composed mostly of text, and begin to develop a good sense of literary criticism in their students.

Using a Story Mountain as a Graphic Organizer

Teachers can use the story mountain described below to draw a visual representation of the rise and fall of action on a story.

The teacher:	The students:
explains that talking about what happens in a story is like taking a hike up a mountain, resting at the top, and then coming down the other side.	listen to presentation.
draws an outline of a mountain or large triangle on the chalkboard or overhead transparency.	draw a similar graphic in their journals or portfolios.

```
                    Climax
                 Event
               Event
             Event
          Problem
       Setting              Resolution
```

asks, "What is the setting for the story?"	answer, "In the country," or similar response.
writes students' answer inside triangle next to "setting."	follow teacher model.
continues questioning, "What was the problem?"	answer, "Fox needed his tail back," or similar response.
continues questioning until all elements of the story have been recorded.	
explains that the group has just made a model that can be used for almost all of the books they will read and enjoy in the Caldecott Club.	are able to demonstrate mastery of this skill in subsequent books.

Discussion Questions and Student Art Activities

The discussion questions relate to both the story (S) and the pictures (P).

1. (S) Why do you think the old woman punished the fox so violently for drinking her milk? In other stories you know, which characters generally carry knives or other weapons? Tell about one of these stories, and compare it to *One Fine Day.*

2. (S) This is an Armenian folk tale. We are beginning to learn a lot about the countries of Eastern Europe. Find Armenia in an atlas or on a globe and then research some of the customs and cultural traditions of the country. You will need to go to the library media center or to the public library. In a short paragraph, share your findings about the climate of Armenia, and what kind of plants and animals are found there.

3. (S) Dramatize this story by selecting actors to play each of the characters in *One Fine Day*. You may use costumes, or draw masks to represent each character. You will also need some props (jug, water, seeds, grain, etc.). This production can be done as a Reader's Theater with a narrator reading the story while the actors pantomime the action. Present your play to another group.

4. (S) On each page, the tail-less fox has a different expression. He smiles, smirks, frowns, and expresses many other emotions, depending on which character he is asking for help. Choose a student to be the fox and have that student show the same facial expressions. Other students must guess which character the fox is asking for help by studying each facial expression.

5. (P) Oil painting is not generally considered an appropriate art experience in the primary grades, but similar effects can be achieved using tempera (poster paint) in liquid form. Students may design and paint their interpretation of the events (or additional imaginative events) in *One Fine Day*.

Additional Student Activity for *One Fine Day*

Objective: Students will use tempera to paint a picture that portrays action and movement of characters similar to the ones in *One Fine Day*.

Materials: 12" x 18" drawing paper, tempera paint sets, and brushes.

The teacher:	The students:
explains the properties of paint:	listen to presentation on tempera and observe demonstration.

1. Tempera is free flowing and easily controlled.
2. Tempera is opaque; one color can cover another.
3. Colors are vivid and can be mixed to produce many tints and shades.

The teacher:	The students:
4. Tempera should be diluted for best consistency.	
5. Tempera may be brushed, stippled, sponged, dripped, and spattered.	
explains painting strategies:	observe and practice painting strategies.
1. Use only assigned paint station where jars of a variety of colors are available.	
2. Take only one jar of paint at a time, return it to the paint station when finished, and then take another color.	
3. Wait for your turn if the color you want is in use. Do not use paint from another station.	
4. Place paint jars toward the center, not the edge of the table.	
5. Do not paint a color on top of another *wet* color.	
distributes materials, explains assignment, assists where needed.	use tempera paints to create a picture in the style of Nonny Hogrogian.
gives ample time for the project and collects paintings for critique.	add paintings to their portfolios when paintings are returned with critique.

UNIT 2: ROBERT McCLOSKEY

Biographical Information

Twice winner of the Caldecott Medal for his outstanding picture books, *Make Way for Duckling* and *Time of Wonder,* Robert McCloskey recently received a singular honor and homage to his work. As a spin-off from the popular duck family story, a sculptor fashioned a family of bronze ducks in the style of McCloskey and had them placed in the Boston Public Gardens, where children have admired and played on them for many years. In the summer of 1991, during a visit to Moscow by President and Mrs. Bush, a copy of the *Make Way for Ducklings* piece was installed in a Moscow square for Soviet children to enjoy in much the same way as their American counterparts. Children's art and literature transcends politics, and the Robert McCloskey story of a duck family who wanted a home with some privacy is a universal theme.

Growing up in Hamilton, Ohio, Robert McCloskey was always interested in drawing. He submitted an entry to a *Scholastic* art competition in 1932, and won a scholarship to the Vesper George School in Boston. There followed many years of art work in various media from bas relief to murals to puppet design. Mr. McCloskey derived many of his ideas for plots and illustrations from his boyhood home in Ohio, but he was equally comfortable with stories set in Boston, New York, or Maine. In a 1970 interview, he confided that most of his fan mail contains pictures of ducks "from California to Scandinavia, from Holland to Turkey."

A favorite story about McCloskey describes his insatiable desire for realism, which was so great that he purchased four ducks to observe their behaviors. Because the artist lived in a crowded apartment in New York City, neighbors in nearby apartments complained about the noise. "No effort," says McCloskey, "is too great to find out as much as possible about the things you know you are drawing." This philosophy pervades all of McCloskey's artistic efforts.

Make Way for Ducklings (Caldecott Medal, 1942)

Art Notes

The medium selected by the artist is sepia-toned lithographic pencils on grained zinc, a process called stone lithography. The pictures are monochromatic, using shades of the same sepia throughout the book. By varying the shading, the artist achieves a fine sense of texture and depth in the pictures. Architectural integrity is achieved through the replication of well-known Boston landmarks, and the maturing ducks are drawn from feathery emergence to teenage gawkiness. The double-page spreads enable the artist to use broad strokes and still maintain infinite detail. *Make Way for Ducklings* has truly become a classic children's book, and many artists have chosen McCloskey's style to interpret their own stories. It is interesting to compare the monochromatic work of Chris Van Allsburg with that of Robert McCloskey.

The Story

Mr. and Mrs. Mallard, searching for a desirable place to raise a family, reach Boston, and find it an ideal location to establish residence. But the busy traffic of city streets is a deterrent, so Mrs. Mallard selects an island on the Charles River near the Public Gardens. In this idyllic environment, eight little ducklings are born and gently reared by their parents. Mr. Mallard, a curious father, decides to explore the area, and leaves Mrs. Mallard in charge of the ducklings after promising to meet the family at the Public Gardens pond. When the mother duck is satisfied that the ducklings have learned enough survival skills, she takes them to Boston. But Mrs. Mallard had not anticipated the notorious Boston traffic. Fortunately, a friendly policeman, comes to their aid, stops traffic, and manages their journey to the safety of the Public Gardens pond. There they find both a tiny island and Mr. Mallard.

Discussion Questions and Student Art Activities

The discussion questions relate to both the story (S) and the pictures (P).

1. (S) How does the author-artist show us the time and place in the story?
2. (S) The theme of *Make Way for Ducklings* can be considered one of the conflict between nature and society. Find examples in the book that show this theme. List them in your journal or portfolio.
3. (S) Write a short paragraph about how Robert McCloskey uses setting and characters to enrich the story. You may begin with one of these prompts:
   • This story happened at a time when policemen walked a beat, and streetcleaners used brooms.
   • This book is a fantasy story even though Robert McCloskey shows a *real* city, Boston, and *realistic* ducks.
4. (S) What are the reality aspects of this book? What are the fantasy aspects of it? Give examples in two columns. Head one column "Real" and the other column "Fantasy."
5. (S) The author has the ducks talk but only to each other. When the ducks are communicating with people, they quack. Why do you think Robert McCloskey chose this way? Give reasons for your answer.
6. (S) What other Caldecott Medal books use the theme of nature against society?

7. (P) The artist uses eye-level viewpoints in many of the pictures in *Make Way for Ducklings*. How does this help the reader get more involved with the action in the story? Write a brief paragraph describing three pictures in the book that have an eye-level point of view.
8. (P) Some art critics say that children enjoy books illustrated in one color and white if the figures stand out enough and express action and vitality. Do you think that *Make Way for Ducklings* is this kind of book? Why or why not?

Time of Wonder (Caldecott Medal, 1958)

Art Notes

Robert McCloskey devoted three years to the creation of watercolor paintings for *Time of Wonder,* which is set at his island home in Penobscot Bay, Maine. Representational art establishes a real sense of place, but the watercolors are definitely impressionistic in their portrayal of the outdoors suffused in color and light. The artwork is reminiscent of French Impressionistic painting—of Pissaro, Monet, and Van Gogh. Conversely, the design of *Time of Wonder* has influenced other artists, for example, the work of Chris Van Allsburg in *Polar Express.* With a column of text on the left, and one-and-a-half page picture spreads, McCloskey's mastery of picture book design is reaffirmed in the work of Van Allsburg.

The Story

Time of Wonder is a charming family story set on a known and loved island in Maine. During the height of the summer vacation season, rocks are warm, children swim, and bays are busy with sailboats, speedboats, and fishing boats.

Nature is at peace. The hummingbirds are in the garden, the dolphins frolic after boats, and the tides are predictable. But at summer's end, when most of the vacationers have left, nature reestablishes its power and force. The story builds in suspense, as storm preparations are made hurriedly but thoroughly, and the island family organizes to withstand the wind, salt spray, and blinding rain.

As the hurricane rages, the family sings familiar songs, plays games, and finally—the storm spent—goes to bed. In the morning, surveying the storm damage becomes an adventure, with overturned trees becoming a natural playground. As the family packs to return to their winter life in the city, there is a sense of sadness in leaving a much-loved place, even as the family looks forward to a return to the island.

Discussion Questions

1. What kind of scenery do you think would look best in watercolor?
2. How could you use watercolor to create a feeling of hot weather, cold weather, or storm?

Student Art Activities

Robert McCloskey's wonderful command of watercolors offers an opportunity to teacher or library media specialist to share a rudimentary lesson in using watercolor for illustration. Elaine Wallace (1990), Art Supervisor for Prince George's County Public Schools, offers the suggestions listed below. This basic set of instructions can be used when an art teacher is not available for consultation.

Objectives: Students will identify the properties of watercolor painting, be introduced to proper watercolor painting techniques, and use the techniques to do a watercolor painting.

Materials: Watercolor paper or heavyweight (90) white drawing paper, watercolor sets and brushes, water containers, paper towels, pitchers, pails.

The teacher:	The students:
displays the pictures in *Time of Wonder* and describes the properties of watercolors.	write the properties of watercolors in their journals or portfolios.
explains the properties of water colors: diluted, transparent, applied from light to dark, and able to dry very quickly.	listen to presentation.
explains that students will use watercolor techniques to paint a landscape, seascape, or other composition in the style of *Time of Wonder.*	listen to presentation
distributes art materials and sets standards for the activity.	

The teacher:	The students:
explains that organization for neatness is extremely important.	
has students open paint box and examine colors, then drop water on each cake to soften paint.	perform operations as demonstrated.
shows how to dip brush in water and place tip of brush in paints until brush is full of color.	practice after instruction.
gives ample time for students to experiment and find out what happens when paint meets paper.	
gives students handout for their portfolios listing application of watercolor techniques:	use handouts to guide their watercolor experiences.

1. The amount of water determines strength of color (more water, lighter color).
2. Light colors should be painted first, then dark over light.
3. The paper serves as white, so plan where white should be.
4. Leaving flecks of white in a painting creates freshness.
5. When painting, lay the paint on and leave it alone. Never keep repainting a spot; it only makes the paper rough, and muddies the colors.

introduces two techniques of watercolor painting: wet-into-wet, and the wash.	observe demonstration.
explains that wet-into-wet involves making paper wet before beginning to paint.	practice techniques.

1. Fill clean sponge with clear water, beginning at top of the paper, make strokes across the surface until the entire paper is wet. Do not scrub. Turn paper over and repeat on the other side.

The teacher:	The students:
2. Apply the wash with a brush full of paint, working quickly from the top of the paper with horizontal strokes. Mix enough paint and carry the paint from one end of the paper to the other.	
3. To achieve a graduated wash, begin with one or two strokes of full color brushed across the top of the paper. Succeeding strokes are done by dipping the brush in water only and brushing it across the paper. As more water is added the wash becomes lighter.	
gives students time to design and execute a watercolor painting in the style of Robert McCloskey and critiques completed paintings.	design and execute a watercolor painting in the style of McCloskey and keep paintings in their portfolios.

UNIT 3: MARCIA BROWN

Biographical Information

Marcia Brown's versatility of style in illustrating three Caldecott Medal books in three different art media may have originated in her childhood; each year at Christmas, she received new "paints, crayons and large pads of drawing paper." She recalls that "Christmas morning would find us making paper dolls and painting pictures of sturdy red barns with angels or fairies hovering overhead. Sometimes my parents joined us, for drawing seemed most natural for the whole family to do. We all loved to read and listen to stories."

Home was a parsonage in a series of New York towns, since her father was a minister. Although Marcia Brown had the typical career plans of most teenagers—to be a doctor, an opera singer, or a painter, it was the third choice that drew her, first to the Woodstock School of Painting, and later, to New York's Art Student League.

In an essay in *Lotus Seeds: Children, Pictures and Books* (1986), Marcia Brown describes her work:

The life of an artist is one of constant preparation. He almost never feels that he has realized his aim. When a book is finished, he is usually just beginning to feel how it might have been. Stacks of trial drawings and rejects attest to many efforts to find the right way to say what one has to say. One develops the technique necessary to express one's feelings about the particular book in hand. Sometimes this takes several months of drawing into a subject until one is ready to begin the actual illustrations. People often ask me how much time it takes to make a book. Five days, five months, three years—as long as is necessary to get down one's ideas and feelings about the book.

Once a Mouse.... (Caldecott Medal, 1962)

Art Notes

This is a book with limited text, but with strong woodcut illustrations that offer only the detail needed to tell the story. As writer and illustrator, Marcia Brown is able to lead us through the story by calling attention to what will be happening next. Writing about her art work in *Once a Mouse...*, Ms. Brown states:

> Though the words of the fable are few, the theme is big. It takes a certain amount of force to cut a wooden plank, and a definite decision. Wood that lived can say something about life in a forest. An artist can make his own color proofs in printers' inks, can mix his colors and give an approximate formula to a printer. Even though the transparent colors on an offset press are different from the thicker ones used at home, this proving can be of enormous help in seeing what one will get.
>
> Each artist has his personal feelings about his way of working, and the finished book is what is to be judged as successful or not, but in my own books I like every color to be cut on a separate block in order to maintain the optical unity of the medium. (1986)

The colors chosen by Marcia Brown are the soft earth tones of green, rose, tan, and gold that evoke the colors of sunset in an Indian forest.

The Story

In a forest in ancient India, a turbanned hermit sat thinking. But his thoughts about big and little were interrupted by a tiny mouse, about to be eaten by a crow. The hermit, in an act of kindness, turns the mouse into a cat that frightens the crow. When the cat is then frightened by a larger cat, the hermit changes his pet into a dog, then a larger dog, and finally into a huge royal tiger. Each change is made to protect the animal from a larger predator. But pride causes the royal tiger's return to mouse status, and the story ends with the original mouse scurrying into the forest, while the hermit returns to his thoughts.

This fable from the Indian *Hitopadesa* has been retold by Marcia Brown. The original version was used by rajahs as a "mirror for princes," to instruct their sons in the dangers of pride.

Discussion Questions

The discussion questions relate to both story (S) and pictures (P).

1. (S) What do you think is the moral of this fable? Write the moral in one brief sentence.
2. (P) The color red is gradually introduced into the illustrations to indicate the presence of danger. At what part of the story does Marcia Brown stop using red? Why do you think the artist used a special color to convey a certain emotion?

Student Art Activities

An art activity relating to this author and book may be added to the student portfolio. The objective of the activity is to have students create a "woodcut" of their own design, using a similar process to the one used by Marcia Brown. Materials needed include styrofoam plates or packaging trays from the grocery store, pencil, brayer, tempera paint or inks, colored construction paper or art paper.

The teacher:	The students:
distributes art materials to the group.	
explains the project, writing directions on an overhead or chalk board.	listen, and follow directions.
1. Draw a picture on the styrofoam plate or package, using a firm pressure on your pencil.	
2. Using a brayer, roll paint or ink evenly over the styrofoam.	
3. Place a sheet of art paper on the styrofoam, press firmly but gently.	

The teacher:	The students:
4. Lift the art paper. The print that appears on the reverse side of the art paper resembles a woodcut. 5. Let the print dry completely. 6. Mat or frame the picture to include in the Caldecott art portfolio.	

Once a Mouse.... is a form of literature known as a fable. In the activity outlined below, students will describe the characteristics of the fable, and write and illustrate an original fable using a familiar moral.

The teacher:	The students:

summarizes the characteristics of a fable on the chalkboard or overhead projector:
 	
   • short and dramatic
   • characters are animals or inanimate objects that act like humans
   • has a stated moral at the end
	copy characteristics in journals or notebooks.

asks students to write an original fable as a group writing experience, using a familiar moral such as "Slow and steady wins the race," and a story map as a graphic organizer. (A model for a story map appears in Chapter 5.)	contribute ideas for an original fable.
leads the group, helping them develop a story line for their original fable.	compose the fable, using stated fable characteristics as guidelines.
writes the final version of the fable on chalkboard or overhead projector, or uses a word processing program to enter the story on the computer.	
distributes art materials to illustrate group fable.	make an individual illustration for the fable.

Cinderella (Caldecott Medal, 1955)

Art Notes

In illustrating *Cinderella,* Marcia Brown researched the art of eighteenth-century Europe. This art was characterized by much emphasis on costume, landscape backgrounds, and the many trappings of an elegant and supposedly enviable life style. In Brown's pictures, the use of wavery pencil-line and colored crayon combine to evoke a recollection of eighteenth-century court life. Pastel colors for Cinderella, bright and almost garish ones for the wicked stepsisters, a hint of gold and silver in the castle drawings, and soft earth-tones for the pumpkin patch are brilliant achievements in the hands of a careful and well-read artist. The paintings of French artists Fragonard and Boucher are possible resources for Marcia Brown's *Cinderella* pictures.

The Story

Marcia Brown translates the familiar fairy tale by Charles Perrault. The colloquial narrative, e.g., "He (the prince) invited everyone who was anyone, including our two young misses, for they cut quite a figure in the land," brings a lilting, musical cadence to the text. The story unfolds magically as the fairy godmother works her spells, Cinderella enchants the prince at the ball, the slipper is lost, and finally the happy denouement as slipper, Cinderella, and the prince are reunited.

The language of the text flows mellifluously in complete agreement with the dreamlike quality of the wavery pen-line and colored crayon illustrations.

Additional Cinderella variants include the Italian one, in which the heroine, Zezolla, is banished to the kitchen and renamed Cat Cinderella, or *La Gatta Cenerentola.* In this version, a date tree grows into the shape of a woman, and the fairy godmother comes out of the tree to get Cat Cinderella dressed for the ball. At the ball, La Gatta Cenerentola drops "the richest and prettiest patten you could imagine." (A patten was a kind of high-heeled overshoe that fine ladies wore when they went out.) When the king orders all the females in the kingdom to return to the palace for a try-on, "the moment it came near Zezolla's foot, it darted forward of itself to shoe her." The king makes Zezolla his queen, and the sisters, "livid with envy, crept quietly home to their mother."

In the Scottish version of Cinderella, first written down in the sixteenth century, there is a lot of violent action by the wicked stepmother. Rashin Coatie, who has lost her slipper at the king's party, is unaware that her stepmother has cut off the heel and toes of her own daughter so that the slipper would fit, and the stepsister would be able to marry the prince. But on the way to church for the wedding, a little bird sings: "Minched fit, and pinched fit/ Beside the king she rides,/ But braw fit, and bonny fit/ In the kitchen neuk she hides." The bird's song brings to the prince's attention that the stepsister is not the right bride, and he gallops back to get the rightful slipper owner, Rashin Coatie.

(In the Scottish version, as in the Chinese, an animal is killed and buried by the vicious stepmother; the bones are dug up, and proceed to grant wishes. But in the Scottish version, the prince spies the beautiful Rashin Coatie in church.)

The Brothers Grimm version has Aschenputtel plant a hazel twig at her mother's grave and water it with her tears. (This is similar to the date tree that grows in the Italian version). The hazel tree promises to grant Aschenputtel's wishes. When a three-day festival is announced, and Aschenputtel wants to go, the wicked stepmother sets several tasks: Aschenputtle must pick a dish of tiny lentils out of accumulated ashes in two hours; then two dishes of lentils must be sifted out. Finally, the birds come to Aschenputtel's aid, and the hazel tree gives her beautiful gowns and slippers of silver and silk, with golden slippers for the third evening. In this version, the prince has put tar in the driveway and Aschenputtel loses her slipper in the gummy pitch. The story continues in the usual manner, to the happy-ever-after ending, but in the Grimm version, the storytellers have the birds come down and peck out the eyes of the wicked stepsisters while they are on their way to the wedding!

Comparable Cinderella variants exist in other cultures, and it is interesting to investigate the folklore similarities and differences.

Another way in which this comparison of folk variants of the Cinderella story can be used is through a computer-generated program with a drawing tool. Slippers from each culture can be drawn on the screen with a brief description of the cultural variation (a Greek sandal, a Chinese tiny slipper, a patten, etc.).

Discussion Questions and Student Art Activities

The discussion questions relate to both story (S) and pictures (P).

1. (P) How does Marcia Brown use colored crayon and pen-line to create a fantasy-type picture?

2. (S) In the story, a very good man deliberately chooses a cruel and haughty woman with two self-centered daughters as his wife. Why do you think all of the versions of Cinderella begin this way? Give reasons for your answer.

3. (S) What does the story tell us about the fashions of the time that the story is set in? Find examples in the book about the hairstyles, the fabrics, and the design of clothes at that time. See if you can research information about costumes and customs of the eighteenth century by using the the library media center's material on the history of costume.

4. (S) What made Cinderella trust her fairy godmother? Do you think that Cinderella had seen her godmother before? Give reasons for your answers.

5. (S) How would you describe Cinderella's personality? Make a web with Cinderella's name in the center box and her character traits "webbing" out from this central point. According to Bromley (1991), the literary web "used as an instructional tool in the classroom is a graphic representation or visual display of categories of information and their relationships."

6. (S) Why do you think that a second ball was held, even though the invitation only mentioned a single party? How would the story have been different if:
    *   Cinderella's father had married a nice person.
    *   Only one ball had been held.
    *   The glass slipper had been broken by trying to force it on a larger foot.
    *   The fairy godmother had not given Cinderella such strict instructions.
    Choose one of the possibilities and write a scene about it.

7. (P) Many of the pictures in Cinderella have humorous and funny touches. Find some examples of humor in the illustrations and share them with the group.

8. (P) Cinderella is always shown in a beautiful, pastel illustration. Why do you think the artist chose special colors for each character in the story?

9. (S) Most of the stories that Marcia Brown illustrated are found in the section of the library media center labeled 398.2. What kind of stories are in this section of the library media center?

Student Art Activity/Multicultural Cinderella

Objective: After evaluating the Caldecott Medal version of Cinderella translated and illustrated by Marcia Brown, students participate in a guided study of Cinderella variants to learn to infer similarities and differences in folk literature.

The teacher:			**The students:**	

reads or shares in storytelling versions of Cinderella from Egyptian, Chinese, Filipino, Italian, and Scottish cultural traditions.

listen to the stories, or read them independently.

leads students in developing a comparison chart as a graphic organizer.

participate in the design of the graphic organizer.

may want to use the following chart as an example.

	Egyptian	**Chinese**	**Filipino**	**Other...**
Setting	court of the pharoah in ancient times	court of the emperor in in ancient times	country festival	(Greek) ancient Athens
Characters	*Rhodope,* a court lady; the pharoah; and an eagle	*Beauty;* a wise elder; a step-mother; a magic fish; the emperor	Maria; a stepmother; a crab; a hand-some young man	a prince; a beautiful girl
Conflict	an eagle carries off a sandal	stepmother kills the magic fish that grants wishes	cannot go to the festival because she has to wash clothes	beautiful girl drops her sandal in a horse trough
"Magic" intervention	none	Beauty digs up fish bones and prays for wishes that are granted	crab appears in river, announces that it is the spirit of Maria's dead mother; grants wishes	none
Climax/ Resolution	owner of slipper is found; marries pharoah	emperor discovers Beauty at slipper try-on; they marry	after the festival, young man traces lost shoe to Maria; they marry	prince weds beautiful girl

10. (S) Composers have been intrigued by the story of Cinderella. Rossini wrote an opera called *La Cenerentola,* and the Russian composer Prokofiev wrote a beautiful ballet score for Cinderella. Locate record-ings, audiotapes, or a video of these musical settings, and share them as a musical background for the fairy tale.

Shadow (Caldecott Medal, 1983)

Art Notes

Shadow is perhaps the most controversial Caldecott Medal book. Critics have addressed both the content and the artistic techniques used by Marcia Brown in designing and illustrating this mysterious and exotic poem. Artistically, the illustrations are carefully planned collages with cut and pasted forms. Some of these forms were cut from black paper, some carved from wood blocks and printed in white on tissue paper. The backgrounds for these forms are a combination of washes and blotting of paper to produce special effects. All of these techniques are beautifully combined in an artistic whole. The criticism arises from the connotations the shapes, cutouts, and colors evoke. Although Lyn Lacy (1986) applauds Brown's artistic strength in her powerful use of light and dark, she nevertheless has some serious points to make about the illustrations and their character.

> [The visual images] use unrelenting darkness itself in pictures of Africa and its people. Questionable backlighting of all figures presents black silhouettes in which human detail is disintegrated except for whites of the eyes. Blackness represents repugnant squirming creatures and staggering inhuman forms...black figures against black shadows march or leap or creep menacingly through high grass. All these uses of black and unearthly white have negative connotations as artistic symbols.

Lacy concludes her analysis of the illustrations in *Shadow* by suggesting that the sophisticated content of the poem is beyond the comprehension of most children, and that the pictures may inadvertently give rise to the fears most children have—of darkness, of the supernatural, and of night itself.

Other critics complain that by choosing to illustrate only primitive figures in a wild environment, Marcia Brown presented damaging pictorial ideas that may foster stereotyping, and actually damage black children's self-images.

This third Caldecott Medal Book illustrated by Marcia Brown is a challenging and serious addition to a unit dedicated to outstanding contributions in the field of children's book illustrating.

The Story

In all cultures and civilizations, it is the task of the storyteller to explain natural phenomena in creative interpretations. In this story told by shamans in Africa, the qualities of the shadow are explored, defined, and explained in terms of reality. The changing size, color, and configuration of Shadow are followed through the day, from sunrise to sunset, and described as a watcher, a mysterious companion, a trickster, or a blind entity when no light is present.

The story is a free verse translation of a poem by the French writer, Blaise Cendrars. In the introduction to Cendrars' book (1982), Marcia Brown writes:

> What is Shadow?. . . Out of the fire that called forth the many images of Shadow, came the ash that was the sacred bond to the life that had gone before.....The eerie, shifting image of Shadow appears where there is light and fire and a storyteller to bring it to life.

Discussion Questions and Student Art Activities

The discussion questions relate to both story (S) and pictures (P)

1. (S) The book begins by telling the reader negative qualities of Shadow—what Shadow is *not*. Make a chart or poster with two columns—one, describing what Shadow *is,* and what Shadow is *not.*
2. (S) How is Shadow brought to life, according to the story?
3. (S) Research shadows by choosing nonfiction books that explain what a shadow is. Write a brief report on your findings.
4. (S) Why are shadows so fascinating? Prepare a video interview in which Shadow appears in silhouette and expresses itself orally.
5. (P) Marcia Brown uses a mixed-media style of illustration in *Shadow*. If you were going to illustrate this poem, which art media would you use? Give reasons for your choice.
6. (P) Create a shadow puppet play based on the book, *Shadow.* You can make thin cardboard cut-outs of figures in the story, attach the cut-outs to a wire or stick, and move them across the stage of the overhead projector. Use colored cellophane to achieve the same effects that Marcia Brown used as a background for your shadow puppet silhouettes.

UNIT 4: BARBARA COONEY

Biographical Information

Barbara Cooney has some good advice for teachers and students who study the art work of Caldecott Medal-winning artists: "You can learn more (about art) by just looking—by looking to see how another artist has done something. Unfortunately, you can't always figure it out."

The winner of two Caldecott medals for her outstanding illustrations, Barbara Cooney grew up in New York, but found a home in New England. In addition to her art talent, she is an accomplished gardener, a gourmet cook, and a wife, mother, and grandmother.

Biographers have noted the wonderful domesticity of an artist who works at home—in a home she designed and helped a son to build in Maine. They describe trips between Maine and Massachusetts during the building period, and indicate that her fine sense of duty does not dissipate her time or energy. Barbara Cooney has a Christmas tree that is every child's delight, both in artistry and in magical holiday spirit. Decked with tiny lights and hand-cut cookies in the shape of every imaginable toy or animal, it is a treat to the eye.

In a tribute to Cooney, Constance McClellan (1980) writes: "She has self-discipline, drive and a motivation for independence. She is a very exciting woman, an inspiration to young illustrators and to women everywhere."

Chanticleer and the Fox (Caldecott Medal, 1959)

Art Notes

Brilliant cobalt blue, vivid green, and rich red-brown, combined with a red, ocher, and somber black, are used by Barbara Cooney in *Chanticleer and the Fox.* Her choices in color are presented throughout the book in an alternating system in which black-and-red illustrations are interspersed with five-color pages, providing an overall design for the book that is both lively and cheerful.

Chanticleer exhibits an artful double-page spread, sensitively accommodating the informal text placement. Color is used to best advantage to punctuate a particular point of interest, and as a balancing element, especially when only red is used with black for moments of peril and danger in the text. The artist's fresh, invigorating style is reminiscent of decorative folk art with its attention to detail in costumes, household, and life style, and yet there is homage to the illuminated manuscripts of the middle ages as well. Huck (1987) describes Cooney's "little poor farm of the middle ages with its wattled fence and thatched roof," and the beautiful clear colors and "natural-looking, appealing children," as examples of a well-designed and lovingly produced book.

The Story

The story of *Chanticleer and the Fox* dates from Aesop's times, but the text chosen by Barbara Cooney is the one written originally by Geoffrey Chaucer for his "Nun's Priest's Tale" in *The Canterbury Tales.*

A very poor woman lives in a dilapidated cottage with her two daughters and an assortment of animals. This story concerns the rooster, who is so proud of his beauty, that he *almost* believes what a sly fox tells him about his father (who had a beautiful singing voice). This appeal to the rooster's vanity nearly costs the rooster its life, but the prompt action of the old woman and all the rest of the characters saves the day—and the rooster's life. Wiser now, the rooster is content to enjoy life in the farmyard, surrounded by his adoring hen-harem.

Because the story is told in a formal manner reminiscent of Chaucer, it is probably more interesting to an older picture-book audience. Some critics feel that younger children might view the story in a modern-day interpretation of a kidnapping or child-molesting fable.

Discussion Questions and Student Art Activities

The discussion questions relate to both story (S) and pictures (P).

1. (S) How does the author let the reader know about the character and personality of the widow?
2. (S) This country family led a very frugal life. Find evidence and descriptions in the story that support this. Write a short journal entry about poverty, beginning "Long ago, people who lived in the country were often poor because. . . ."
3. (S) What, in the story, tells us when it takes place? Where? What are some clues to let us know about the time of the story?
4. (S) What kind of bird was Chanticleer? The author-artist needs two pages to introduce the reader to the rooster. Why do you think so much space is devoted to Chanticleer?
5. (S) Why do you suppose Chanticleer put so much faith in what other animals told him? How does Partlet flatter him? The fox?
6. (S) In what other folk tales is a fox outwitted by being persuaded to open his mouth? (Gingerbread Boy)
7. (S) There are two morals in this tale—the fox and the rooster each express one. Which moral do you think best suits the story? Give reasons for your choice in a short journal entry.

8. (P) Find your favorite picture in the book. Write a short journal entry about the picture: how it shows the setting, the characters, and the colors the artist used.
9. (P) Compare the drawings of the fox in Nonny Hogrogian's *One Fine Day* with the fox in *Chanticleer and the Fox.* Which fox seems more realistically drawn? Which fox seems more friendly? Less cunning? How do you think artists decide the way in which they will depict an animal in a book?
10. (P) With a partner, plan a short debate between two foxes: the one from *One Fine Day,* and the one from *Chanticleer and the Fox.* The subject for the debate is: "Getting Along With Others." Try to have a sense of humor in your remarks.
11. (P) When you visit an art museum, ask where the medieval art work is displayed. Study the paintings. How does Barbara Cooney use ideas from fine arts in her Caldecott Medal book?

Ox-Cart Man (Caldecott Medal, 1980)

Art Notes

In *Ox-Cart Man,* Barbara Cooney captures the spirit of early America, and presents it to the reader in homage to the naive primitive style of early American artists, who painted on wood with whatever materials were available. The flat figures, the panoramic landscapes of an uncluttered and beautiful New England countryside, and the scenes of Portsmouth Harbor remind present-day readers of a time before photography, when the only way to communicate with family and friends left behind in other countries and cultures was through a painting sent by way of merchant ships.

This Caldecott Medal book is characterized by formal yet imaginative page layouts, wonderful depth of coloration, and a sensitive use of light and dark throughout. Most of the book depicts New Hampshire rural and Portsmouth marketplace settings with a sharp eye for authentic detail of time and place; even the fallen autumn leaves and delicate spring blossoms reflect the flat shapes and blunt colors used by the American primitive artists. In her book, *Art and Design in Children's Picture Books: An Analysis of Caldecott Award Winning Books,* Lyn Lacy (1986) describes some of the techniques that Barbara Cooney used in *Ox-Cart Man,* particularly her use of light and dark in contrasting illustrations.

When a wonderfully red sunset appears just as the Ox-Cart Man approaches home from the market, it dramatically transforms sky and hills by implying depth and contour. . . . A turn of the page, and one has the welcoming home scene in warmth of the kitchen with exquisite modeling and highlighting of figures gathered around softening firelight. . . . Another turn of the page, and one finds a barn scene in which the Ox-Cart Man carves a yoke while the winter sun casts across the floor and walls a long low shadow that is stunningly unique for such a work in early-American style.

Barbara Cooney has used modern media of acrylics and gesso-board to depict an earlier time in American history.

The Story

A New England farmer and his family work together to do the chores that are necessary for a comfortable and satisfying life. This is a story of time, and how the simple events of a year contribute to the well-being of a rural family. Set in the early 1800s, the story shows, rather than tells, how the farmer prepares to go to market and how his family assists in these preparations. When the farmer starts his long journey to the marketplace, leading the ox loaded with items to be sold, the reader knows intuitively that the farmer will be returning alone. There is a bittersweet quality to the story as the farmer, his tasks of selling and buying competed, kisses the ox on the nose, and leaves on his return journey. He is welcomed affectionately by his family, the few purchases and gifts are shared, and the family returns once more to preparations for the next year's journey. The peace and serenity achieved through the repetition of familiar and necessary tasks is a comforting aspect of the story.

Discussion Questions and Student Art Activities

The discussion questions relate both to story (S) and to pictures (P).

1. (S) How do the illustrations help you understand the story? Write the answer to the question in your journal or portfolio.
2. (S) Barbara Cooney had to do a great deal of research before she made the pictures for *Ox-Cart Man.* Make a list of the *kinds* of books she probably used and record the list in your journal or portfolio. Then visit the library media center and try to locate some books that would be helpful if you were illustrating a book about early American life in New England.

3.   (S) *Ox-Cart Man* describes four seasons of the year, and the jobs that need to be done in each season so that the family can survive and prosper. Make a calendar for the family. Show what items are produced by family members, and when each of the products must be made.

4.   (P) Each of the pictures in the book appears to have been painted on wood. Find art books in the library media center that describe how early American artists painted. You will discover that many of the artists traveled from place to place, painting families or houses on tops of wooden boxes, or leftover scraps of boards from their houses and barns. Write a story about one of these early American artists, using facts that you have located. You may begin, "Today I visited the village of Salem, where the Snow family asked me to paint their portraits in exchange for room and board . . . ."

5.   Try to get a small piece of wood to draw on. Compose a picture, using magic markers, paint, or crayon. Be sure to sign and date your picture. Save it in your portfolio to display in a Caldecott gallery.

UNIT 5: LEO AND DIANE DILLON

Biographical Information

Both Leo and Diane Dillon studied to become artists at the Parsons School of Design and the School of Visual Arts in New York, but each brought to their creative and talented work a background formed at opposite ends of the United States: Diane, in California; Leo, in New York. Shortly after finishing school, they were married, and began working as free-lance artists, exploring a wide variety of artistic fields: book jackets and illustrations, advertising, posters, record album covers, and magazine illustrations. They also experimented with a number of different styles and techniques, and developed a unique and complex way of addressing a task.

They have been teachers, as well as full-time artists and illustrators. About the making of *Why Mosquitoes Buzz in People's Ears*, Leo and Diane Dillon (1976) have said:

> When each animal tells his version [of the events], rather than repeating what actually happened, we exaggerated his story as he might have when retelling it. The antelope, who had a very small part when the lion sent him off to get the owl, begins to ham it up to get more attention. The little red bird watches everything, and when the story is

over, flies away. He could be compared to the storyteller who gathers information and passes it on to the next generation. Needless to say, we had fun doing this story.

Why Mosquitoes Buzz in People's Ears (Caldecott Medal, 1976)

Art Notes

In this retelling of an African folk tale, Leo and Diane Dillon have used watercolor and pastels in strong, soft colors and in bold, stylized compositions inspired by the designs of African textiles. Areas of color are separated by a white line of varying depth that also describes the detail and becomes an integral part of the design.

The artists use a two-page spread to introduce the characters, and there are no borders on the pages. Characters in the story are defined by their colors: the iguana is green; the snake purple; the rabbit soft gray; the monkey brown; the owl multicolor gold, orange, and tan; the lion tawny gold; and the birds are brilliant, exotic colors.

When the Dillons are working together on a book, they completely blend their individual styles. Either Leo or Diane establishes the chosen style of illustration and makes the initial drawings, while the other supplies the colors. The basic drawings in *Why Mosquitoes Buzz in People's Ears* were done in pencil on tracing paper, which was then rubber-cemented to a heavier paper. One area, such as an animal, or several areas of similar color, were cut out of the tracing paper, and the cutout portions were lifted off. These areas were then painted with watercolors, gradually built up through repeated applications with an air brush to produce variations of shading and hue. Where additional texture was called for, pastel was rubbed on with cotton or a spatter technique was used. When the color was right for a certain area, but the surrounding area was yet to receive color, the artists masked the completed portion with an adhesive-backed paper, cut to fit exactly. After additional color was applied, this sticky paper was lifted off. This process was repeated until all desired areas had been colored. The black areas were painted in india ink. The remaining tracing paper, which covered the areas to be left white, was removed, and the entire painting was sprayed with a clear fixative. For the night pictures, another spray of blue or purple was used as a last glaze to give darker shading.

The Story

Iguana is forced to put sticks in his ears to avoid the tall tales of a pesky mosquito. As a result, the iguana is unable to hear python when he speaks to him, and this miscommunication leads to a series of events culminating in the death of a baby owl. When mother owl returns home and finds the dead baby, she is so sad she refuses to "wake the sun" any longer. Consequently, the earth remains dark until lion summons all the animals to a council, and the events leading up to owl's refusal to bring daylight are revealed and traced back to the pesky mosquito. When all of this is explained to mother owl, nature's balance is restored and the moral of the story is expressed in terms of mosquito-swatting through the ages.

Discussion Questions and Student Art Activities

The discussion questions relate both to story (S) and to pictures (P).

1. (P) This book is set in West Africa. How do the artists show us this?
2. (P) Have the students compare remnants or small scraps of African print fabrics with the illustrations in the book.
3. (P) How do the double-page pictures move the story?
4. (S) Can you find words to describe the animals' characters? Introduce a junior thesaurus or *Webster's New World Thesaurus* if students have not used a thesaurus before. Explain that the word thesaurus is a Latin word for "treasure house", and that a thesaurus is a treasure house full of words. In this brainstorming activity, students first describe the character of the animals in the story, and then find words that identify the animal. (Examples: *iguana*—cranky, grumpy, disagreeable; *snake*—worried, anxious, insecure; *rabbit*—fearful, timid; *crow*—overreactive; impulsive; *monkey*—thoughtless, active imagination; *owl*—maternal, sad.
5. (S) Which do you think was the strongest character in the book? Give reasons for your answer.
6. S) Do you think the monkey *knew* that he had accidentally killed the owl? Why or why not? Find evidence in the story.
7. (P) How many ways does the artist show the sun setting? (Getting smaller, changing color from flame to pale green, looking downward.)
8. (P) How do the artists use *eyes* as a visual clue to what is happening in the book? (When animals are sleepy, their eyes are slits and downcast. Eyes can appear questioning, curious, fearful, or suspicious.) Describe a scene in the book that portrays emotions through a picture of the *eyes*.

9. (P) What kind of art materials did the artists use for the pictures in this book? How can you tell? (Watercolors and pastels.)
10. (P) In what way does the artist use pictures of birds in the story? (Focusing attention on larger characters, splashes of color).
11. (S) Repetition of sounds is an important part of the story. How are the sounds appropriate for the animals? Give examples. ("Wasuwasu" for the snake, "krik, krik, krik," for the rabbit.)
12. (S) This book has a surprise ending. Why do you think the authors chose that kind of ending?

Additional Art Activities

1. The animals pictured in this book are stylized or fanciful. Research the animals described in *Why Mosquitoes Buzz in People's Ears* and prepare a chart or poster showing what the animals realistically look like. Include information about the habits of each animal.
2. Design a mural showing the sequence of events in the book. Start with the iguana, add the snake, and continue the story, using colorful paper, fabric, three-dimensional effects, and other materials to make your mural lively and true to the book.
3. This story is good for a reader's theater. Work with a group, assigning roles of animals to members of the group. Have a narrator read the parts of the book that advance the action. Make simple masks or costumes for the characters.
4. Using the information in the *Arts Notes* section, try to create a new picture for the book. You may not have all of the materials that the Dillons used, but you can achieve similar effects with available materials. You may wish to design your extra illustration to be used as a book cover.

Ashanti to Zulu (Caldecott Medal, 1977)

Art Notes

Each of the pictures in this book include a man, a woman, a child, their living quarters, an artifact, and a local animal as part of the composition. The art work for the book is a combination of pastels, watercolors, and acrylics. The frames surrounding the pictures are done in black ink and watercolor. The interwoven design at the corners of each frame is based on the Kano Knot, which symbolizes endless searching, a design originally used in the city of Kano in northern Nigeria during the sixteenth and seventeenth centuries.

The Story

This book is a collection of cultural and traditional practices of 26 African peoples. Each page shows a large bordered painting of one of the peoples, and there is a short paragraph describing a custom, life style, or traditional story told by the group. The composition of the pictures reflect African values or philosophies.

Each illustration should be carefully studied, because the artists have included details important to the peoples shown in the picture: housing, food, crafts, style of dress and ornamentation, jewelry, weaponry, religious practices, and flowers and animals of the region.

Taken individually, the paintings express a life style from each region of Africa; taken as a whole, the illustrations remind the reader of the vastness of the African continent and the variety of the African peoples.

Discussion Questions and Student Art Activities

The discussion questions relate both to story (S) and to pictures (P).

1. (S) If you were preparing a report on one of the peoples of Africa, how would you use the pictures and information in this book?
2. (S) There is a labeled map of the continent of Africa in the back of the book. The labels represent the peoples described in the book. Use this map and a world atlas to locate the African nations where the peoples came from. Make a poster showing both the countries and peoples of Africa. You can also use a world almanac for current political boundaries.
3. (S) The author and artists used many resources in designing this book. Plan a visit to a local museum of natural history to see exhibits of the peoples of Africa.
4. (P.) The Dillons are two people working like one artist. Working with a partner, design and construct a diorama based on one of the peoples described in *Ashanti to Zulu.*
5. (S) How do you think the illustrators found out about the customs and traditions of each of the peoples in *Ashanti to Zulu?* Make a list of books and resources you think they may have used.
6. (S) Using pictures in this book as a guide, make a paper doll and dress it in a costume of its peoples. You may use a plastic doll if you like.
7. (P) Elaborate jewelry was important to African peoples. Create a necklace, bracelet, or other jewelry, using beads, wire, and chains. You may draw and color an original design for jewelry.

8. (S) Wedding ceremonies are important in the African culture. Locate descriptions of weddings and/or bridal traditions. Make a chart that compares and contrasts these rituals. (The Ndaka and Sotho peoples have particularly interesting wedding customs.)

9. (P) Plan and present a Pageant of African Peoples. Each student selects a letter of the alphabet and interprets that African people in costume, using the book illustrations as a resource. Each participant may read the information that accompanies the picture. The Pageant may be presented to other classes, or as a part of an African American History Celebration.

UNIT 6: CHRIS VAN ALLSBURG

Biographical Information

Trained in fine arts at the University of Michigan and the Rhode Island School of Design, Chris Van Allsburg has displayed his sculpture and drawings in galleries and museums. When he illustrated his first book for children, *The Garden of Abdul Gasazi*, it was critically acclaimed and given several major book and artistic awards.

"In my elementary school, we had art twice a week. I loved those days," remembers Van Allsburg (1986). He also recalls that his passion for art underwent a profound transition when he realized that peer pressure can be very strong in the sixth grade. "Certain peer pressures encourage little fingers to learn how to hold a football instead of a crayon. Rumors circulate around the schoolyard: Kids who draw or wear white socks and bring violins to school on Wednesdays might have cooties." But by the time Chris Van Allsburg entered college, he had begun to enjoy art for fun. It took him five years to get his undergraduate degree because, as he puts it, "I never let liberal arts courses get in the way of making art."

Van Allsburg earned a Bachelor of Fine Arts from the University of Michigan and a Master of Fine Arts degree from the Rhode Island School of Design. He has twice won the Caldecott Award and has also received recognition for his Honor Books. In all of his books, he suggests through his beautiful pictures that a fantasy adventure need not be entirely over just because the book itself is closed.

Jumanji (Caldecott Medal, 1982)

Art Notes

Chris Van Allsburg worked in black-and-white to create the illustrations for *Jumanji*. He used a soft black pencil and "dust" made by grinding up the graphite in pencils, sort of like eye shadow. By using pencils and pencil shavings artistically he created depth and texture in the illustrations. He involves the reader in a strong sense of space in the picture through the placement of figures or objects in the picture. Pictures are drawn from the perspective of someone viewing the action from above, or from an angle. Readers feel pulled into the picture, or like someone observing Peter and Judy's activities through a one-way mirror. Attention to light and shade, characterization, and a variety of shapes and sizes used for composition contribute to the overall surrealism of the story. Each drawing is given equal import, and each picture appears on the righthand side of the page, with a formal white border. In this way, the eye is drawn first to the illustration, and then to the text, centered on the white lefthand page.

The Story

"Jumanji, a young people's jungle adventure especially designed for the bored and the restless," reads Judy. She and her brother Peter have found a board game in the park and have decided to take it home and play the game. When the game comes to life as each child takes a turn, some disastrous incidents occur. By following directions *exactly,* the children are able to get out of the game and hide it in the park for the next unsuspecting game players to find. *Jumanji* has been called a "twilight fantasy," and this is perhaps an apt description, for most dreams take place and are recalled in the dusky gray-black light of twilight.

Discussion Questions and Student Art Activities

The discussion questions relate both to story (S) and to pictures (P).

1. (S) The book has been called a surreal story. Look up the dictionary meaning of the word surreal. Then compose a paragraph explaining why, or why not, the story is surreal.
2. (S) Why do you think the author makes Peter and Judy follow the directions so carefully?
3. (S) What might have happened if Judy had not rolled a 12 and the game had continued?

4. (S) Write a scene for the story describing what would have happened if the children had not read the directions and tried to quit part way through.

5. (P) Using the book, *Jumanji,* design and make a game board to be used with game pieces, dice, or a spinner. Make sure that the directions are complete and can really be followed. You may use the events in *Jumanji* or create your own fantastic adventure.

6. (P) What kind of video game could be produced using *Jumanji* as a model? If you have access to a computer and a drawing program, design a game similar to *Jumanji* that can be played singly or with a partner.

7. (P) Use clay or other sculpting materials to make models of the animals that appeared in the jungle game, Jumanji. Use the figures as part of a three-dimensional *Jumanji* game.

8. (P) Save the shavings from your pencil sharpener until you have enough to fill a small cup. Then, crush the shavings until a fine dust is formed. Use this material to create a single picture for a Chris Van Allsburg Appreciation Gallery. You may choose any subject matter. The finished picture should look similar to the drawings in the book, *Jumanji.*

The Polar Express (Caldecott Medal, 1986)

Art Notes

Chris Van Allsburg has chosen acrylics in full color to illustrate this book. But the glorious evocations of a snowy winter night are achieved through a brilliant use of light and color. The two-page spreads contribute to the immediacy of the journey through woods, over mountains, and the arrival at a mid-twentieth century architectural setting for the North Pole. There are elements of pointillism in the painting of the hundreds of elves massed in the town square to see Santa Claus present the first gift of Christmas.

The Story

A young boy whose confidence in the spirit of Christmas has been shaken, awakes late on Christmas Eve to hear a large steam engine in the street outside his room. Invited to join other children on the train, the boy travels through time and space to the North Pole, where Santa Claus is preparing to leave on his long journey through the world. One child is to receive "the first gift of Christmas," and Santa Claus selects the young boy. The boy asks for one of the silver bells from Santa Claus' sled, and it is graciously given to him. But when the children board the train for the return to reality, the boy discovers that he has lost the bell. On Christmas morning, the young boy finds the bell under the tree, but only he and his sister can hear its sound. The story reminds us that the fantasy world of children is fragile and easily lost in maturity.

Discussion Questions and Student Art Activities

The discussion questions relate both to the story (S) and to pictures (P).

1. (S) Where do you think the train is coming from? Why is the narrator the only person from his neighborhood invited to go on the Polar Express?
2. (S) When the boy is asked what he wants as a gift, he asks only for a sleigh bell. Why do you think he asked for this simple gift? Is there any evidence in the story to suggest that a bell is a valuable present? Where?
3. (P) How does the artist paint Santa's helpers? Are they recognizable as real? If the story did not tell us that the blobs were crowds of elves, could the reader tell? Give reasons for your answers.
4. (S) Why do you think the boy's parents could not hear the bell?
5. (S) Do you think this is the story of a dream? Why or why not?
6. (S) Why do you think the author chose a train as a means of transportation to the North Pole? If you were the author, what kind of transportation would you have picked? Give reasons for your answer.
7. (S) How old do you think the boy is when this mysterious event happens? How old is he when he tells the story? Give reasons for your answer.
8. (S) Write a story in which a girl is the person invited on the Polar Express. What would be different, if anything, in her choice of gifts?
9. (P) How does the artist put light into the picture, even though his story takes place at night?
10. (P) What differences in colors are there between the snowscene pictures and the pictures showing the indoors?
11. (P) What are some of the architectural features of the North Pole? Visit a gallery or art museum and look for examples of American art work from the early twentieth century. How are these paintings like the illustrations in *Polar Express?*
12. (P) Edward Hopper was an American artist who painted night scenes in which the viewer is looking into a lighted place. What kind of feelings do you have when you look at paintings like these?
13. (P) The last picture in the book is small and framed in the center of the last page. Why do you think that the artist or author decided to make this contrast?

The Mysteries of Harris Burdick

Additional Art Activities

Another book by Chris Van Allsburg is *The Mysteries of Harris Burdick*. In the introduction, we are told that the book contains 14 pictures from stories written by Burdick. The narrator tells us that many people have written stories to go with the pictures. Now it's your turn. Look at the pictures. Find one you like a lot, read the caption, and then write a story, poem, or script that goes with the idea and picture. For example, the first picture shows tiny globes of light coming through an open window into a boy's bedroom. Could the light blobs be aliens from another planet?

This book is a wonderful opportunity to use cooperative learning in an art and literature setting. Each group selects a picture (with title and caption) and writes the story. The imaginative results are shared with other groups and lend themselves to dramatization and media activities.

UNIT CLOSURE

A Caldecott Gallery of Art

When the students complete the units in "The Caldecott Club," they will have portfolios and journals with examples of art techniques used in favorite Caldecott books. Select a location for a Caldecott Gallery in which student work may be displayed. Pictures may be mounted and framed; stories, poems, and essays may be displayed, also.

Invite other classes to visit the Caldecott Gallery, and have individual students from the Caldecott Club serve as docents, or tour guides for the art exhibit. Parents may be invited to visit the gallery for a special tour, with juice and cookies served afterwards. Local newspapers and cable television producers are often happy to be invited to special events at school, and will showcase student work through the media.

When the exhibit of Caldecott-inspired student work closes, all work is returned to the artists and writers.

Extending the Caldecott Art Experience

Field trips to local museums and galleries can be an enriching extension of the Caldecott Club units. Students may be prepared for taking these trips in several ways.

One effective way is to suggest similarities between the works of artists in museums and galleries and illustrations by artists in Caldecott Medal books. If it is not possible to visit art museums or galleries, a similar comparison can be made by using art reference books from the library media center collection, or art prints may be ordered from vendor catalogs.

The following short list offers a comparison between Caldecott Medal authors and their specific books which resemble well-known artists and their paintings, sculpture, or other art pieces. This list may stimulate brainstorming efforts of teachers and students to develop a permanent document to be used as part of the arts and enrichment curriculum of the school.

An Art Match: Fine Arts and the Caldecott Medal Artists

Caldecott Book	Comparable Painting
Marcia Brown's *Shadow*	Makande peoples, Face Mask in the National Museum of African Art, Washington, DC
Robert McCloskey's *Time of Wonder*	Winslow Homer's "Breezin' Up," and Eugene Boudin's "On the Beach, Dieppe, 1864"
Caldecott Book	**Comparable Painting**
Robert McCloskey's *Make Way for Ducklings*	Winslow Homer's "Right & Left," National Gallery of Art, Washington, DC
Marcia Brown's *Cinderella,*	Boucher's "Madame Bergerat" and "The Swing," Pietro Longhi's "Blindman's Buff," National Gallery of Art, Washington, DC

STUDENT RESOURCES

Nonny Hogrogian:
Always Room for One More, Caldecott Medal, 1966
One Fine Day, Caldecott Medal, 1972

Robert McCloskey:
Make Way for Ducklings, Caldecott Medal, 1942
Time of Wonder, Caldecott Medal, 1958
Blueberries for Sal, Honor Book, 1949
One Morning in Maine, Honor Book, 1953
Journey Cake, Ho! Honor Book, 1954

Marcia Brown:
Cinderella, Caldecott Medal, 1955
Once a Mouse..., Caldecott Medal, 1962
Shadow, Caldecott Medal, 1983
Stone Soup, Honor Book, 1948
Henry Fisherman, Honor Book, 1950
Dick Whittington and His Cat, Honor Book, 1951
Skipper John's Cook, Honor Book, 1952
Puss in Boots, Honor Book, 1953

Barbara Cooney:
Chanticleer and the Fox, Caldecott Medal, 1959
Ox-Cart Man, Caldecott Medal, 1980

Leo and Diane Dillon:
Why Mosquitoes Buzz in People's Ears, Caldecott Medal, 1976
Ashanti to Zulu, Caldecott Medal, 1977

Chris Van Allsburg:
Jumanji, Caldecott Medal, 1982
The Polar Express, Caldecott Medal, 1986

PROFESSIONAL RESOURCES

Bader, Barbara. (1976). *American Picture Books: From Noah's Ark to the Beast Within.* New York: Macmillan.
Bromley, Karen d'Angelo. (1991). *Webbing with Literature: Creating Story Maps with Children's Books.* Boston: Allyn and Bacon.
Brooks, Susan W. and Susan M. Senatori. (1985). *See the Paintings! A Handbook for Art Appreciation in the Classroom.* Madison, WI.
Brown, Marcia. (1986). *Lotus Seeds: Children, Pictures and Books.* New York: Scribner.
Cendrars, Blaise. (1982). *Shadow.* Translated and illustrated by Marcia Brown. New York: Scribner.
Ciancola, Patricia. (1981a). *Illustrations in Children's Books, 2d ed.* Chicago: American Library Association.

————. (1981b). *Picture Books for Children, 2d ed.* Chicago: American Library Association.

Commire, Anne, ed. (1985). "Interview with Robert McCloskey." *Something About the Author: Facts and Pictures About Authors and Illustrators of Books for Young People, Vol. 39.* Detroit: Gale Research Co.

Dillon, Leo and Diane Dillon. (1976). Caldecott Acceptance Speech.

Elleman, Barbara. (1986). "Picture-Book Art: Evaluation." *Booklist,* June 15.

Hickman, Janet and Bernice C. Cullinan, eds. (1989). *Children's Literature in the Classroom: Weaving Charlotte's Web.* Norwood, MA: Christopher Gordon Publishers.

Hopkins, Lee Bennett. (1970). *Selections from Books Are by People.* New York: Scholastic Magazines, Inc.

Huck, Charlotte. (1987). *Children's Literature in the Elementary School,* 4th ed. New York: Holt, Rinehart, and Winston.

Janson, H.W. and Samuel Cauman. (1982). *History of Art for Young People, 2d ed.* New York: Abrams.

Kingman, Lee, ed. (1968). *Illustrators of Children's Books: 1957-1966.* Boston: Horn Book.

————. (1978). *Illustrators of Children's Books: 1967-1976.* Boston: Horn Book.

————. (1988). *Illustrators of Children's Books: 1977-1986.* Boston: Horn Book.

Klemin, Diana. (1966). *The Art of Art for Children's Books: A Contemporary Survey.* New York: Clarkson N. Potter, Inc.

Lacy, Lyn Ellen. (1986). *Art and Design in Children's Picture Books: An Analysis of Caldecott Award Winning Books.* Chicago: American Library Association.

Levy, Virginia K. (1988). *Let's Go to the Art Museum.* New York: Abrams.

Parnes, Sidney. (1990). *Better Thinking and Learning.* Baltimore: State Department of Education, Division of Instruction.

Perkins, David. (1988). *Dimensions of Thinking: A Framework for Curriculum and Instruction.* Alexandria, VA: Association for Supervision and Curriculum Development.

Sims, R. (1982). *Shadow and Substance: Afro-American Experience in Contemporary Children's Fiction.* Urbana, IL: National Council of Teachers of English.

Wallace, Elaine. (1990). *Dreams, Fantasy and Imagination: A Painting Unit.* Upper Marlboro, MD: Prince George's County Public Schools.

Worsham, Antoinette M. and Anita J. Stockton. (1986). *A Model for Teaching Thinking Skills: The Inclusion Process. (PDK Fastback 236).* Bloomington, IN: Phi Delta Kappa Educational Foundation.

3

The Cleary Club

INTRODUCTION

Beverly Cleary is universally recognized and loved for her childrens' books by teachers, parents, library media specialists, and bookstore personnel. But even more important are the ranks of children who have read and enjoyed her stories. Her fans trade personally owned copies of her books, borrow stacks of them from public and school libraries, and enjoy the companionship of reading together, with peers or parents. Cleary's stories remain relevant to children, and even though Ramona is now over 30 years old, her anxieties, temper tantrums, curiosity, and genuine kid behavior still captivate readers. Cleary's readers are grateful for a writer who has the ability to convey the way children feel and act in interesting stories peopled with likeable characters. There will probably come a time when one of Beverly Cleary's audience of early readers will do a longitudinal study of Henry Huggin's maturation as part of a doctoral dissertation. After all, Henry would be over 40 years old now! In a 1990 *Booklist* interview by Ilene Cooper, Ms. Cleary describes a review in which she is commended for "updating" the themes of her books by having Ramona's father lose his job. Cleary responded that she was able to write about the change in life style in the Quimby household because many years ago, during the Depression, her father had lost his job, too.

Young readers have developed a kinship and close relationship with Beverly Cleary, and trust her so completely that their requests for "another Cleary Book" are acknowledgments of their confidence in her ability to continue to provide lively books, with conversation and action moving at a concise, brisk pace. Characters who find themselves in the everyday predicaments that the readers have experienced, plots that move quickly and suspensefully to a satisfactory conclusion, and settings that are as familiar and comforting as the readers' own homes—these are the qualities that Cleary brings to her books, and the reasons why "Cleary books" are universally welcomed and enjoyed.

Building on the existing foundation of familiarity and affection for the books and characters invented by Cleary, educators can develop a lively and highly motivated framework for a unit in literary arts. One such plan is "The Cleary Club."

In this model, children are involved in a contract arrangement, by which they agree to read a certain book as a group experience, and to design and to develop independent activities and projects based on that book. They also agree to read other books by the same author as an independent activity, and to keep a journal of their thoughts and responses to the books they read. In return for these commitments, the students are awarded membership in "The Cleary Club," with all the rights and privileges of membership. Tangible privileges include a breakfast or luncheon in which all of the menu selections are chosen from family meals or special occasions described in various Cleary books. "Beezus Quimby's Birthday Cake" is always a popular choice—even without the baked-in Bendix doll!

The goal for the program is to have students enjoy reading for pleasure, and to extend this reading enjoyment beyond the classroom. By selecting the books written by Beverly Cleary and by using the organizational structure of a club, this goal should be comfortably met. A second goal is to have students learn the techniques of group discussion. For many children, this will be an introduction to the skills of brainstorming, and teachers should decide what will be the ground rules for student-leader interaction.

In a whole language or literature-based approach to the teaching of reading, many techniques and methods are available from which to choose. Creative teachers will combine strategies from different models and develop one that is custom-made for their students.

"THINK-PAIR-SHARE"

Dr. Frank Lyman of the University of Maryland suggests a cooperative learning strategy known as "Think-Pair-Share" (1991). In this model, students are taught to use a new response cycle in answering questions. The technique is easy to learn and can be used across many grade levels and group sizes. Dr. Lyman identifies the components of think-pair-share as follows:

- Students *listen* while the teacher poses a question.
- Students are given time in which to *think* of a response.

- Students are then sometimes cued to *pair* with a neighbor and discuss their responses.
- Finally, students are invited to *share* their responses with the whole group.

Students are given the time to think about what their own responses might be before someone answers the question and the group moves on to the next one. There is an opportunity to phrase a response mentally, and sometimes to discuss the answer verbally with a partner before being asked to share publicly. Student involvement is high, because each student gets a chance to share ideas with at least one other person in the group. The desire to be a contributing member of a group is very strong at the elementary school level, but it is sometimes inhibited by a fear of being laughed at or ignored by one's peers. This method generally works well because it encourages achievement, self-esteem, and acceptance by the group.

Most experienced teachers will admit that student time on task is directly related to the amount of involvement the student has in any given activity. When a student has a partner, and the two have decided on a response that they think is appropriate, the energy generated within the group is palpable. In addition, the wait time frequently leads to more thoughtful answers and better recall of information.

Teachers can also benefit from wait time, if they have confidence in their own powers to manage a group discussion. One of the benefits to teachers through the management of the "Think-Pair-Share" model, according to Dr. Lyman, is time to concentrate on asking higher-order questions, observing student reactions, and listening to student responses.

CORE THINKING SKILLS

In *Dimensions of Thinking: A Framework for Curriculum and Instruction* (Association for Supervision and Curriculum Development, 1988), another suggestion for group discussion management is described. The difference between critical thinking and creative thinking is stressed. Both thinking processes involve an understanding of *metacognition,* which refers to awareness and control of one's thinking, a thinking-about-thinking component.

Inherent in this model is an emphasis on the core thinking skills. The core thinking skills are the enablers of thinking, according to the Association for Supervision and Curriculum Development. Briefly stated, these core thinking skills include:

- *Focusing:* defining the problem and setting goals.
- *Information-gathering:* observing and formulating questions.

- *Remembering:* storing and retrieving information (recall) in long-term memory.
- *Organizing:* comparing, ordering, classifying, and representing.
- *Analyzing:* identifying attributes, relationships, and patterns; identifying main ideas and logical fallacies.
- *Generating:* inferring, predicting, elaborating.
- *Integrating:* summarizing and restructuring.
- *Evaluating:* establishing criteria and validating or confirming data.

This strategy is more individually oriented, and works well in a guided independent study of the works of specific authors. Elements of the model, however, lend themselves to group discussion techniques. Remembering the reasons why Ramona did not want Beezus and Mary Jane to take her to school on the first day can lead to a spirited discussion of first-day incidents as students recall personal experiences.

COOPERATIVE LEARNING

Cooperative learning is a method of organizing a classroom learning environment so that students at all levels of performance interact, working together in groups toward a common goal. Instead at competing as an individual against every other member of the class, the group is given the responsibility for creating a learning community where all students participate in significant ways. Initially, the teacher is the task setter, explaining the task in meaningful terms. In the model presented in this chapter, cooperative learning strategies are used.

Students are grouped and regrouped as reading and analysis of *Ramona the Pest* progresses.

Teaching Strategies	
The teacher:	**The students:**
creates and maintains an environment for group activity.	incorporate contributions of all group members.
takes care of physical arrangements.	create an effective working group.
facilitates recording of group responses and decisions.	discuss amicably and consider alternative points of view.

The teacher:	The students:
assists if needed.	reach a working consensus with other students.

Research findings presented by Jay McTighe and Barbara Reeves in the Maryland State Department of Education document "Better Thinking and Learning" (1990), indicate that

> teachers who employ cooperative learning methods promote learning because these collaborative experiences engage students in an interactive approach to processing information, resulting in greater retention of subject matter, improved attitudes toward learning, and enhanced relations among group members.

UNIT OBJECTIVES

Through the "Cleary Club," students will be able to:

- recognize that each Beverly Cleary book is composed of chapters.
- describe how each chapter advances the action of the plot, provides a logical progression or sequence of events, and contributes to the rising action of the plot.
- answer specific comprehension questions about the plot, characters, and setting of the book.
- participate in discussions of episodes in the book.
- predict events or a plot line on the basis of chapters previously read.
- perform activities designed around themes and characters of the book.

Teaching Strategies

1. The teacher:	The students:
explores with the students the idea of dividing a book into chapters.	offer theories and explanations.
asks, "Why do you think authors arrange their books by chapters?"	may respond in the following ways: "So the readers will have an idea of what's going to happen next."

1. The teacher:	**The students:** *(cont.)*
	"To keep readers interested in finishing the book."
	"So you only read a little bit of the book at a time."
	"As a plan or outline for the book."
	"To remind you where you were when you stopped reading."
asks students to open their books to the contents page and read the chapter headings silently.	read the page silently.
uses one of the questioning techniques for discussion.	
asks, "What do we know about this book so far?" "Who is going be the main character in the book?" "What are reasons for your answer?" "After reading the chapter titles, which chapter do you think you might like best?" "Which chapter sounds like Ramona might have some troubles?"	respond appropriately, using group discussion techniques.
assigns Chapter 1 to be read silently and explains that a group discussion of each chapter will follow.	read assigned chapter.
	record in journal a summary of the discussion about the reasons for the Table of Contents in a book.

2. The teacher:	**The students:**
explains that students will be placed in discussion groups and	decide on a group leader and recorder for each

2. The teacher:	The students: (*cont.*)
asks each group to appoint a and recorder.	discussion group. (*Note:* Student cooperative learning groups should be changed after each chapter so that interaction among peers is varied.)
distributes cards with discussion questions to consider, based on contents of each chapter.	conduct a discussion.
circulates to observe group dynamics and to assist where necessary.	
gives adequate time for groups to complete task.	
reassembles class for oral report on responses to the chapter questions.	present their group's consensus and participate in summarizing the chapter.

3. The teacher:	The students:
explains that since there are so many interesting episodes in each chapter, students may choose activities to complete from a selection on cards.	select an activity and complete it successfully.

UNIT ON BEVERLY CLEARY

Biographical Information

Beverly Bunn Cleary, originally of Yamhill, Oregon, had a childhood very similar to the endearing characters that people her books. Her memoir, *A Girl from Yamhill* (1988), describes a family caught in the Depression but retaining solid values of honesty, morality, and the Protestant work ethic.

Beverly Cleary recounts an incident that occurred in seventh grade where the school librarian also taught reading. For the first time, she was given an assignment to write a letter in which she and the other students in the class were to use their imaginations. Ms. Cleary writes, "All my life, Mother had told me to use my imagination, but I had never expected to be asked, or even allowed to use it in school."

Following this opportunity, Beverly Cleary was told to write an essay about a favorite book character. Since she had so many favorites, Ms. Cleary created a story about a girl who travels to Bookland and meets many characters from fiction. The author relates in her memoir: "I thought Journey to Bookland was a poor story because the girl's journey turned out to be a dream; and if there was anything I disliked it was a good story that ended up as a dream."

However, the teacher disagreed: "When Beverly grows up, she should write childrens' books."

When Beverly graduated from high school, opportunities for a college education were limited by the national economy. But her father supported her desire for a college education by letting her move to a distant cousin's home in California to attend a local community college. Her preparation for college was an extensive course in cake-baking, one of the tasks she was to assume in return for room and board.

Beverly Cleary never changed her mind about careers or writing. Undergraduate school at the University of California, Berkeley, was followed by graduate school at the University of Washington in Seattle, where she specialized in library services to children.

Marriage to Clarence Cleary and a family life that provided material for the childrens' books she wrote, and continues to write, round out a truly remarkable chronicle of an observant and talented writer. Beverly Cleary writes now for second-generation readers, as Ilene Cooper points on in a recent *Booklist* interview: "Yes," answers Ms. Cleary, "but the yardstick is still me—I think even today children feel very similarly about the things that happen to them. The emotions don't change that much."

Ramona the Pest

The Story

Ramona Quimby "was a girl who could not wait. Life was so interesting she had to find out what happened next."

That's how readers feel about *Ramona the Pest*. The chapters move so quickly through Ramona's first days in kindergarten. From the first day, when she and Howie were taken to school, Ramona always had high expectations. It wasn't *her* fault that Susan didn't like her curls "boinged," or that Davy's shirt buttons flew off when she chased and caught him. Ramona certainly couldn't have predicted that Miss Binney, her beloved teacher, would get a sore throat and that she, Ramona, would be taken to the principal's office for hiding on the playground to avoid the dreaded substitute. And even though Ramona eagerly awaited a rainy day so she could show off her new red boots, she certainly hadn't planned to get stuck in the mud and need to be rescued by Henry Huggins.

But Ramona was a girl who knew herself well. When she couldn't promise *not* to boing Susan's curls anymore, she recognized that the alternative was suspension from kindergarten.

A lost tooth, a kind teacher, and a family that loved and accepted Ramona for herself come together to provide a happy ending.

Discussion Questions for Chapter 1: "Ramona's Great Day"

1. What was the "great day" for Ramona?
2. Why did Ramona want her mother to take her to school, instead of having Beezus take her to kindergarten?
3. Why do you think Ramona was so impatient to go to kindergarten?
4. What was the first direction that Miss Binney gave to Ramona?
5. Why did Ramona think she must stay in her seat?
6. Have you ever been confused by words that have several meanings? Make a list of some of these kinds of words. (e.g., "weight" and "wait").
7. So far, which of the kindergarten students would you like to have for a friend?
8. Ramona was preparing to make a "great big noisy fuss" when Miss Binney sent her to time-out. What happened to make Ramona change her mind?
9. Do you think Ramona is going to like kindergarten as much as she hoped? Why or why not?
10. What positive things and what negative things happened to Ramona on her "great day."

Activity Suggestions for Chapter 1: "Ramona's Great Day"

1. Ramona made a mistake on the first day of school when she misunderstood Miss Binney and thought she would get a "present." Write about a time when you made a mistake at school and were embarrassed. You may start your story: "One mistake I don't want to make in school this year is...."
2. Draw a picture of Ramona as you think she looked on the first day of school. Write a short characterization of Ramona under the picture, like a caption in a yearbook or newspaper. List Ramona's good qualities, but you may also include some of her faults.
3. Write a paragraph about a present you have received. You may begin your story: "My favorite present was...."

4. Ramona thought the words to the song Miss Binney taught the class were "dawnzer lee light." Research "The Star Spangled Banner" and prepare a report on how it became our national anthem.
5. Ramona thought "Gray Goose" was a good game because she got to run. Select a game you like to play and write the directions for playing it. You may wish to use an outline of the steps to keep directions in correct sequence.
6. One of the funniest parts in Chapter 1 was Ramona's question about *Mike Mulligan and the Steam Shovel.* Write an answer for Miss Binney to tell the kindergarten that you feel would be satisfactory to them.

Discussion Questions for Chapter 2: "Show and Tell"

1. What happened to make Ramona realize that Miss Binney understood Ramona's pride in her doll?
2. When Miss Binney tied the ribbon on Ramona's old rabbit, Ramona thought of many ways she could use it. List some of the things Ramona thought of. Can you add additional things to do?
3. Why do you think both Howie and Ramona wanted the ribbon so badly? Which character do you think deserved it more: Howie or Ramona? Give reasons for your choice.
4. Howie and Ramona agreed to a plan so that Ramona could have Miss Binney's gift ribbon. Why do you think Ramona wanted the ribbon so badly?
5. The children solved their problem by making a bargain, but the mothers put off making a decision. Do you think kids get along better when their parents do not try to help out? Why or why not?
6. Do you agree with Beezus' feelings about Show and Tell? Why or why not?

Activity Suggestions for Chapter 2: "Show and Tell"

1. Find the part in Chapter 2 in which Ramona thinks about her feelings about sharing. Read it and then write a story about a time you had to share something with a friend or family member.
2. Read the part in Chapter 2 when Miss Binney asks if anyone brought something to show the class. Rewrite the scene as a play with dialogue. How many characters will there be? Will there be a narrator? Where should the scene end?
3. Howie liked to work with tools. Write directions for taking something apart. Tell what tools will be needed, and give step-by-step directions. Make sure the directions are in correct order.

4. Draw two pictures: one of Beezus' doll Chevrolet and one of the chewed-up rabbit Ramona shared with Howie. Use the descriptions of the toys to make your pictures accurate. Be sure to color the pictures. Choose one sentence from the story to describe each toy.

Discussion Questions for Chapter 3: "Seat Work"

1. What were the two kinds of children who went to kindergarten? Which kind was Ramona. Give reasons for your answer.
2. Why do you think Ramona enjoyed chasing Davy so much. How do you think Davy felt about being chased?
3. How was seat work different from the "running part" of kindergarten?
4. What did Ramona expect to learn in kindergarten?
5. How did Ramona make handwriting more interesting?
6. Ramona was pleased when Miss Binney admired her picture. What happened to make Miss Binney cross later?
7. By trying to help Davy, Ramona caused a problem in kindergarten. Have you ever done something you thought would be helpful and have it turn out wrong? Share the experience with your group.
8. Ramona did some creative art work with the letter "Q". Why do you think Miss Binney smiled at Ramona's letter, but became impatient with Davy's "D"?

Activity Suggestions for Chapter 3: "Seat Work"

1. Ramona decorated her initial "Q" so that it looked like a cat. Make an alphabet board using Ramona's ideas for making pictures out of initials.
2. Chapter 3 has some action-packed verbs. Find the following words in your dictionary and write the meaning the word has in the story: scrambled, shrieked, accused, tagged, scurried, scribbled, glared, mussed.
3. Miss Binney changed from a sweet and kindly teacher to a stern one in this chapter. Find the part starting with Miss Binney telling Ramona to sit down. Then perform the short scene as a Reader's Theater. Remember to leave out the description and narrative parts. You will need a narrator, Miss Binney, and Davy. Show how Miss Binney, changed by changing voices.
4. "The more Ramona saw of Davy, the better she liked him." What do you look for in a friend? Write a paragraph describing qualities you admire and why your friends have these traits. You may include what you like to do with friends, and a time when your friend made you feel happy or hurt your feelings.

Discussion Questions for Chapter 4: "The Substitute"

1. What does this chapter title tell us? What do you think is going to happen?
2. How did the children feel when they found out Miss Binney was not at school? Find parts of the story as evidence.
3. Why do you think Ramona decided to hide and not go into the kindergarten room? Do you think she made a good decision? Why or why not?
4. Ramona had lots of different feelings when she was hiding behind the trash cans. What did she feel about herself? the children in her kindergarten class?
5. What kind of a person was Miss Mullen, the school principal? Give examples from the story. What do you think about the way Miss Mullen handled Ramona? What would you have done if you were the principal?

Activity Suggestions for Chapter 4: "The Substitute"

1. The kindergarten children were very confused and anxious when they saw the substitute teacher in their class. Write a paragraph from the *substitute's* point of view. How did Mrs. Wilcox feel about teaching 29 kindergarten students? *Did* she know the rules of the kindergarten? Give reasons for your answer.
2. When Ramona hid herself behind the trash cans she began to feel very sorry for herself. Find the part that begins, "Except for Ribsy, Ramona was lonely." Then have a friend read the paragraph while you act out Ramona's feelings.
3. Prepare an advertisement for a substitute teacher. Include all the things you believe a substitute should know and be able to do.
4. By the end of Chapter 4, we know a lot about Ramona's character. Prepare a *web* describing Ramona. (Her name should be in the center box, and characteristics should be written on lines coming out of the box. Include good and bad habits.)

Discussion Questions for Chapter 5: "Ramona's Engagement Ring"

1. In this chapter, Ramona shows that she is a leader in her class. What are some of the things that happen that prove this?
2. How did Ramona act when she had to wear Howie's old brown boots? How did she act in her new red boots? Find and read aloud the parts of the chapter that describe the two events.
3. This chapter takes place mainly on rainy days. How does the weather make this a funny chapter? List at least three things that happen because of the rain.

4. In the beginning of the chapter, Ramona "shows off" by wearing a pink worm on her finger as an "engagement ring." Who does Ramona finally decide to "be engaged" to? Do you think she made a good choice? Why or why not?
5. Miss Binney again shows her kindness when Ramona gets stuck in the mud. Describe how a teacher was understanding to you during an embarrassing time.

Activity Suggestions for Chapter 5: "Ramona's Engagement Ring"

1. Ramona loved rainy days. Find the part of the chapter describing all the things she did in the rain before Howie arrived to walk to school with her. Then write a journal entry about a rainy day. You may begin your journal entry, "Today is a rainy day. I love rainy days because....But sometimes I don't like rainy days because...."
2. Write a script for a TV news show, consisting of three parts: (a) One part should be the weather forecast. (b) One part should be a news segment about Ramona being stuck in the mud. (c) One part should be an interview with Henry Huggins, who rescued Ramona. Then videotape the news show with friends.
3. Ramona thought that a tow truck might pull her out of the mud. Draw a plan for an invention that could remove people from mud. Describe and label parts of the invention and tell how it works.
4. Ramona got a lot of attention with her "engagement ring." Draw a comic strip about the events in Chapter 5. Be sure to have the comic strip panels show what happened in order (Ramona arriving in her old brown boots, picking up the worm, etc.).
5. When Ramona got her new shoes, she spent a lot of time trip-trapping in them, pretending to be one of the Billy Goats Gruff. Dramatize that scene, using improvisational techniques.
6. Getting new shoes is fun, and getting the *box* is great, too. List as many things as you can think of to do with a shoebox. Then choose one, and do it. (A diorama of a scene from the story is a good choice.)

Discussion Questions for Chapter 6: "The Baddest Witch in the World"

1. Why do you think Ramona decided to be a witch for Halloween?
2. Have you ever scared yourself with a costume and mask? Describe how you felt when you saw yourself in the mirror.

3. Howie's mother always talks as if Howie weren't present. What were some of the reasons Mrs. Kemp was not able to make Howie a pirate costume?

4. When Ramona realized that no one could recognize her behind her witch mask, how did she feel?

5. What did Ramona do to make sure everyone knew who she was? Why was it so important to Ramona that people know who she was?

Activity Suggestions for Chapter 6: "The Baddest Witch in the World"

1. Chapter 6 has a lot of events and characters. Prepare a story map showing what happens in this chapter. You may use this model:

Story Map Model

Title: _____

Setting: [   ]

Problem: [   ]

        Event 1 _____

        Event 2 _____

        Event 3 _____

        Event 4 _____

        Event 5 _____

Solution: [   ]

Characters: _____   _____
                    _____   _____
                    _____   _____

---

2. Design a mask that you think is frightening. You will need to research different kinds of masks. The Fine Arts section of the public library or your school library media center has many colorful and informative books about masks.

3. Prepare a catalog of Halloween costumes. Find pictures of interesting costumes in magazines and other publications. Cut them out and paste them in a notebook with a paragraph about each one and which character in *Ramona the Pest* should wear the costumes.

4. Ramona needed to make a sign that would let everyone know who she was behind the scary mask. Design and make a bumper sticker or a sign that would let people know who you are. (You can use symbols and pictures, too.)

5. Mrs. Kemp tells Mrs. Quimby a long story about why Howie doesn't have a pirate costume. Find that part of the chapter and make a cause and effect chart using what happened to Mrs. Kemp. You may use this model:

Cause and Effect Chart		
CAUSE		EFFECT
When_____did this, this happened_____.		
Next,_____and so_____.		
(Continue the pattern.)		

Discussion Questions for Chapter 7: "The Day Things Went Wrong"

1. When Ramona got a loose tooth, why was she suspicious about the existence of the tooth fairy?
2. Susan calls Ramona a "pest." Why do you think Ramona reacted so angrily? What was the *worst* thing a child could be called in kindergarten, according to Ramona's class?
3. Why does Miss Binney send Ramona home from school?
4. What would you do to punish Ramona if *you* were the teacher? Do you think Ramona's punishment was fair? Why or why not?

Activity Suggestions for Chapter 7: "The Day Things Went Wrong"

1. "Ramona loved Miss Binney for being understanding. She loved Miss Binney for not being cross when she was late for school. She loved Miss Binney for telling her she was a brave girl." Make a list of qualities *you* look for most in a teacher. Think about teachers who have made you feel good about yourself, and why. When the list is complete, prepare a Nomination for Best Teacher in the World, using your list of characteristics in composing the paragraph.
2. Research "teeth" in the library media center. Prepare a short report on why teeth really fall out, and the process of regrowth. Include a section on how to care for teeth properly.

Discussion Questions for Chapter 8: "Kindergarten Dropout"

1. What does Mrs. Quimby mean when she says to Ramona, "Miss Binney may not like some of the things you do, but she likes you"?

2. Ramona overheard Miss Binney call her "bright and imaginative" but also describe her as having a "negative desire for attention," during the conference with Mrs. Quimby. What does Miss Binney mean? Describe five events in the book that are examples of Ramona's "negative desire for attention."

3. Ramona finally has a chance to use the "new word" she learned on the first day of school—"dawnser." Why do you think the author puts this funny scene in the middle of a sad chapter?

4. How does Ramona act after she gets home from school? How do you think you would feel if you were suspended from school?

5. How does Ramona decide to handle going back to school? Is it a realistic solution? Why or why not?

6. How did Mrs. Quimby like having Ramona at home during the morning? Find parts of the chapter to support your answer.

7. What happens to show Ramona that her teacher really cares for her? Is this a satisfactory ending for the story? How would you have the story end?

Activity Suggestions for Chapter 8: "Kindergarten Dropout"

1. Put yourself in Ramona's shoes. Write a diary of events that happened during the time you were suspended from kindergarten. Use the information in Chapter 8 as a guide, but imagine what Ramona would have thought and written in her diary. You might begin, "Something sad happened to me today...."

2. Interview your parents or older relatives about events from their childhood. You can ask permission to record the interviews on videotape or audiotape. You may want to ask if they recall being sent home from school, and how they felt when things went wrong with their friends. Share the interview with your literary arts group.

3. Imagine that you are Ramona. Write a letter to an advice column like "Dear Abby" and describe what has happened to you. Then, imagine you are "Dear Abby," and answer Ramona's letter.

4. Compose a "rap" or rhyming narrative of the "Kindergarten Dropout" chapter. Describe the incidents as they happened to Ramona in the order that they occurred.

5. In Chapter 8, Ramona's whole family comes together. Draw a series of pictures illustrating incidents in which Mr. and Mrs. Quimby, Beezus, and Ramona were doing something together. Make your pictures as detailed and dramatic as possible.

6. If there were to be another chapter in *Ramona the Pest*, what do you think it would be about? What would happen when Ramona went back to kindergarten class? How do you think Susan would greet Ramona's return? Who in the class would be most glad to see her back? If you have access to a computer, use a word processing program to prepare the chapter. Then, think of a good title for the chapter.

7. Beverly Cleary, the author of *Ramona the Pest*, was a childrens' librarian before she became an author. Research information about Ms. Cleary's life and career, and script an interview with the author. The interview may be produced on videotape for viewing by the group.

8. Participate in a panel discussion of the book, *Ramona the Pest*. Using what you have learned about plot, character, and setting, review the book and give reasons for your recommendations based on selections from the book.

UNIT CLOSURE

To close the Cleary Club unit, the teacher can help students organize a Cleary Club Festival or a Cleary Club Museum.

Review of *Ramona the Pest*	
The teacher:	**The students:**
summarizes the story.	participate in discussion when appropriate.
reviews plot, characters, and setting.	
reviews biographical data about author.	
provides a book list for independent reading of Cleary books. (List appears at the end of this chapter.)	use book list to select additional books by Cleary for reading.

The Cleary Festival

For the Cleary Festival, students can select and prepare a menu of Cleary Club foods to be served to guests specially invited to view displays and performances of projects the students have drawn from their Cleary Club portfolios.

Planning and Implementing a Cleary Festival

1. The teacher:
asks students to make notes
in their journals on
specific foods, meals, etc.
mentioned in Cleary books they
are reading.

explains that they will be using
this food list as the basis of the
menu for the Cleary Festival.

provides adequate time for
independent reading.

collects journals and classifies
"Cleary Food Notes" according to
meal courses—salad, main dish,
desserts, types of meals.

groups students by courses in
a cooperative learning
arrangement.

circulates and helps plan menu
when assistance is needed.

leads discussion of menu with the
entire group.

encourages volunteers to design
menu and invitations; to serve
luncheon; to provide food and
dishes.

The students:
take notes as reading
progresses.

read at their own pace.

submit journals for
analysis and evaluation.

participate in group
process.

seek help when needed.

participate in discussion.

select committee.

2. The teacher:
coordinates Cleary Festival with
teachers, cafeteria schedule, and
other school personnel.

asks students to select a favorite
project from their portfolios to
display, perform, or show as part of
a Cleary Museum.

coordinates arrangements for the
Cleary Club Festival.

distributes awards and certificates
for Cleary Club membership.

The students:
prepare for Cleary
Festival.

contribute project.

participate in festival.

accept awards.

The Cleary Museum

The Cleary Museum may be arranged in the library media center, the classroom, or in a section of the building designated as the gallery. Some teachers who have used this model invite parents to attend a special tea or afternoon/evening meeting to view the projects completed by literary arts students. Performance pieces are staged during these meetings. Journals kept by students are returned to them, with encouraging and positive comments about the quality of the work. When the unit is completed, students readily observe the ascending difficulty of both the questions and the activities. As their skills in using the core thinking skills and cooperative learning model improve, they are prompted to try higher-level thinking skills in other areas of literature.

BOOKS BY BEVERLY CLEARY

Beezus and Ramona. Illusrated by Louis Darling. New York: Dell, 1980.
Beezus and Ramona. New York: Avon, 1990.
The Beezus and Ramona Diary. Illustrated by Alan Tiegreen. New York: Morrow, 1986.
Cutting Up with Ramona. Illustrated by JoAn L. Scribner. New York: Dell, 1983.
Dear Mr. Henshaw. Illusrated by Paul O. Zelinsky. New York: Morrow, 1983.
Dear Mr. Henshaw. (Large type edition). Santa Barbara, CA: ABC-CLIO, 1987.
Ellen Tebbits. Illustrated by Louis Darling. New York: Morrow, 1951.
Ellen Tebbits. New York: Avon, 1977.
Ellen Tebbits. New York: Dell, 1979.
Emily's Runaway Imagination. Illustrated by Joe and Beth Krush. New York: Morrow, 1961.
Emily's Runaway Imagination. New York: Dell, 1980.
Fifteen. New York: Dell, 1980.
A Girl from Yamhill: A Memoir. New York: Morrow, 1988.
A Girl from Yamhill. New York: Dell, 1989.
The Growing-Up Feet. Illustrated by DyAnne DiSalvo-Ryan. New York: Morrow, 1987.
The Growing-Up Feet. New York: Dell, 1988.
Henry and Beezus. Illustrated by Louis Darling. New York: Morrow, 1952.
Henry and Beezus. New York: Dell, 1979.
Henry and Ribsy. Ilustrated by Louis Darling. New York: Morrow, 1954.
Henry and the Clubhouse. Illustrated by Louis Darling. New York: Morrow, 1962.
Henry and the Clubhouse. New York: Dell, 1979.
Henry and the Paper Route. Illustrated by Louis Darling. New York: Morrow, 1957.

Henry Huggins. Illustrated by Louis Darling. New York: Morrow, 1957.

Henry Huggins. (Translated into Spanish by Argentina Palacios). New York: Morrow, 1983.

Janet's Thingamajigs. Illustrated by DyAnne DiSalvo-Ryan. New York: Dell, 1988.

Jean and Johnny. Illustrated by Joe and Beth Krush. New York: Morrow, 1959.

The Luckiest Girl. New York: Dell, 1980.

Lucky Chuck. Illustrated by J. Winslow Higginbottom. New York: Morrow, 1984.

Meet Ramona Quimby, 5 books, including *Ramona and Her Family; Ramona and Her Mother; Ramona Forever; Ramona Quimby, Age Eight; Ramona the Pest.* New York: Dell, 1980.

Mitch and Amy. Illustrated by George Porter. New York: Morrow, 1967.

The Mouse and the Motorcycle. Illustrated by Louis Darling. New York: Morrow, 1965.

The Mouse and the Motorcycle. New York: Avon, 1980.

The Mouse and the Motorcycle. New York: Dell, 1980.

The Mouse and the Motorcycle. (Large type edition). Santa Barbara, CA: ABC-CLIO, 1989.

Muggie Maggie. Edited by David Reuther. Illustrated by Kay Life. New York: Morrow, 1990.

Otis Spofford. Illustrated by Louis Darling. New York: Morrow, 1953.

Otis Spofford. New York: Avon, 1990.

Ralph S. Mouse. Illustrated by Paul O. Zelinsky. New York: Morrow, 1982.

Ralph S. Mouse. New York: Dell, 1983.

Ralph S. Mouse. (Large type edition). Santa Barbara, CA: ABC-CLIO, 1989.

Ramona and Her Father. Illustrated by Alan Tiegreen. New York: Morrow, 1977.

Ramona and Her Father. New York: Dell, 1979.

Ramona and Her Father. (Large type edition). Santa Barbara, CA: ABC-CLIO, 1988.

Ramona and Her Father. New York: Avon, 1990.

Ramona and Her Friends. New York: Dell, 1980.

Ramona and Her Mother. New York: Morrow, 1979.

Ramona and Her Mother. New York: Avon. 1990.

Ramona Forever. Illustrated by Alan Tiegreen. Morrow, 1984.

Ramona Forever. New York: Dell, 1985.

Ramona Forever. (Large type edition). Santa Barbara, CA: ABC-CLIO, 1989.

Ramona Quimby, Age Eight. Illustrated by Alan Tiegreen. Morrow, 1981.

Ramona Quimby, Age Eight. New York: Dell, 1982.

Ramona Quimby, Age Eight. (Large type edition). Santa Barbara, CA: ABC-CLIO, 1987.

The Ramona Quimby Diary. Illustrated by Alan Tiegreen. New York: Morrow, 1984.

Ramona the Brave. Illustrated by Alan Tiegreen. New York: Morrow, 1975.

Ramona the Brave. New York: Dell, 1984.

Ramona the Brave. (Large type edition). Santa Barbara, CA: ABC-CLIO, 1990.

Ramona the Pest. Illustrated by Louis Darling. New York: Morrow, 1968.

Ramona the Pest. New York: Dell, 1982.

Ramona the Pest. (Translated into Spanish by Argentina Palacios). New York: Morrow, 1984.

Ramona the Pest. (Large type edition). Santa Barbara, CA: ABC-CLIO, 1990.

The Real Hole. Revised edition. Illustrated by Mary Stevens. New York: Morrow, 1986.

The Real Hole. New York: Dell, 1987.

Ribsy. Illustrated by Louis Darling. New York: Morrow, 1964.

Ribsy. Illustrated by Louis Darling. New York: Dell, 1982.

Runaway Ralph. New York: Morrow, 1970.

Runaway Ralph. New York: Dell, 1981.

Sister of the Bride. Illustrated by Beth and Joe Krush. New York: Morrow, 1963.

Sister of the Bride. New York: Dell, 1981.

Socks. Illustrated by Beatrice Darwin. New York: Morrow, 1973.

Socks. New York: Dell, 1980.

Strider. New York: Morrow: 1991.

Two Dog Biscuits. Revised edition. Illustrated by DyAnne DiSalvo-Ryan. New York: Morrow, 1986.

PROFESSIONAL RESOURCES

Association for Supervision and Curriculum Development. (1988). *Dimensions of Thinking: A Framework for Curriculum and Instruction.* Washington, DC.

Cleary, Beverly. (1988). *A Girl from Yamhill: A Memoir.* New York: William Morrow.

———. (1982). *Ramona the Pest.* Illustrated by Louis Darling. New York: William Morrow.

Cooper, Ilene. (1990). "Beverly Cleary." *Booklist,* October 15.

Laughlin, Mildred Knight and Letty S. Watt. (1986). *Developing Learning Skills through Children's Literature: An Idea Book for K-5 Classrooms and Libraries.* Phoenix, AZ: Oryx Press.

Lyman, Frank. (1991). "Think-Pair-Share: A Cooperative Learning Strategy." Howard County Public Schools and the University of Maryland.

McTighe, Jay and Barbara Reeves. (1990). *Better Thinking and Learning.* Maryland State Department of Education, Division of Instruction.

4

Contemporary Realistic Fiction

INTRODUCTION

"You know that book we're reading in Literary Arts?"

Dialogues in the library media center frequently begin this way. One is expected to respond positively, or at least with, "Hmmmm...give me a clue."

On a recent afternoon, the student was referring to a Walter Dean Myers novel, *Scorpions*. "Look at this," he invites, pulling a clipping from a local newspaper from the paperback he's holding. "It" is an account of a fight between two opposing "crews"—gangs of preteens—on a playground in our city. A gun had been fired, a young man critically injured. "See, it's *exactly* like the scene in this book," the student smiles. "This Myers guy knows what he's writin' about!" he confides, and takes the clipping back. One has the feeling that a critique has just been offered. "This Myers guy" is a credible author of realistic fiction.

This chapter examines contemporary realistic fiction in children's books, concentrating on authors who invent stories that deal with events, emotions, and responses that emphasize the ordinariness of daily life. In literature, as in life, events are frequently related. A knowledge of *how* events are connected in a novel enriches the reading experience. When intermediate-level students (grades five through seven) are invited to explore events in a story either through time-ordered action or through cause-and-effect, comprehension is heightened and literature becomes more meaningful.

For many students, reading about death, either accidental (*Bridge to Terabithia*) or violent (*Scorpions*), may be a first-time experience in literature. Sensitive authors recognize the inexperience of readers in dealing with concepts of dysfunctional families, prejudice, violence, illness, or death, and use their writing skills to create plots that are peopled with realistic characters who *are* able to cope with troubling events in life, or at least know where to seek help.

Conversely, authors of realistic fiction introduce readers to characters who are members of cheerful, upbeat families (Anastasia Krupnik or Bingo Brown) and milieus that are recognizable neighborhood communities. In such settings, writers can create events that are fun to read about because these story lines reflect places and people similar to those in a reader's experience.

Jill Paton Walsh, a respected author of children's books, reflected on the "art of realism," in an essay in *Celebrating Children's Books* (1981). "The first point that one must make about realism, is that it, too, is fantasy. Realistic fiction is about imaginary people, living in imagined contexts, doing what was never done, saying what was never said."

Realistic fiction books that endure have a sense of scene, of character, or of happening. Although students cannot name the elements of fiction, they remember a narrative pace, an emotional involvement with the characters, places described, an aura of danger, or a certain vigor or zest in the development of the plot.

Edna Johnson, in a foreword to *Anthology of Children's Literature, 4th edition*, speaks of the awareness of children to the "wholeness" of a book. Johnson points out that children are natural literary critics. "They welcome the presence of theme, idea, motif, and revelation when these are inherent in the story....Subtleties of approach, the sustaining of a mood are understood."

And children come to regard particular authors as special friends and confidantes. In selecting authors for in-depth study in a literary arts curriculum, many prolific writers suggest themselves for consideration. This chapter highlights the books of Walter Dean Myers and Betsy Byars, as representatives of multicultural authors who have written realistic fiction on many levels of readability for students in grades five through seven.

The difference in reading difficulty is also a new experience for many students, accustomed to the pace of Matt Christopher in his sports stories, or Beverly Cleary in her books. The concept that the same author who wrote *Scorpions,* Walter Dean Myers, also wrote the fun-filled *Moondance* stories is hard to grasp. In the classroom, books are usually presented developmentally, with the science textbook introducing concepts in a gradually ascending hierarchy. But in an integrated literature program, students are encouraged to select books that extend across a wide range of student reading abilities.

The seminar setting for book discussion and the individual reading conference introduced in this chapter enable teacher and student to explore the range of ideas, themes, and skillful presentation that different authors bring to their body of work.

"At first I thought that the writer wrote an easy book, to kind of get you interested, and then as the author got famous, the books got harder," one student wrote in a journal entry. "But now I know that authors just write about the next good idea they get, and if the characters are older or do more dramatic things, it's because that's just the way they are."

Again, the literary arts curriculum has two strands: reading for enjoyment, and reading to build necessary skills. Questions to stimulate quality thinking are analyzed, and student activities related to the author's body of work in realistic fiction are suggested. A group of questions that explore literary analysis are included as a means of evaluating students' understanding of foreshadowing, irony, and figurative language. A model for conducting individual reading conferences with students, and a structure for a student-teacher seminar discussion is described.

CRITERIA FOR REALISTIC FICTION

Paula Kay Montgomery (1977, p. 90) offers a group of questions that readers and evaluators should ask themselves when reading realistic fiction. Her suggestions are arranged by narrative, from theme through tone. They are valid considerations and appropriate to use with students as they explore books designated as realistic. Criteria of plot, characterization, style, and setting are highlighted in this chapter:

1. *Plot:*
- Is the action expressed in a series of interrelated forces?
- Are the incidents part of a well-knit plan appropriate to the other story elements?
- Do the events follow one another in a logical progression?
- Is there a logical and orderly progression from one action to another?
- Are the actions plausible?

2. *Characterization:*
- Is the character convincing?
- Do characters convey individuality?
- Do the characters lend themselves to reader identification?
- Is there believable character development?

3. *Style:*
- Is there originality in the author's expression of the story?
- Is there clarity, order, and unity to the writing?
- Have exact words been used to describe setting? actions?

4. *Setting:*
- Does the setting support the story?
- Are descriptions incorporated smoothly into the story?

These questions may be given to students during the introduction to the study of realistic fiction. As students read, either in a guided setting or as individuals, access to these criteria may provide a helpful guide.

The purpose for reading realistic fiction should be to guide students to recognize fiction as a literary form, and to apply literal, interpretive, and critical thinking skills to a selection. Fiction should *not* be used as a forum for amateur psychotherapy. Again, Jill Paton Walsh has some salient comments to make in "The Art of Realism" (1981):

> Though it is possible to learn from books of fiction, it is not possible to teach with them; though it is possible for a book to heal psychic wounds, it is not possible to use books for the practice of psychic medicine....
>
> To know with whom readers will identify in a book you have to know how they see themselves. That will often not be how we see them.

ENTRY LEVELS FOR A UNIT ON REALISTIC FICTION

Depending on the degree of literature immersion that students have experienced in the primary grades, teachers and other guides may consider three different entry levels for studying realistic fiction.

First, if students have had little experience with formal response to literature, the entry level should be a format in which all students read the same book and participate in a series of class discussions of the book with the teacher as discussion leader. This chapter provides a model for students at Entry Level 1, using Betsy Byar's Newbery Award-winning book, *Summer of the Swans*. The guided reading format establishes a rapport among readers and provides an environment for the exchange of ideas about the plot, characters, and setting of a book that all have read. Once students feel comfortable at this level, groups can go on to the second level of book discussion: the small-group seminar and the individual reading conference.

If students have had previous experience in a literature-based curriculum, teachers may decide to start directly at the second entry level. In this model, students read independently from a choice of contemporary realistic fiction by selected authors, and discuss their reading with other students who have read the same books independently, or engage in a one-to-one conversation with an adult (teacher or volunteer) who has also read the selected book. Ideas for using this method are offered using selected books written by Walter Dean Myers.

From this second level of entry, groups can proceed naturally to the third entry level: an enrichment unit dedicated to the study of characterization and other elements introduced with contemporary fiction but extended to include literary analysis, writing, drama, and art.

When students begin to recognize techniques authors use to create well-rounded, believable characters, and are able to become involved with these characters on an emotional level, two things happen. Readers see a similarity between conflicts faced by fictional characters and problems they, too, face; and students are able to make tentative connections from contemporary fiction that emphasize the universal themes that permeate all good literature.

Entry Level 1: Guided Group Discussion

Chapter 3 provides the foundation for book discussion, developing a taxonomy of thinking skills through careful questioning. In preparing for the guided discussions, teachers may wish to consider the following list of questions.

Questions to Stimulate Quality Thinking

1. *Knowledge*: Identification and recall of information.
   - Who, what, when, where, how _____?
   - Describe_____.
2. *Comprehension:* Organization and selection of facts and ideas.
   - Retell_____in your own words.
   - What is the main idea of _____?
3. *Application:* Use of facts, rules, principles.
   - How is_____an example of_____?
   - How is_____related to_____?
   - Why is_____significant?
4. *Analysis:* Separation of a whole into component parts.
   - What are the parts or features of_____?
   - Classify _____ according to_____.

- Outline/diagram/web_____.
- How does_____compare/contrast with_____?
- What evidence can you list for_____?

5. *Synthesis:* Combination of ideas to form a new whole.
   - What would you predict/infer from_____?
   - What ideas can you add to_____?
   - How would you create/design a new_____?
   - What might happen if you combined_____with_____?
   - What solution would you suggest for_____?

6. *Evaluation:* Development of opinions, judgments, or decisions.
   - Do you agree_____?
   - What do you think about_____?
   - What is the most important_____?
   - Place_____in order of priority.
   - How would you decide about_____?
   - What criteria would you use to assess_____?

Entry Level 2: Seminars and Individual Reading Conferences

This unit of study of the books written by Betsy Byars may be developed in several ways. Using the model proposed is an opportunity to either review, or introduce, the dynamics of group book discussion. When the group process for literature discussion is comfortably in place, teachers may wish to explain the method of individual book conferences following a group experience.

In a literature-based reading program, independent reading must be given *status,* as an integral part of the day—not just something for students and teachers to do when all the "important" work is done. The literature-based, whole-language approach to teaching reading is designed to develop positive, skilled lifelong reading habits, and to guide students to recognize, analyze, interpret and evaluate literary works.

When individual reading conferences are utilized, the emphasis should be on teacher (or volunteer adult) and student as colleagues, brought together by mutual enjoyment of reading books by a favorite author.

Before a program based on individual reading conferences can begin, teachers must consider two important aspects: (1) the practical one of record-keeping, organization, and management, and (2) the guidelines for discussion or interviewing techniques that are consistent throughout the program.

Among the practical elements is a decision on how records will be kept. One model used in a literary arts curriculum has students keeping records of books read in their reading journals, not as a competitive device to see who reads the most books, but as a frame of reference for a discussion with library media specialist, teacher, or adult volunteer. The students record the title of the book, the date the book was completed, and special points to be brought out in discussion: plot development, characterization, and literary qualities that make the book enjoyable or problematical.

In turn, the teacher maintains anecdotal records in the teacher journal, with brief annotations about students' responses to the books read, their levels of understanding, their use of higher-order thinking skills in analyzing plots and themes, and their strengths in reading skill development.

At the end of the unit, the student reading journals are collected and evaluated in two areas: content and mechanics. This twofold determination enables both teacher and students to see progress over a period of time, and accountability is maintained as a factor in the ubiquitous, but necessary grade.

A second practical consideration is availability of books that are necessary for a group study of the work of a single author. Paperback collections should contain multiple copies of selected authors' books. Careful planning between library media specialist, teachers, and administrators must be a major consideration. Budget constraints and the need for a balanced library media collection need to be addressed in planning the literary arts curriculum. Solutions to this problem are often found through book fair profits, fund-raising efforts, and other money-generating means. When a staff and faculty are truly committed to a whole-language approach to teaching reading, financial matters can be amicably addressed.

One other factor needs to be considered in planning independent reading conferences, and that is the idea of *incentives.* In earlier chapters, incentives were group-oriented events such as celebrations, festivals, art showings, and special meals.

Motivating readers continues to be a strong goal in the literary arts program, but food rewards are no longer of primary importance. Instead, reading can often be encouraged by awarding stickers, paperback copies of a student's favorite book, a field trip to hear a familiar author, or other imaginative incentives devised by teachers and library media specialists. One library media specialist who spent summers at the ocean accumulated many sharks' teeth, and distributed them as tokens or prizes as part of a "Shark Club Reading: We Devour Books!" For landbound readers whose major knowledge of sharks was through the excitement of the film *Jaws!,* this was a considerable incentive to read voraciously.

A series of case studies in Joellie Hancock and Susan Hill's *Literature-Based Reading Programs at Work* (1987) describes a set of questions that are appropriate for discussion in an individual reading conference. These questions are intended to stimulate the student reader to think about the book and apply higher order thinking skills to an analysis of plot, character, and setting. Questions include:

- What does the author want to share with you? (Plot and theme)
- What are the people in the story like? (Characters)
- Which character do you like? Why?
- Is there any character you dislike? Why?
- Does the (central) character change through the story?
- Do you like the ending? Why? Why not? (Resolution)
- Did any part of the story surprise you? Why? Why not? (Conflict)

It may be helpful to post a suggested list of questions that may be addressed during an individual reading conference. Such questions provide students with guidelines for notetaking in their reading journals and assist them in arriving at a conference both prepared and confident.

Kathleen Graham, in *Literature-Based Reading Programs at Work* (1987), suggests a format for the individual reading conferences. Graham approaches the reading conference using six points of reference.

Rapport between the adult interviewer and the student reader is critical; the interviewer must make the child feel at ease. Usually a simple welcoming, friendly comment is enough to establish this rapport.

Sharing emphasizes the dialogue aspects of the conference. Adult leaders must make a commitment to listen actively to the student's personal response to a book and to guide the discussion to succeeding points through appropriate comments.

Questioning enables the teacher or library media specialist to ask one or more searching general questions about the author's message or point of view which will, in turn, give the student the opportunity to discuss the theme of the book, the author's voice.

Oral reading gives the student an opportunity to share a favorite short, self-selected passage from the book by reading aloud. This option provides a comfortable forum for sharing dialogue or narrative from the book in a lively, animated way.

The provision for *records* of the reading conference are similar to other methods described previously.

Closure is assured through *encouragement and guidance,* in which the adult participant takes time to discuss the student's future reading plans and perhaps offer suggestions about other titles by the same author.

The individual reading conference as part of a literature-based reading program offers a wide range of positive outcomes. By including volunteer parents as conference participants, students are given role models from an adult community who demonstrate a love for reading as a lifetime pleasure. By explaining the modified whole-language approach to teaching reading through literature, teachers and library media specialists can offer suggestions to parents for working reading into family life by encouraging and praising their children's efforts. When a parent becomes aware of the growth in reading skills that is made possible by surrounding their children with appropriate literature, by reading aloud to them, by reading along with them, by discussing the stories they read with them, and by listening to their children's ideas, that parent becomes an active participant in developing the intellectual growth of their children. They also realize that parenting may extend to the classroom with vigorous, positive results.

Entry Level 3: Advanced Literary Analysis

Teachers may wish to introduce a vocabulary of literary analysis by using the sound filmstrip sets produced by Pied Piper Productions. These programs have an excellent explanation of the elements of fiction, and use examples from books and stories that are familiar to most students.

After viewing the filmstrips, the terms protagonist, antagonist, plot, character, setting, conflict, climax, resolution, and voice may be defined and summarized on the chalkboard or overhead projector, and students may record these defined terms in their reading journals.

For this unit, students should have a bound composition book in which to record information about their reading and writing assignments, and for their personal responses to contemporary realistic fiction. Throughout the unit, assignments will include journal writing, and it should be made clear to students that there is a difference between a *personal* journal and a *reading* journal.

Definition of Literary Terms

Plot: The series of events in a story.

Conflict: A problem or struggle necessary for plot development. The series of events that precipitates conflict are called the rising action. Conflict in a story or book involves the protagonist in a struggle with *external* forces, such as nature or other persons, or with *internal* forces within themselves.

Characters: The *protagonist* is the central character. The *antagonist* is an opposing character or force.

Characterization: Characters must be *developed* in a story, exhibiting many human traits or emotions. For a character to be credible, there must be a unity of character and action. The way a writer creates and develops a character's personality is called *characterization*. This important element of fiction usually includes four major types of characterization:

- *well-rounded* , in which a character is developed fully
- *flat,* one-dimensional, or not fully developed
- *static,* remains the same throughout the story
- *dynamic,* changes as the story develops and builds to a climax

Setting: The time and place in which the events in the story happen is called the setting. The setting may be:

- *integral,* necessary for the development of the story.
- *incidental,* simply a background or backdrop for the story.

Climax: The climax, or turning point, is the high point of interest in the plot of a story. It is the moment when the outcome of the story becomes clear. The climax usually involves an important discovery, decision, or event.

Resolution: The *falling action*, in which the various plot turns are resolved in a satisfactory conclusion.

Irony: A contrast between what is expected and what actually exists or happens.

Foreshadowing: The technique of hinting about something that will occur in a story. Foreshadowing creates suspense by providing details that will be integral to later events in the book.

Voice: Voice, or point of view, refers to how an author chooses to narrate a story. Works of fiction may be told from a first-person point of view or a third-person point of view. In a book told from the first-person point of view, the narrator is a *character* in the story. The author-character uses the first person pronouns *I* and *we* in describing events. In a book told from the third-person point of view, the narrator is usually outside of the story (as an omniscient but unseen presence.) The narrator uses the third-person pronouns *he* and *she*.

UNIT 1: BETSY BYARS

Biographical Information

Betsy Byars has written 25 books for young people. Most of them are classified as contemporary realistic fiction. She is both a prolific writer and an enduring one. She began her writing career publishing magazine stories and articles but soon concentrated on writing for children as her own children were growing up. Now she is known principally as a novelist. In 1971, Betsy Byars was awarded a Newbery Medal for the book, *Summer of the Swans.* She says she gets her ideas from newspapers, magazines, and from people she knows, and she is known especially for her way of incorporating current trends smoothly into her books.

Her books are aimed at middle grade readers, with characters and settings that are appealing and appropriate. Her contemporary realistic fiction frequently falls into the problem novel category, dealing with topics like child abuse (*The Pinballs*), or overuse of popular TV (*The TV Kid*), or wife abuse (*Cracker Jackson*).

Byars is known for creating memorable characters. Her characters are invented but intensely credible. Her exposition of character is very skillful. Denise M. Wilms (1985), assistant editor of *Booklist,* comments

> Personalities are built up layer by layer through dialogues and monologues that spotlight critical moments in the present or in the past. These are often off beat and their novelty increases their effectiveness at making highly individualized characters.

Betsy Byars develops her plots with tight focus, believable conflict, and a dramatic, moving climax. Because plotting is so essential to a book's development, she works with dedicated and professional skill to keep the reader involved. Wilms notes that plotting in Byars' books seems to grow inevitably out of character.

> It is a measure of her skill that plot can't be easily considered apart from character. Therefore, the plot is never predictable: you never know which way it's going to turn. Yet it isn't quirky or devious; it *seems* like it's just an outgrowth of [a character's] thought and emotions.

Betsy Byars is a thoughtful storyteller. She is able to depict problems that children know about, or difficulties that they may have experienced, in a way that the reader can understand and perhaps learn from. And, although the plots may not be funny, there is a great deal of quiet, understated humor that readers relate to and enjoy. The reader senses that Byers is a writer who already knows a great deal about children. As storyteller, she has an authentic voice that is both compassionate and understanding towards a child's emotional development. Betsy Byars has mastered her craft, and her impact on contemporary realistic fiction for chidren is strong.

Unit Objectives

This unit will enable students to:

- analyze plot, setting, theme, and characters developed in the book.
- analyze what makes characters credible.
- predict the effect of an event or action on the plot of the book.
- create a video drama or reader's theater script and perform it.
- practice higher-order thinking skills in book discussion.

Teaching Strategies	
1. The teacher:	**The students:**
introduces the book as a story about a girl who feels she has a lot of personal problems.	
leads brainstorming discussion about the kinds of problems students have in their lives and lists problems described on chalkboard or overhead projector.	participate as appropriate
asks students if a lot of the problems mentioned are common to most students.	use brainstorming ideas to compile list.
has students copy list into reading journal, and explains that as they read the book, they should relate Sara's problems to those on *their* list for discussion later.	copy lists from chalk-board or overhead.
2. The teacher:	**The students:**
reads aloud or gives time for silent reading of chapters or designated pages.	read chapters or pages assigned.
gives students "milestones" or dates when chapters will be discussed. (This can be in the form of a calendar with discussion days circled.)	plan reading schedules to complete chapters for discussion.

Summer of the Swans

The Story

The summer that Sara was 14, she spent a lot of time crying about her perceived big feet, skinny legs, her nose, and even her shoes, which she had accidentally dyed a hideous shade of "puce." Her self-centered adolescent behavior is relieved only through her genuine affection for her younger brother, Charlie, who is mentally handicapped and does not speak, as a result of a devastating illness in early childhood. After Sara takes Charlie to see some lovely swans on a nearby lake in the woods, Charlie becomes confused and tries to find the swans by himself. He becomes hopelessly lost in the woods, and the entire community is mobilized to help find the little boy. During the crisis of Charlie's disappearance, Sara learns that Joe Melby, a classmate, is not the villain she had supposed, and she also learns some valuable lessons about family connections.

*Discussion Questions and Activities (*Summer of the Swans, *pages 1-46)*

1. When the story begins, Sara is listing all of her shortcomings. Which two of her physical characteristics do you think bother her most? (Knowledge)
2. How does Wanda feel about her sister's problems. Find evidence in the chapter that show the reader how the two sisters get along together. (Application)
3. Why does Sara say that it has been the worst summer of her life? (Knowledge)
4. In your journal, write about the things that would make a summer miserable for you. You may begin: "When summer comes, I'm not going to...." Or you might write, "This will probably be a miserable summer because...." (Synthesis)
5. How does the author let us see Sara's patience with her little brother, Charlie? (Comprehension)
6. Who do you think cares more for Charlie—Wanda or Sara? Give reasons for your answers. (Analysis)
7. In what ways do you think a family would be affected if one of its members were mentally handicapped? (Evaluation)
8. Sara's statement: "If you look cute, you *are* cute; if you look smart, you *are* smart; and if you don't look like anything, then you *aren't* anything," expresses the way she feels when the story begins. How would you respond to Sara? Write a journal entry that would show the "other side" of an attitude like Sara's. (Evaluation)

9. Why is Sara so certain that Charlie will enjoy seeing the swans? How does Charlie show his fascination with the swans? Why do you think Sara feels so strongly about the swans? (Comprehension, application)
10. Why do you suppose Sara starts to cry while she is watching the swans? (Evaluation)

*Discussion Questions and Activities (*Summer of the Swans, *pages 47-92)*

1. What advice does Wanda give Sara about feeling good about oneself? (Knowledge)
2. What had happened to Charlie when he was three years old? (Knowledge)
3. Select partners to dramatize the scene between Wanda and Sara (pp. 48-50.) The scene may be performed as a reader's theater. (Comprehension)
4. How does the missing button on Charlie's pajamas affect the plot of this book? Why is this event significant? (Application)
5. The author uses voice to let us know what Charlie is thinking and feeling. Find two examples of point of view in this chapter that illustrates how the all-knowing narrator functions in a book. (Analysis)
6. Write a journal entry based on the scene in the book when Charlie realizes that it is a cat and not a swan, that he sees in the yard. In your paragraph, try to describe the feelings that Charlie has when he sees the cat in the bushes.
7. Make a map showing the route Charlie traveled when he left his house. Use the narrative description on pp. 58-64 to help you visualize the locale. Share your map with members of the group and compare ways in which a reader interprets information. (Analysis)
8. How did Sara react to Charlie's disappearance? What were Aunt Willie's feelings? (Knowledge)
9. Where did Sara think Charlie had gone? (Knowledge)
10. What kind of a friend is Mary? Find three examples in this chapter that show the qualities of her friendship. (Comprehension)
11. Sara describes having a "something wrong" feeling. Have you ever had that kind of experience? Try to recall the events that caused the feeling and then write about it in your journal, either in poetry or in narrative form. (Analysis)
12. When Aunt Willie blames herself for Charlie's disappearance, she shows her love for him by assuming guilt. Do you think that this way of dealing with a crisis is a common one? Give reasons for your answers. (Evaluation)

13. What was the relationship between Charlie's birthday photograph and the watch? (Comprehension)
14. What makes Sara think that Joe Melby stole, and then returned, Charlie's watch? (Analysis)
15. What kind of person is Sara's father? Find passages in the chapter that describe him, both through physical and personality traits. (Analysis)
16. Why do you think Sara's father virtually abandoned his family? (Analysis)
17. Why does Aunt Willie find excuses for the behavior of Sara's father, Sam? (Analysis)
18. With a partner, perform the scene between Joe Melby and Sara (pp. 89-90) as reader's theater. If you have access to video equipment, you may wish to produce the scene as a video segment. (Synthesis)

*Discussion Questions and Activities (*Summer of the Swans, *pages 93-142)*

1. What really happened to Charlie's watch? Do you think that Mary did the right thing to remain silent about Joe Melby's involvement? Why or why not? (Knowledge, Evaluation)
2. Why do you think Sara is embarrassed to talk to Joe? (Comprehension)
3. Predict what will be the future relationship between Sara and Joe. (Synthesis)
4. What are Charlie's emotions when his watch breaks? (Knowledge) Describe the scene visually in an illustration in your journal. (Synthesis)
5. In your journal, write an explanation for what Sara meant when she said (p. 119): "I have cried over myself a hundred times this summer. I have wept over my big feet and my skinny legs and my nose. I have even cried over my stupid shoes, and now when I have a true sadness there are no tears left."
6. When Joe Melby offers to let Charlie wear his watch, what does this show about his character? (Application)
7. As Sara saw the swans fly overhead, she excitedly pointed them out to Charlie. What was Charlie's reaction? (Analysis)
8. How does Sara react to Joe's invitation to the party? (Knowledge)
9. Do Sara's feelings about her father change in the book? Find evidence to support your position. (Analysis)
10. How does Sara's personality grow and change through the book? (Comprehension, Analysis)
11. What were the two events that led to a change in Sara's personality? (Comprehension)

12. Sara had a vision of life as a series of flights of steps. In your journal, draw a visualization of Sara's image, placing characters on the steps according to her description.

Additional Discussion Questions and Activities

1. Respond in journal entry form to one of these statements: (a) Sara is more accepting of her responsibility toward Charlie. (b) Sara's family's attitude toward Charlie is based on love, not pity. (c) Sara learns to cope with her adolescence. (d) Sara learns to adjust to her home situation.
2. Create a collage from magazine pictures and real objects that expresses the setting for *Summer of the Swans.*
3. Design and produce a travel brochure about the West Virginia country where Sara lived. Use Byar's descriptive passages from *Summer of the Swans* as text for your brochure.
4. Research illnesses that might cause a condition similar to Charlie's. You might want to begin your research with spinal meningitis, Lyme's disease, or Rocky Mountain spotted fever, which are prevalent in mountainous regions.
5. Research the habits and behaviors of swans. At one point, Sara describes the swans as "mute." Is this true? Prepare a short illustrated report for your group.
6. There are no chapter headings in *Summer of the Swans.* Imagine that you and members of your group are editors, and it is your job to find titles for each chapter for a Table of Contents. You will need to review the episodes in each chapter to make sure that your titles capture the main idea.
7. Who is the protagonist in the story?
8. The main characters are in conflict with either nature, humans, or themselves. What kind of conflict is depicted in this book? Is there more than one major conflict?
9. Prepare a graphic organizer showing events, climax, and resolution. Use a story map or story mountain to show these elements of fiction.
10. Students may now refer to the lists, which they generated through brainstorming at the beginning of the unit. Using their lists as "Column 1," they may match comparable problems discovered in *Summer of the Swans* as the content for "Column 2." This comparison provides a satisfying closure for students, who recognize that a good book generally reflects their own interests and problems.
11. Symbolism is an undercurrent in this book. The mute swans are symbols for the voiceless Charlie; the choice of location of the swans—the beautiful university pool versus the wooded lake in a natural setting—

suggest the choices available to Sara. Depending on the level of the students considering the novel, the teacher may decide to include the concept of symbolism as part literary analysis.

12. Deciding on the theme, or message, of a book is sometimes difficult for students in the intermediate grades. With teacher guidance, students may arrive at the message about life or human nature that the writer presents in a work of fiction. There may be one or more themes. Books in which themes must be figured out by the reader through careful reading and thinking are generally most successful. Themes implicit in the book, *Summer of the Swans,* include:

- adjusting to a new way of life
- coping with adolescence
- accepting personal sadness
- learning to cope with a mentally handicapped child
- developing a sense of responsibility
- developing self-esteem.

Students may suggest other themes in addition to these.

UNIT 2: A BETSY BYARS SAMPLER

Authors of contemporary realistic fiction for young persons use the elements of fiction subtly but powerfully to create strong books that have both emotional and intellectual appeal to readers. Betsy Byars is adept at characterization, and particularly in developing characters that grow and change in positive ways. She is also skillful in presenting situations and events in a story that have a resemblance to the problems that readers encounter in their own lives. When readers recognize these similarities, there is an emotional bonding with the book's characters. A story that evokes curiosity, laughter, sadness, or fear encourages a reader to experience a genuine interaction with characters and the events that affect their lives.

In a literature-based curriculum, a book discussion format may involve teacher, volunteer adult, and reader in a literary analysis of the elements of a story or in critical judgment of the quality of a book. In addition, emotional and personal responses to a book and interpretations of the author's intentions are given status as worthy considerations in an objective analysis of a book.

The summaries of four books by Betsy Byars provided below may serve as a tool to familiarize both discussion leader and students with plot, character, setting, and special qualities that the author brings to a book.

Students may select books to read and to discuss based upon similarities between book character and themselves.

Maintaining consistency in reading conferences while avoiding boredom through sameness is a sensitive area for the person developing literary arts units based on the works of a single author.

A reading conference should be a social interaction with language. The manner in which questions are phrased can convey a message to the reader. Are questions essentially the same, even though the book is different? Or does the questioner offer another way of looking at a situation, event, or character in a book? The National Council of Teachers of English (NCTE, 1988-1989) points out that teachers not only bring their expertise and authority to interactions with students, they also precipitate change by nudging and questioning to stimulate thinking and enable students to ask their own questions and seek answers. In a well-planned reading conference, students are given time to articulate and revise what they know about an author and how that author writes. Some student objectives that are valid and may be incorporated into questioning plans for a book discussion are:

- to discuss how problems encountered may help to develop character traits.
- to analyze what makes characters credible.
- to predict what will happen to a character.
- to conclude how conflict is important to plot development.

Specific questions for discussion are not given. Questions will frequently evolve naturally because of the enthusiasm of the reader and the active listening skills of the questioner. Betsy Byar's novels provide a means for readers to experience the lives of her fictional characters, to gain a better understanding of people, and to participate in the pleasure of reading.

Cracker Jackson

The Story

Betsy Byars wrote *Cracker Jackson* 20 years after she wrote the Newbery Award book, *Summer of the Swans,* yet she retains the wonderful freshness and awareness of things that are important to young persons. In this book, Jackson "Cracker" Hunter is an eleven-year-old who lives with his divorced mother. Until recently, he had been cared for by a very young, very Southern care giver named Alma, but Alma has married Billy Ray, a mechanic in a local garage, and Cracker is struggling with the usual problems of school and relationships.

Cracker's mother is a flight attendant and has divorced Cracker's father because "he was never serious." But the divorce is amicable, and Cracker looks forward to his father's weekly phone calls. Cracker's mother is very much concerned with propriety and manners and worries about Cracker's safety and well-being to an inordinate degree, according to Cracker.

Problems arise when Cracker recognizes signs of physical abuse in Alma, with whom he has stayed friends. He enlists his friend, Goat, to try to find out whether Billy Ray is beating Alma, and together, the two boys discover a sordid story of abuse, not only of Alma, but of Nicole, her infant daughter. Although Cracker and Goat try to resolve the problem by "driving" Alma and Nicole to a shelter for abused women, they are frustrated when Alma decides to return home to Billy Ray. Ultimately, Cracker's mother takes control of the situation, but only after Alma has been brutally beaten, and Nicole (dropped by Alma during the beating) suffers a concussion.

The story concludes with Alma and Nicole going to a shelter for abused spouses, where Alma has a job in the preschool nursery, driven there this time by Cracker's parents.

There is a lot of humor in the book, particularly in segments involving Goat and his outlandish behavior. "I am in deep trouble," his phone conversations to Cracker from the closet usually begin. Betsy Byars has a sure ear for the dialogue of young persons, and she is especially good in characterizing boys. This book deals with a serious problem, and there is an agonizing poignancy in a story in which a young boy sees injustice and brutality and tries to deal with it in a manly and dignified way.

The Burning Questions of Bingo Brown

The Story

Harrison "Bingo" Brown is a student at Eleanor Roosevelt Middle School with a preadolescent's generic fear of conversations or relationships with persons of the opposite sex. Bingo also has a healthy fear of Billy Wentworth, the class clown and resident Rambo clone. When their teacher, Mr. Markham, distributes journals to the students and directs them to fill the pages with free writing, compositions, illustrations, and their thoughts, Bingo is pleased, because he has already decided his future lies in writing science fiction novels. He has three in progress and plans to write to Ray Bradbury as part of an assignment.

Mr. Markham, called "Mr. Mark" by his students, is a young and imaginative teacher who becomes a flawed character through his immature decision to involve the children in a letter-writing campaign to his girlfriend, and, subsequently, to an invented person who is contemplating suicide.

The "burning questions" of the title are based on Bingo's plan to fill his journals with burning questions for which he has few answers. They include questions about love (he has fallen in love with three girls in ten minutes based solely on their career plans), adult problems, and peer pressure.

The setting for the book is the classroom of Eleanor Roosevelt Middle School, where Bingo, Billy, Melissa, Harriet, Mamie Lou, and other characters experience an assortment of experiences under the care of their teacher, Mr. Markham. When an older student wears a tee shirt to school that has a vulgar message, the school principal, Mr. Broehler, bans *all* tee shirts that have "ABC's." Bingo misinterprets his mother's suggestion that the students rebel and join forces to wear message tee shirts in defiance of the principal's new rule. Billy Wentworth, in his Rambo mode, assumes leadership of the rebellion, but at the moment of confrontation at the front door of the school, the principal does not appear and the coup fails.

The plot reaches a climax when Mr. Markham is critically injured in a motorcycle accident, and Bingo and Billy, visiting the scene, decide that the "imaginary" friend that they had written to was really their teacher with suicidal tendencies. But when Bingo and Melissa are selected to visit Mr. Markham in the hospital, Bingo decides that Mr. Markham may have tried to kill himself but has now opted for life. Relieved, Bingo goes back to the burning question he had been neglecting: If one is holding hands with a girl, who decides when to let go?

Betsy Byars creates real characters who interact exactly like the preadolescents that they are. Their causes, their crushes, their dubious attempts at humor, and, above all, their self-centered absorption in how they are perceived by their peers are portrayed in sympathetic style.

Adult characters in the book are less well-defined. Dad sells insurance and travels a lot; Mom is a curious blend of former flower child and rigid conformist. It is the character of Mr. Markham that is somewhat baffling— his pseudo-cynicism with his students and his depression combined with a manic sense of urgency are difficult emotional states for young readers to appreciate.

Bingo Brown and the Language of Love

The Story

In this sequel to *The Burning Questions of Bingo Brown,* Mr. Markham has returned to Eleanor Roosevelt Middle School, but Melissa, Bingo's girlfriend, has moved to Bixby, Oklahoma.

The plot involves the grudging but emerging friendship between Billy Wentworth and Bingo, and Bingo's struggles to achieve maturity. Billy's family moves into the house next door to Bingo, and Bingo fears the worst. Meanwhile, Bingo's parents have forbidden him to use the phone because he ran up a large long-distance bill with seven calls to Oklahoma. In order to repay the money for the phone bill, Bingo is required to fix dinner for the family for 36 nights. Much of the action of this story is centered in Bingo's home during Bingo's eleventh summer.

Bingo's mom has gone to work as a realtor, and Bingo realizes that he has fallen out of love with Melissa. Meanwhile, Cici, one of Melissa's friends is introduced as a character. In a busy plot, Cici develops a crush on Bingo, Billy likes Cici, Bingo's mother becomes pregnant, and Bingo and his father are left to fend for themselves while his mother flees to *her* mother's home. Through it all, Bingo maintains his summer journal, but instead of "burning questions" he is recording "Trials and Triumphs." For a while there are only trials, but by the end of the book Bingo is able to record a number of triumphs.

> He had fallen out of love with Melissa, suffered, then discovered his suffering was in vain. He loved her more than ever. He had been deserted by his mother, learned that he was to become a brother and that his father was to become his mother. He had not fallen apart, as some people would, at discoveries of this nature. He had received five letters from Melissa, had been caught in the kitchen and in the living room with Cici, and had handled the ensuing misunderstandings with considerable dignity. Most important of all, he had learned to dog-paddle in the mainstream of life.

Once again, Betsy Byars leads the reader toward an affection for the central character of Bingo Brown. From total self-absorption in mousse and moustache development, Bingo begins to grow into a responsible person learning the "language of love," even if it *is* directions on how to reheat a casserole.

Bingo Brown, Gypsy Lover

The Story

The story takes up where the reader left Bingo in *Bingo Brown and the Language of Love.* Mom is now seven months pregnant, Bingo is once again corresponding with Melissa in Oklahoma, and characters introduced in earlier stories play together in a repertory setting: Grammy is a major character in this book, while Cici and Billy Wentworth are minor figures.

The conflict arises from Bingo's need to find an appropriate gift for Melissa for Christmas. She has written to him and indicated that she is sending him a present he is "going to love," and so Bingo feels challenged to find the perfect gift for her for no more than $3.59, his total savings. In Melissa's letter to Bingo, she also alludes to a book she and a friend are reading together, *Gypsy Lover,* and confesses that instead of using the gypsy hero's name (Romondo), she inserts "Bingo" into the narrative.

When Bingo attempts to find this romantic novel, he encounters a new character, Boots, who is certain that her older sister has the book, *Gypsy Lover,* and that she will share it with Bingo. It is apparent that Boots would like to initiate a mixed-sex relationship with Bingo, but he heroically resists. Finding a pair of earrings on the sale counter that he thinks would be perfect for Melissa, he hurriedly purchases them, mails them with a semiromantic Christmas card, and waits for Melissa's package to arrive. When it does, Bingo is mystified. "It's a piece of cloth with handles," he reports to his parents, who, for once, do not make fun of him. Actually, the gift is a notebook carrier, and in her note Melissa emphasizes her certainty that Bingo is going to be a famous writer and she will have contributed to his success by providing him with a carrier for his manuscripts.

The book reaches its climax when Bingo's mother goes into premature labor and is taken to the hospital. Bingo realizes that the jealousy twinges he had felt completely fade when he is faced with a genuine life-or-death crisis. Bingo stays with his grandmother during these stressful days and the two develop an affectionate rapport. Baby Jamie is born safely, and Bingo becomes a worried protector and big brother. As the story concludes, the family is about to take the baby home to its new life, and Bingo once more records his triumphs toward successful maturity.

The characters are realistic and funny, and they interact with Bingo in dialogue that is typically preadolescent. Betsy Byars takes a universal practice like the reject gift drawer, and writes a witty and believable chapter in which Billy Wentworth gives his beloved Cici a bottle of Brut instead of a vial of perfume. The scene in the hospital in which Bingo observes new babies being stuffed into soft red Christmas stockings for their trips home is vivid, affectionate, and moving. "The baby was awake, and seemed to actually enjoy being a stocking stuffer," Bingo observes.

The setting in suburbia gives a vivid picture of neighborhoods where a K-Mart and the upscale mall are both reachable by bike.

Betsy Byars seems to be inventing an entire community peopled with likeable characters doing real things and coping with the vicissitudes of life, in much the same way that Beverly Cleary created Henry Huggins and his friends. The difference lies in Bingo's hormonal levels, and this is what makes the Bingo series such a comfortable step up from Henry for young readers.

Student Activities

Although the thrust of this unit is an individualized program of book discussion to promote an understanding of literary elements, readers enjoy the opportunity to do projects or participate in creative extensions of the author's books. Many activity books suggest possibilities that are fun and involve groups in cooperative experiences. A list of "Professional Resources" for literature-based activities using contemporary realistic fiction for children appears later in this chapter.

Below are some activities specific to the books of Betsy Byars that have proven workable and popular in a modified whole-language approach to literature.

1. A panel discussion in which students promote their favorite Byars book is a lively and entertaining way for readers to express themselves. In the panel discussion, each participant introduces a character from a Byars book that seemed most believable to them. The participant should describe the person and give at least two situations in the book that contributed to his or her credibility. After all participants have presented their favorite character, listeners (or viewers) vote on which member of the panel was most persuasive.

2. A favorite format for video is the talk show, in which a group of students participate in a discussion based on a single theme, e.g., similarities between characters in different Byars' books, or similiarities in conflict (self against self, society, nature, another person) found in books by Betsy Byars, or various themes found in books by Betsy Byars. A host guides the discussion and leads questioning from the audience.

3. Media saturation may have positive outcomes by providing readers with formats for literary activities. The celebrity interview, a magazine filled with feature stories about the author's characters, or a newspaper published with news stories created from situations in some of Betsy Byars' books are popular choices. Comic books or strips are an artistic way to interpret plot incidents in Byars' books. The ubiquitous advice column also provides a model for interpreting problems and conflict experienced by characters in Byar's novels.

4. A brainstorming session in which students imagine themselves part of an advertising campaign for the books of Betsy Byars is an energizing experience. Posters may be designed and produced, commercials may be written and produced in both video or print formats, and endorsements for products by Byars' characters could be made.
5. The design of a tee shirt relating to Byers' books can be both a fashion and a literary statement. Depending on resources available, students may create a message and illustration for one of their favorite Byars' books. If the tee shirt is designed on poster board, it may be cut out and taped to a wire clothes hanger for display. In some instances, students prepare cotton tee shirts and wear them as part of a "Betsy Byars Demonstration," similar to the one described in *Cracker Jackson*.
6. Readers enjoy developing activity books or literary experiences based on their reading. A group may brainstorm ideas for individual publications or projects.

UNIT 3: WALTER DEAN MYERS

Biographical Information

In an essay published in *The Washington Post*, September 8, 1990, author Walter Dean Myers reminisces about his high school experiences. It is a poignant and sensitive self-revelation that leaves the reader with an intense admiration for the person that Myers *was* then, and *is* now. Titled "Least Likely to Succeed," the essay describes a young black man, identified as not only bright but college-bound, and therefore welcomed at Stuyvesant, a college-preparatory school. There, to Myers' intense embarrassment, he found that poverty governed his future. He did not have the fees required for college applications, he did not even have the money for gym shorts, and so, in anger and desperation, Myers began skipping school. He "hung out" in Central Park, reading Camus, Balzac, Thomas Mann, T.S. Eliot, and Eugene O'Neill.

He blamed his parents for being poor and dreamed of a day when his father would get a raise or hit a number, or when some magazine would publish one of the poems he had submitted. He writes:

> What I thought I needed was for somebody to give me the magic key to life. What I really needed was somebody who had experienced the same pain, who had been as poor and who wore his ethnicity with as much discomfort and who had somehow found an answer, or at least a way to ease that pain.

Even as Myers deliberately chose to remove himself from an educational setting, he recognized the consequences of this choice. The idea of being drawn into "the deadening pool of anonymous African-Americans [sic] male laborers was a frightening thought."

The essay continues with Myers describing a scene that took place in June of his senior year in high school.

> I did not go to the park that June day in 1954. I went to school instead. It was over. Graduation had come and gone....Now the doors were locked. I stood at the door, realizing what must have happened, then quickly walked away down the familiar streets, streets I could navigate even through my tears, to the subway and then home to Harlem.

The essay concludes with a summary of Myer's route to becoming an author. He served in the military and worked in a series of dead-end jobs, yet the promise he had showed at 16 did not go away. He continued to read—and write—and felt a sense of accomplishment that he was "doing something with my mind," as he puts it. He confesses:

> On that June day outside Stuyvesant, I feared that I had been found out, that I was really no different from the thousands of other black kids destined to failure. What I eventually discovered was that I *was* like all of those other black kids, but my language and writing skills would allow me to take advantage of some of the breaks that would come my way. Whatever success I find in life will be the result of those abilities, a little luck and the constant, painful memory of a locked school door.

This personal memoir of a black writer's perceptions about his own prospects is an excellent portrait of Walter Dean Myers. He has been interviewed by many writers; he has described his books in detail; and he has a prodigious output of novels written for many audiences with widely divergent reading and maturity levels. But Myers always comes back to his personal conviction that reading and education are the only way up and out for *anyone,* not just the black brothers. Stephanie Zvirin interviewed Walter Dean Myers in *Booklist* in 1990. She asked him about this philosophy, and Myers responded:

> I really feel kids can make comebacks once they reach a certain maturity if.... IF they have reading ability. I've done hundreds of interviews in prisons and rehab centers, and I think being able to read and process information makes the difference between people who succeed after their first encounter with the law and those who fail. If intervention for someone like Jamal [in *Scorpions*] is through education, he will make it. If education is neglected, he won't.

Although Walter Dean Myers has strong and serious personal convictions, his stories are touched with humor and insight into the personalities of young persons. His books, *The Young Landlords, The Mouse Rap,* and *Me, Mop and the Moondance Kid,* are spirited and affectionate accounts of kids doing very kid-like things, whether it is forming a dance group to perform in the park or participating in sports.

Myers is one of the most popular and versatile authors writing for young people today. He has been awarded the Coretta Scott King Award three times for his "outstanding, inspirational, and educational contribution to literature." His books cross color and genre lines to convey an underlying message of concern for children and adolescents. "I think I have a responsibility to the children I'm writing for," he states. "My responsibility is to be their voice and to give them their images,...and when I get to...my more personalized books, I think in terms of writing the black experience."

Unit Objectives

This unit will enable students to:

- identify setting and describe its importance.
- track the order of events.
- describe the relationships among characters.
- analyze a character's motives.
- infer the theme of a book.
- locate significant details.
- identify the point of view.
- analyze the use of irony as an element of fiction.
- explain the effects of expressive language in dialogue.

Teaching Strategies	
The teacher:	**The students:**
introduces Walter Dean Myers' *Scorpions* as an example of the realistic fiction "problem" novel.	
reviews the discussion held previously in which students developed their own "problems list."	participate in reviewing their "problem list" recorded in journal.

The teacher:	The students:
asks students to predict (based on the summary) what some of the problems might be in *Scorpions*.	read summary and make predictions orally.
allows time for students to record predictions in their reading journals.	record predictions.
follows the process for directed reading and book discussion used for *The Summer of the Swans*.	participate appropriately.

Scorpions

The Story

Jamal Hicks lives in a Harlem apartment with his mother, a domestic worker, and his younger sister, Sassy. Jamal's older brother, Randy, is in prison, and the family is trying to find ways to raise money for an appeal. Randy, the leader of a Harlem gang called the Scorpions, shot a storekeeper during a robbery. His friend, Mack, a minor drug figure and crack addict, has just been released from prison for a similar offense. The premise of the story is that Jamal must now assume the leadership of the Scorpions, taking Randy's place. When Jamal protests that he is only 12 years old, Mack explains that is the reason he's been selected; members must be under 16 so they don't testify in court or get tried as adults. Mack gives Jamal a gun to seal the deal.

Jamal tries to get along, do his homework, and not cause his mother additional worry. But the school principal has him targeted as a troublemaker, and even a teacher whom Jamal admires only views him as a grunt worker. When Jamal gets a job on Saturdays in a neighborhood store, he feels the first pride of a job well done. But members of the Scorpions terrorize the store owner, and Jamal is fired.

This plot proceeds like a Greek tragedy. Fights at school, the stabbing of Jamal's older brother, and other events lead up to a climactic scene in which Tito and Jamal go to meet members of the Scorpions to tell them that neither Jamal nor Tito want to be involved. The boys are carrying the gun to return to Mack, but panic when Mack and his cohorts draw knives. While Jamal struggles, Tito fires the gun, killing one and injuring another of the Scorpions. The boys get away, but Tito is consumed with guilt and is physically ill from the knowledge that he has killed someone. Jamal is persuaded to have his mother sign a paper authorizing the school nurse to give him dylantin or some sort of anti-hyperactivity medication.

While Jamal and Tito try to decide what to do about the fatal confrontation at the playground, Mack comes to Jamal and claims that he has wasted Angel and Indian. He tells the boys that it was a showdown to see who would head the Scorpions. Relieved, Jamal permits Mack to believe his fantasy. Tito confesses a version of the killing to Abuela, and the two of them plan to return to Puerto Rico. Jamal is left alone with the fearsome knowledge that for a while he had been glad to have a gun. Mrs. Hicks sums up the sadness of their lives when Mr. Staunton, her employer, refuses her a loan for Randy's lawyers. "'Lord, when am I going to learn that my problems don't belong to nobody but me?'" Mama started rocking back and forth. "'Lord, when am I going to *learn?*'"

Discussion Questions and Activities

1. What does the reader learn about Jamal in the opening chapters? About Sassy, his sister? About Mama? About Randy?

2. Describe the apartment where Jamal lives, using information given in the book to support your description. Record the description in your reading journal. You may include a sketch.

3. A great deal of the action of the story takes place in Jamal's apartment. Design a stage set that could be used for a play based on *Scorpions*.

4. Do you agree or disagree with Jamal's thoughts: "Jamal got back to school on time, making sure to walk past Mr. Davidson so the principal would notice that he wasn't late. Mr. Davidson didn't say anything. That was what was wrong. When you did something wrong, everybody put their mouth on you. Then when you did something good, everybody acted like it wasn't anything special." Record your response in your reading journal to discuss with your group.

5. Write a paragraph in your journal expressing your feelings about how teachers and principals communicate with *you* during the day. You may choose to do a time-ordered composition as Myers does, describing a school day from morning till afternoon.

6. Jamal describes Tito to Mack as "my home boy." What does Jamal mean? Randy describes Mack as "my ace." What does this tell us about relationships among peers?

7. Mack explains why the Scorpions don't want Randy as their leader. What explanation does he give for their decision?

8. What can you infer from Jamal's reluctance to become leader of the Scorpions?

9. How does Tito's family life compare with Jamal's? What do you think is the greatest contrast? In your journal, describe your own family life. What characteristics, if any, are similar to Tito's family? Jamal's family?

10. Do you think Sassy is typical of most younger sisters? Why? Why not? Give evidence from the story for your opinion.

11. Characters in *Scorpions* learn about life through their experiences. What conclusions about education could Jamal come to from his contacts with teachers and Mr. Davidson, the principal? The school nurse? Write a monologue in which Jamal explains why he feels "disrespected," or *dissed* in school. Write the way you think Jamal would talk.

12. What effect does the sight of Jamal with a gun have on the other Scorpions? How does Jamal's attitude, as leader of the Scorpions, change when he gets the gun?

13. Why does Jamal think there will be trouble if the Scorpions find out that he has a part-time job?

14. Why did Mr. Gonzalez fire Jamal from his job? Do you think Jamal deserved to be fired? Why? Why not?

15. Tito says that the wasted people in the park looked like "thrown-away people." What do you think Tito meant?

16. What reasons did Jamal give Tito for wanting to keep the gun? What events changed Jamal's mind?

17. Jamal's love of art leads to a parting gift for Tito. Why do you think Tito first refused the gift, and then accepted it?

18. If you get newspapers and magazines at home, scan them for one week for news about gang violence similar to that described in *Scorpions*. Do you think the media deals fairly with accounts of violence? Why? Why not? Prepare a position paper in which you explain your feelings about violence, its causes, and possible prevention measures.

19. If your public library or media center has a videotape or audio recording of *West Side Story,* by Leonard Bernstein, schedule a presentation of this musical drama with your teacher and literary arts group. Then compare the characters in *Scorpions* with those in *West Side Story.*

Decision-Making Model

Problem	Goal(s)
Dwayne wants to fight Jamal.	Jamal wants to frighten Dwayne so the confrontations stop.

Alternatives	Pros & Cons
Jamal could go home directly from school.	+ avoid the fight for the present.
	- lose respect of his peers.
Jamal could change the location of the fight to some place away from school	+ avoid trouble with principal.
	- there would be no control over combatants to end fight.
Problem	**Goal(s)**
Jamal could leave the gun at home and fight with fists.	+ no one would be accidently wounded.
	- Jamal would lose the fight.
Jamal could agree to let a "paying audience" watch the fight.	+ Jamal would not be able to use the gun.
	- Jamal could intimidate Dwayne by pretending to be willing to shoot him.
Decisions	**Reason(s)**

Note: This model may be used as a graphic organizer for analyzing other books.

Additional Discussion Questions and Activities

1. From which character's point of view is the story told?
2. Why do you think Walter Dean Myers chooses the narrator's voice (third person) instead of letting Jamal tell his own story in a personal (first person) narrative?
3. Jamal's older brother, Randy, is in prison. In the book, we only find out about him through other characters. How can the reader piece together Randy's character from these descriptions?
4. Tito Cruz is Jamal's best friend. How does Walter Dean Myers convey the feelings of friendship between Jamal and Tito? Find passages in the book that show this friendship. In your journal, write how Tito would

describe Jamal. Then write a paragraph telling how Jamal would describe Tito. Use evidence from the book to support your statements.

5. As the story develops, Randy becomes a stronger character, affecting the lives of his family members in many ways. Why do you think he is able to have such an impact when he is away in prison and never actually appears in the book?

6. Create the character of Randy to present as a dramatic monologue. Use the information that other characters in the book give the reader about Randy in writing your script. You may present your monologue to the rest of the group and have the group decide who best conveys the character of Randy.

7. Use the decision-making model, above, and chapters nine and ten of *Scorpions* to analyze the events that occur.

8. What does Mrs. Hicks mean when she tells Tito: "Me and your grandmother, we try our best, but God knows it's hard. We say things we don't mean because to say the things we mean is just too hurtin.'" When you have organized your thoughts about the meaning of these lines, try to express them in a poem. Record your response in your reading journal.

9. The climax of the story is the action-packed scene in the park when Tito and Jamal confront Indian and Angel. How would a television newsperson describe the meeting? Write a short script in which the newsperson interviews bystanders who may or may not have observed the shooting.

10. Why do you think that Mack claims responsibility for the shooting? Is this turn of plot foreshadowed anywhere earlier in the book? Find evidence for your answer if you agree that the author has used foreshadowing to predict this.

11. Jamal and Tito have very different reactions after the shooting. Tito becomes physically ill, but Jamal accepts the event calmly. Is Jamal's remorse only because of the loss of his friend, Tito? Why do you think the author shows us this difference in character? Which character do you think has the most appropriate response to violence? Give reasons for your answers.

12. Walter Dean Myers uses the literary element of *irony* effectively in this book. Irony is a contrast between what is expected and what actually exists or happens. When Jamal becomes almost robotlike after the school nurse begins to give him an antihyperactive medication, it is as if the author is telling us that this is how society deals with perceived differences. The irony arises because, in trying to avoid a drug dependency, Jamal has one forced on him. Try to find other examples of irony in *Scorpions*. Record these episodes in your journal in a case study format.

UNIT 4: A WALTER DEAN MYERS SAMPLER

Walter Dean Myers brings a spirit of sincerity and empathy to his books. Although most of his stories are topical and current in their plots and characters, there is always an underlying strand of honesty and conviction. He is an author skilled in depicting events on the street, and in the ethnic neighborhoods where his books are set.

His commitment to his readers is very strong. His special gift is an ability to communicate his message and philosophy verbally as well as through the written word. Readers enjoy the story line in his books, but perhaps more importantly, gain a sense of validation for their own cultural diversity.

To successfully implement the literature-based curriculum, it is imperative to listen to authors like Walter Dean Myers. Students have diverse backgrounds, which reflect a variety of cultural heritages. When students come to a book discussion group, participate in a cooperative learning activity, or meet with teacher or library media specialist for an individual reading conference, they bring with them their different language proficiencies, their learning styles, and their own authority and expertise.

The two books summarized below are examples of the way in which Walter Dean Myers uses this cultural diversity to validate and challenge students' representations of the world.

The Mouse Rap

The Story

The plot is developed in a first-person, hip-rapper narrative by The Mouse (Freddie), a very likeable teen who loves basketball, hanging out, and music. His friends share his interests in sports and girls. When The Selects, a group of girls who like to dance, want to enter a contest in the park, they discover that they need to enter as a mixed group, so the girls try to persuade Omega, Toast, Styx, and The Mouse to join them in an MTV-like production number. When the boys are reluctant to participate, Sheri appeals to her grandfather. He was once a peripheral member of Siegel Brothers mob, and he still has a friend, Sudden Sam, who is purported to know where a large amount of cash has been stashed away in a Harlem building. The cash is the result of a bank robbery during the mob reign, and because so much time has passed, it is announced that the money will belong to the finder. Sheri is convinced that the publicity generated by finding the money will help The Selects with their competition in the park contest.

The subplots are germane to the main story: budding romance between Beverly and The Mouse; the distrust Mouse feels for his recently returned father; the pick-up basketball games in the park with their somewhat darker symbolism; the humorous homage to Tiger Moran, Katie Donahue, and other aging members of an old-fashioned gang.

Each chapter opens with a rap, hinting at what is to come, and even giving the beat for its recitation. The book could be slow going for the reader who is not familiar with the rhyming, Muhammed Ali style prose and there are a lot of allusions to trendy clothes and food. Myers narrative seems natural because the character of The Mouse is developed so sympathetically: his confusion over values, gender, and all the other troublesome and complicated aspects of growing into maturity.

In reading the book, one sometimes wishes for a glossary. For example:

- "We tubed out for a while." (watched TV)
- "She invites me over to her crash to tube." (her apartment to watch TV)
- "I switched the Brain Box to Truly Deep and did some heavy grinding." (thinking)
- ". . . she's so fly she's almost airborne." (She's pretty.)

The narrative is almost a tour de force by the author, as if he were testing himself to see if the rap-narrative could be sustained throughout the book. And except for an occasional lapse into standard English, Myers is consistent with his literary voice.

The book is visually lively, set in the parks and streets of Harlem; however, the setting does not elicit the "mean streets" concept, just a neighborhood where people live and get by the best they can. One senses the caution and fear of violence among the residents of the neighborhood, but it is subtly integrated into a story of universal appeal—average kids looking for adventure. As a multicultural study, the panorama of characters include African-Americans primarily, but there are senior citizens, Hispanics, Asians, and even Eastern Europeans.

Hoops

The Story

Lonnie Jackson lives for pick-up games of basketball. He's exceptionally talented, so when an opportunity comes for his team to participate in a tournament where he might be discovered by college scouts (a way out of Harlem), he is all for it. But when he finds out that the team's coach is to be Cal Jones, a wino he has almost stepped on at the park basketball court, he has second thoughts about the tournament.

The plot of the book revolves around Lonnie's growing respect and affection for the mysterious Cal. It is Cal who brings Sweet Man Johnson, a famous professional basketball star, to the team's practice, and it is Cal who becomes Lonnie's advisor and male role model.

When the team begins tournament play, subplots of gambling intrigue, point shaving, and the ugly and violent side of basketball blend to a tragic finale, in which Cal outsmarts Tyrone and refuses to throw the game. For this, Cal is stabbed and left to die, Mary-Ann is injected with a near-fatal drug overdose, and Aggie, Cal's long-time companion, comforts the grieving Lonnie. The book ends on a hopeful note, with Lonnie encouraging yet another group of youngsters to play their best.

The characters are realistic; poverty is all-pervasive; and the seemingly unstructured lifestyle of Lonnie and his friends is described in a matter-of-fact style. The women characters in the book join a Grecian chorus of sad and grieving figures, mourning the loss of possibilities for success and achievement, and even for a normal life with a partner. The girls are all willing to sleep with the guys, and there is a troubling sense of a lack of commitment on the part of the black males that permeates this novel. Yet, the characters are likeable, and the reader wants to see these characters fight their way up from oppression and despair.

The New York setting is true to the present, with neighborhoods lively day and night.

Student Activities

1. Walter Dean Myers' books are fun to read because they have much detail about clothes, food, sports and other subjects that interest readers. Using a "What's Hot......What's Not" format, design a list using the "hot" items from books by Myers. For example:

IN	OUT
Nikes and Reeboks	Shoes without commercials
Bike helmets	Beepers
Leather jackets	Gold chains

2. Using a "Sports Machine" format or similar sports talk show plan, script a series called "Heroes in High-tops," using characters from Myers' books as guests in an interview format. Select a host for your series, and produce a video pilot of your new show. Present the pilot program to your group for critique.

3. Research the substance-abuse prevention programs that are available in your area. Prepare a list of hot-line numbers that students could use to get information and help for drug-related problems.

4. Research materials available in your school library media center or public library on substance abuse. Consider marijuana, crack cocaine, heroin, tobacco, and alcohol. Prepare a chart showing the harmful effects of these drugs and offer recommendations for substance-abuse prevention.

5. In a story written from first-person point of view, the narrator's personality can be revealed through actions, words, and thoughts. What is the main way the author reveals Jamal's personality in *Scorpions?* How would this story be different if it were narrated by another character? Choose one of the characters from a Walter Dean Myers book (for example, *Me, Mop, and the Moondance Kid*) and summarize the events in a chapter from that character's third-person point of view.

BOOKS BY BETSY BYARS AND WALTER DEAN MYERS

Byars, Betsy. *Animal, The Vegatable, and John D. Jones.* New York: Delacorte, 1982.
———. *Bingo Brown and the Language of Love.* New York: Viking Penguin, 1989.
———. *Bingo Brown, Gypsy Lover.* New York: Viking Penguin, 1990.
———. The *Blossoms and the Green Phantom.* New York: Dell, 1987.
———. *The Burning Questions of Bingo Brown.* New York: Viking Penguin, 1988.
———. *Cartoonist.* New York: Viking, 1978.
———. *Cracker Jackson.* New York: Viking Penguin, 1985.
———. *The Cybil War.* New York: Viking, 1981.
———. *The Eighteenth Emergency.* New York: Viking, 1973.
———. *The Glory Girl.* New York: Viking, 1983.
———. *Goodbye, Chicken Little.* New York: Harper and Row, 1979.
———. *The House of Wings.* New York: Viking, 1972.
———. *The Night Swimmers.* New York: Delacorte, 1980.
———. *The Not-Just-Anybody Family.* New York: Delacorte, 1986.
———. *The Pinballs.* New York: Harper and Row, 1977.
———. *The Two-Thousand-Pound Goldfish.* New York: Harper and Row, 1982.
———. *The TV Kid.* New York: Viking, 1976.
Myers, Walter Dean. *Adventure in Granada.* New York: Viking, 1985
———. *Ambush in the Desert.* New York: Viking, 1986.
———. *Fast Sam, Cool Clyde, and Stuff.* New York: Viking, 1975.
———. *The Hidden Shrine.* New York: Viking, 1986.
———. *Hoops.* New York: Delacorte, 1981.
———. *The Legend of Tarik.* New York: Viking, 1981.
———. *Me, Mop, and the Moondance Kid.* New York: Delacorte, 1988.
———. *Motown and Didi: A Love Story.* New York: Viking, 1984.
———. *The Mouse Rap.* Viking, 1990.

————. *The Nicholas Factor.* New York: Viking, 1983.
————. *The Outside Shot.* New York: Delacorte, 1984.
————. *Scorpions.* New York: Harper and Row, 1988.
————. *Won't Know Till I Get There.* New York: Viking, 1982.
————. *The Young Landlords.* New York: Viking, 1979.

PROFESSIONAL RESOURCES

Bauer, Caroline Feller. (1983). *This Way to Books.* New York: H.W. Wilson.
Coger, Leslie Irene, and Melvin R. White. (1982). *Reader's Theatre Handbook,* 3d ed. Dallas, TX: Scott, Foresman.
Coody, Betty. (1983). *Using Literature with Young Children,* 3d ed. Dubuque, IA: William C. Brown.
Goodman, Kenneth. (1986). *What's Whole in Whole Language?* Portsmouth, NH: Heinemann Educational Books.
Hancock, Joellie and Susan Hill, eds. (1987). *Literature-based Reading Programs at Work.* Portsmouth, NH: Heinemann Educational Books,.
Johnson, Edna, ed. (1970). *Anthology of Children's Literature, 4th ed., revised.* Boston: Houghton Mifflin Company.
Laughlin, Mildred Knight, and Letty S. Watt. (1986). *Developing Learning Skills through Children's Literature: An Idea Book for K-5 Classrooms and Libraries.* Phoenix, AZ: Oryx Press.
Monson, Dianne, and Day Ann McClenathan, eds. (1979). *Developing Active Readers: Ideas for Parents, Teachers and Librarians.* Newark, DE: International Reading Association.
Montgomery, Paula Kay, and H. Thomas Walker. (1977). *Teaching Media Skills: An Instructional Program for Elementary and Middle School Students.* Littleton, CO: Libraries Unlimited.
Myers, Walter Dean. (1990) "Least Likely to Succeed," in *Washington Post Education Review*, Sept. 8, 1990. Washington, D.C.: The Washington Post.
National Council of Teachers of English. (1988-1989). *The English Coalition Conference: Assumptions, Aims, and Recommendations of the Elementary Strand.* Urbana, IL.
Sloan, Glenna. (1984). *The Child as Critic.* 2d ed. New York: Columbia Teachers College Press.
Spolin, Viola. (1983). *Improvisiation for the Theater: A Handbook of Teaching and Directing Techniques.* rev. ed. Evanston, IL: Northwestern University Press.
Walsh, Jill Paton. (1981). "The Art of Realism," in Hearne, Betsy and Marilyn Kaye. *Celebrating Children's Books: Essays on Children's Literature in Honor of Zena Sutherland.* New York: Lothrop, Lee and Shepard.
Wilms, Denise M. (1985). "Cracker Jackson," *Booklist*, October 2.
Zvirin, Stephanie. (1990). "The Booklist Interview: Walter Dean Myers," in *Booklist*, Feb. 15, 1990. Chicago: American Library Association.

5

Shifting Levels of Fantasy

INTRODUCTION

"Keeping track of these secondary worlds is really tiring," Mark complained.

"Yeah, especially when you can't keep track of the real one very well, either," observed Sharon. "Personally, I *prefer* fantasy," she added. "In the real world, there's always Mr. Kenyon and detention; in fantasy, if you get in trouble, you can just drop through a time warp or call up a dragon."

Fantasy literature is, by definition, a narrative that involves some violation of what are commonly accepted as the laws of reality. Magical objects, ancient swords, powerful rings; the fantasist writes of these impossibilities with skill and a sure knowledge that people will read with the "willing suspension of disbelief," that Aristotle, the Greek dramatist, described.

Susan Cooper writes, in a reflective essay, "Escaping Into Ourselves" (Hearne and Kaye, 1981):

> When we depart from our own reality into the reality of the book....we're going out of time, out of space, into the unconscious, that dreamlike world which has in it all the images and emotions accumulated since the human race began. We aren't escaping out, we're escaping in, without any idea of what we may encounter. Fantasy in the metaphor through which we discover ourselves.

In this chapter, fantasy literature is explored through metaphor and other figurative language. The fantasies of Laurence Yep and Lloyd Alexander are read. Literary analysis highlights the authors' strengths in using figurative language to design secondary worlds of high fantasy, myth fantasies, and travel to other worlds. Figurative language is language that communicates ideas beyond the literal, or actual, meanings of the words.

In a comprehensive study of the *Chronicles of Prydain,* Tunnell and Jacobs (1990) assess the continuing popularity of Lloyd Alexander's fantasies and conclude that there are four characteristics that may explain why these books find so many readers: (1) credibility, (2) tension, (3) humor, and (4) hope.

Other talented and popular authors of fantasy literature are also considered in this chapter as their work impacts the imaginative and creative thinking skills of the readers.

This multilevel consideration—reading for plot, character, and setting, as well as for an appreciation of symbolism—is a meaningful progression for young readers and may indeed be a tiring process.

However, most readers in the middle grades are already familiar with fantasy, sometimes referred to as low fantasy, through White's *Charlotte's Web* or Seldon's *The Cricket in Times Square.* The *Ralph* stories of Beverly Cleary provide an excellent introduction to this type of fantasy. In low fantasy, characters are often talking animals who take on human characteristics while remaining true to their species. Low fantasies are often based on eccentric characters who find themselves in ridiculous situations. These stories have simple plots with an element of magic that are set entirely in the primary world—the world of perceived reality.

Low fantasies are generally humorous and accessible, providing an excellent developmental ladder to the more complex fantasies at the other end of the continuum. A broad range of books defined as high fantasy are often as serious as the low fantasy books are humorous. These high fantasies are complex narratives, drawing upon ancient roots—myth, legend, and spiritual beliefs. These books are located entirely in an imagined secondary world with an invented geography, with exotic and imaginative flowers and plants, and with laws of nature of their own. These are stories of high adventure and enchantment, quests for magical objects, self-discovery, and the battle between good and evil. These dramatic scenes are played out upon wide but well-defined landscapes and the consequences are universal in their impact. Middle Earth, Narnia, Earthsea, and Prydain are fully realized secondary worlds.

There is another level of fantasy that does not have a convenient label. These are the stories that the literary arts student, Sharon, referred to as "time warp stuff." In these books, there is a collision between primary and secondary worlds, and the borders are not always strictly divided. In these stories, characters are transported across time and space, and past may interact with present day. These fantasies are built on many of the universal themes of high fantasy: the coming of age, the quest for wholeness and home, and the fact that yesterday and tomorrow are part of today. Madeleine L'Engle writes in this style with great success. When Sandy and Dennys Murry inadvertently stumble into one of their father's experiments, and find themselves in the arid desert of Noah and his family, the ensuing *Many Waters* is created.

Because the best fantasies captivate our minds and our hearts simultaneously, through the ingenious blending of profound ideas and complex issues, it is often a difficult genre for readers. Students enjoy the adventure, the quest, the excitement of the story line, but only the more reflective reader will wonder about the symbolism in the book.

Skills of evaluation, provocative questioning, creative reading, listening, and writing , as well as visualizing, are embedded in the units of study.

Authors who devote their writing primarily to the invention of fantasy have given considerable thought to their choice of subject matter. Not only do they create characters and worlds for these characters to inhabit, they also provide a philosophy for these characters to support. This quality that sets books of fantasy apart is the second level of meaning that readers may be taught to look for—significance, symbolism, allegory, a moral, a message, a lesson. Discovering meaning is not a simple process. But when it *is* discovered by the student, the book itself gains a value that may outlast the short time span during which a young reader is available to the author or teacher.

"Its [fantasy's] gift is, like the gift of poetry, to create an extension of reality, to intensify and expand the realization of experience, to shape and sharpen the sensibilities. In short, to keep alive man's sense of wonder" (Johnson, 1977). This is a quest in itself, for both teacher and reader.

Definition of Literary Terms

A helpful guide for the study of fantasy has been suggested by Frank E. Williams in his book, *Classroom Ideas for Encouraging Thinking and Feeling* (1970). This model draws on both the critical and creative thinking areas, and combines an examination of the author's style, themes, and philosophy with a study of literary or figurative language techniques. Some of the literary terms that describe these techniques are defined below.

Allegory: An expression through symbolic figures and actions of truths or generalizations about human conduct or experience.

Analogy: A form of logical inference that if two or more things agree in some respects they will probably agree in others. In fantasy, these analogies are frequently stated as the agreement between literary format and philosophy.

Hyperbole: An exaggeration for emphasis. For example, "A Fflam is always valiant! I've slashed my way through thousands...of warriors."

Metaphor: An indirect comparison between two unlike things that have something in common. For example, "The stars are candles in the sky."

Onomatopoeia: The use of words to imitate sounds. For example, fizzed, hissed.

Paradox: A statement that seems contrary to common sense, and yet is perhaps true. For example, the princess in waiting, Eilonwy, in the *Chronicles of Prydain* is portrayed as an airhead, but it is she who generally produces the most sensible suggestions to solve a problem.

Personification: The technique of giving human qualities to an object, animal, or idea. For example, "The ice talked, grinding its teeth."

Simile: A comparison using "like" or "as." For example, "Gurgi, miserable as a wet owl...."

CRITERIA FOR FANTASY

Six criteria for well-written fantasy are as follows:

- It must be believable. The impossible must seem completely plausible.
- It must have consistency and logic acceptable to the reader.
- It must have an original concept. It must be unique, inventive, and mysterious.
- It is predicated on an acceptance that the logic of the real world may be suspended through imagination.
- It usually includes imaginary characters, curious occurrences, strange people in strange lands, or time travel and transformation.
- It is based on a theme that expresses a universal truth.

1. Plausibility

Zena Sutherland describes the elements of fantasy in *Children and Books* (1986):

> The special quality of fantasy is that it concerns things that cannot really happen or that it is about people or creatures who do not exist, yet within the framework of each story there is a self-contained logic, a wholeness of conception that has its own reality. If it does not, it fails.

Lloyd Alexander, Susan Cooper, Laurence Yep, Madeleine L'Engle, and other authors of fantasy manipulate the characters, setting, and time in their books in order to create plausible and believable fantasy. Their secondary worlds are other planets, another world within this planet, or one like it. These writers of fantasy have other powerful tools in supernatural characters or the manipulation of time.

2. Consistency

Popular authors of fantasy novels are able to establish a premise at the beginning of the book, a sort of inner logic for the tale, and at the same time, provide boundaries to contain the fantasy. The reader must be able to recognize the author's frame of reference both within and without the boundaries of the fantasy world.

3. Originality of Concept

Authors of fantasy recognize that the function of their genre is to interpret human experiences with memorable and penetrating symbols or images, and to attempt to explain some of the ways in which the human heart and mind deal with hidden realities.

> The great fantasies, myths and tales are indeed like dreams: they speak from the unconscious to the unconscious, in the language of the unconscious—symbol and archetype. Though they use words, they work the way music does: they short-circuit verbal reasoning, and go straight to the thoughts that lie too deep to utter.....They are profoundly meaningful and usable—practical—in terms of ethics, of insight, of growth. (Tunnell and Jacobs, 1990)

4. Logic

The secondary worlds created by authors of fantasy books must be disciplined creations with clearly marked boundaries. These worlds have their own laws and limits. A successful fantasy will have perfect logic. Lloyd Alexander offers these comments about the logic of fantasy:

> Writers of fantasy must be, within their own frame of work, hardheaded realists. Happenings should have logical implications. Details should be tested for consistency....What seems so free in fantasy is often inventiveness of detail rather than complicated substructure. [There must be]....elaboration—not improvisation. (Tunnell and Jacobs, 1990)

5. Plot, Character, and Setting

The components of fantasy are expanded or extended to include both the real world and imaginary worlds. The protagonist in fantasy is generally an "Everyman," involved in a quest or search, or in a struggle between good and evil. In the *Chronicles of Prydain*, Lloyd Alexander depicts the character Taran's quest to discover his destiny. As Taran grows to maturity, he faces many adventures with the help of his companions, characters that support the protagonist. Antagonists are larger-than-life representations of evil, in conflict over ideology. High fantasy has a strong relationship to the Middle Ages in many of its settings, with dragons, knights, mythical beasts, gnomes, unicorns, and trolls wandering through a setting both strange and mysterious.

The skillful author of fantasy knows that the reader can accept all kinds of characters so long as the secondary worlds are carefully and vividly described. Effective fantasy combines the strange and the familiar and, while it may be unreal, it is never untrue.

6. Themes

Although the particular quality of fantasy is the emphasis on theme, wise authors never let theme overwhelm the plot. A theme expresses a universal truth and emerges easily without being labeled as truth or moral. Potent themes related to universal desires, conflicts, and values pervade fantasy and give the genre its particular power. Fantasy illuminates the constant struggle of good and evil within our world and within each of us, and enables readers to decide their place within the broader sphere of space and time. The cycle of life and death, the importance of love, friendship, and sacrifice, and the creatures that give order to the universe all provide forums for the author of fantasy to celebrate the beauty and wonder of the natural world. The themes of fantasy do not deal with a specific problem in a specific time; instead they deal with universal questions set apart from the real world.

ENTRY LEVELS FOR A UNIT ON FANTASY

Entry Level 1: Guided Discussion of a Fantasy Novel

Teachers and media specialists may wish to review and reinforce strategies for literary evaluation of an author's work by using a guided questioning method designed specifically for the study of fantasy. Graphic organizers can be used on a more sophisticated level, delineating fantasy worlds and realistic worlds that exist simultaneously in many fantasy novels.

The Black Cauldron, one of Lloyd Alexander's fantasy novels in the *Chronicles of Prydain,* is developed as a unit for Entry Level 1.

Entry Level 2: Independent Reading Contract for Fantasy Novel

If the scope and sequence of reading and literary skills has been developed in students by following the instructional methodology in previous chapters, the ideal progression is one that leads directly to the independent reading contract.

Students and instructors may decide to use the independent reading contract model as an individualized approach to the fantasy novel. For many students who are voracious readers and who anticipate a good read in every book they select, the opportunity to read widely in an author's body of work is a wonderful gift.

A reading contract is an agreement between teacher and student in which the student agrees to perform certain tasks from a menu of reading activities, and the teacher agrees to award points or grades for the successful completion of the agreed-on task within a determined time limit. In its simplest form, the reading contract provides space for the student to enter the number of activities he or she thinks is reasonably possible to complete in the alloted time. Another space is provided for the number of points or grade the student intends to earn. The contract is then signed by the student and the teacher and a copy is given to the student, with the original retained by the teacher.

Generally, the teacher has already provided a menu of possibilities from which the students may choose. Each item is accompanied by the number of points or grade for which that particular activity is valued. There are many commercial forms of independent reading contracts available, but teachers may prefer to design their own form to meet the particular needs of the literature unit. In using an approach to literature through authors, the independent reading contract is a valid tool for assessing not only the comprehension, but the level of thinking skills of the individual student.

Components of the independent reading contract give students the opportunity to experience the interaction of reading, speaking, listening, and writing as reasoning and communicating acts. And the contract gives teachers documentation for assessing the work of students through portfolios of their writing, extended oral and written responses to reading, logs or records of reading in class and outside class, and oral one-to-one conferences.

A model for a menu of choices for an independent reading contract using the works of author Lloyd Alexander might look like this:

Model of Menu Choices

You may contract for one or more activities from the menu below. The points and grade value are in parentheses after each activity. This contract is valid for six weeks from the date of signing.

1. Read one of the books of the *Chronicles of Prydain* and schedule an appointment for a reading conference to discuss plot, characters, and style. (10 points, Grade Value=C)

2. In addition to the above, bring to the reading conference a poster or other graphic description that you consider to be an exciting invitation for others to read the book. (15 points, Grade Value=B)

3. Read one of the books of the *Chronicles of Prydain* and prepare a portfolio to submit that includes a description of the main characters in the book, drawings or illustrations of the main characters, and a brief essay on how you think Lloyd Alexander built on events in previous books to furnish excitement and adventure in the book you read for your contract. (15 points, Grade Value =B)

4. Read two additional books of the *Chronicles of Prydain* and make an appointment for a reading conference. Be prepared to compare and contrast the plots of the two books, describe any growth or maturity in the characters through the two books, and how the author has used setting in the two books. (20 points, Grade Value=A)

5. Read two additional books by Lloyd Alexander. Submit a portfolio that contains an Activity Book of at least 20 pages based on the events, characters, and fantasy elements of the Alexander books. In your portfolio, include an essay of at least 500 words on the style of writing of Lloyd Alexander, and reasons why you think he continues to be such a popular writer. (20 points, Grade Value =A).

When teachers and library media specialists demonstrate confidence in their students by offering them a custom-designed independent reading program, bonding occurs. In effect, teacher and student meet at a common level of reading enjoyment.

GRAPHIC ORGANIZERS

According to Frank Smith of the Maryland State Department of Education, "the difference between good and poor learners is not the sheer quantity of what the good learner learns, but rather the good learner's ability to organize and use information." Research projects conducted in cooperation with the Maryland State Department of Education have shown that teachers who utilize graphic organizers with their students promote learning because knowledge that is organized into holistic conceptual frameworks is more easily remembered and understood than unstructured bits of information.

Graphic organizers exist in a variety of forms. Traditionally, teachers have used the web as a visual method for organizing information. In webbing, a central concept is surrounded, or webbed, with supporting characteristics or data so that a pictorial web emerges to show a complete semantic structure.

Jay McTighe (1989), education specialist in the Division of Instruction Language and Learning Improvement Branch of the Maryland State Department of Education, defines graphic organizers as a means for providing a visual, holistic representation of facts and concepts and their relationships within an organized frame.

They have proven to be effective tools to aid learning and thinking by helping students and teachers to represent abstract information in more concrete form, depict relationships among facts and concepts, relate new information to prior knowledge, and organize thoughts for writing.

In addition to the web, graphic organizers may include the concept map, sequence chain, story map, main idea table, flowchart, character analysis chart, comparison table, criteria grid, decision making chart, and analogy model.

Teachers and library media specialists may decide to use the suggested activities in introducing the use of graphic organizers for analyzing fantasy books or other literary genre.

Objectives

Graphic organizers will be used:

- before instructional activities, such as reading a chapter of a book, or viewing a film, to activate prior knowledge, to provide a conceptual framework for integrating new information, and to encourage student prediction.
- during instruction, to help students actively process and reorganize information.
- after instruction, to summarize learning, encourage elaboration, help organize ideas for writing, provide a structure for review, and assess the degree of student understanding.

In the literature on learning, four major graphic representation strategies are found. (1) A *networking strategy* requires students to depict the relationships among the concepts or ideas in a passage of text in the form of a diagram using nodes for concepts and links for relationships. The cognitive map (web) is such a graphic organizer. The web helps readers organize relationships between and among characters in a book, or relate plot developments in an organized manner. (2) A *mapping strategy* requires students to use a set of predetermined symbols to represent how ideas in a textual passage are related. The symbols may indicate that one item is an example of another, is caused by another, occurred before another, and so on. A sequence chain, compare and contrast Venn diagram, comparison table, character analysis chart, or analogy model are graphic organizers that let readers organize and summarize their thoughts about what is occuring on several levels of a fantasy book. (3) A *concept mapping strategy* requires students to identify elements of the content of an episode or chapter of a book, then note these elements in order from general to detailed, moving from top to bottom of a page. Then all items are linked by lines marked to indicate the type of relationship connecting the items. Examples of this type of graphic organizer are the story map, the extended story map, the main idea table, and the decision-making model. (4) An *iconic strategy* allows students to create personalized representations through drawings or sketches. A storyboard is an example of this kind of graphic organizer.

It is important to note that in all instances students must be taught to use the strategy.

Activities

Here are a variety of models of graphic organizers that will be used in understanding and interpreting the fantasy books of Lloyd Alexander and Laurence Yep. They may be used for analyzing the way authors invent characters, plan plots, and involve readers in the events and episodes of a book. Tape or glue these models into your journal to use as examples of graphic organizers in studying the books of selected authors.

1. Use the models of graphic organizers shown here to guide the reading of books by Lloyd Alexander or Laurence Yep. Decide which model would be most helpful in interpreting plot, character, and setting for both the realistic and fantasy elements of the book. Fill in the information about the story, the characters, and the sequence of events as you read each chapter.
2. Prepare an oral presentation with visual support material (graphic organizers) describing the way Lloyd Alexander uses characters' conflicting ideas to advance the action in his books.

3. Summarize the plot of one of Lloyd Alexander's books using a story map or extended story map to provide visual reference.
4. Select one of the books written by Laurence Yep and prepare an oral presentation on the way in which Yep uses the dragon symbol in his fantasy books. An analogy model, compare and contrast Venn diagram, or a character map may be used as visual support for the presentation.
5. Using a decision-making model, select an episode from one of Lloyd Alexander's books in which an important decision influenced the direction of the plot and describe the occurrence, including the consequences and alternatives for the decision.
6. Authors often use graphic organizers as outlines for their fiction stories. Use the model for a story map, or a main idea table, and sketch an idea for a book of your own. You may need to use the model for a character map to extend your ideas. Then, use the outline you have prepared to fully develop your original story.

UNIT 1: LLOYD ALEXANDER

Biographical Information

A recruitment advertisement on television features medieval knights dressed in armor for battle, facing off across a giant chess board while a chorus chants ancient runelike themes and cymbals clash: Viewers are being asked to consider the U.S. Marine Corps in the elitist context of "a few good men."

How many generations of idealistic young persons have been fascinated and moved by Arthurian legend? What is the mystique of Excalibur or the powers of the wizard Merlin?

Lloyd Alexander developed a lifelong fascination for hero tales and fantasy from a boyhood in Philadelphia spent haunting bookstores for ancient mythic tales. Armed with a garbage-can lid, like Oscar the Grouch, Alexander set out to do heroic deeds in a decidedly traditional neighborhood.

Ironically, Alexander found his actual Arthurian fantasyland during World War II when he was stationed in Wales. A real war waged around him, but for Alexander the people and landscapes of Wales were reinventions of all that he had read during those quiet Philadelphia evenings.

When the war ended and Alexander stayed in Paris to go to school, his urge to write and to set up his own medieval world peopled with heroic knights, or humorous bards, or failed poets was strengthened. Returning to

Cognitive Map (Web)

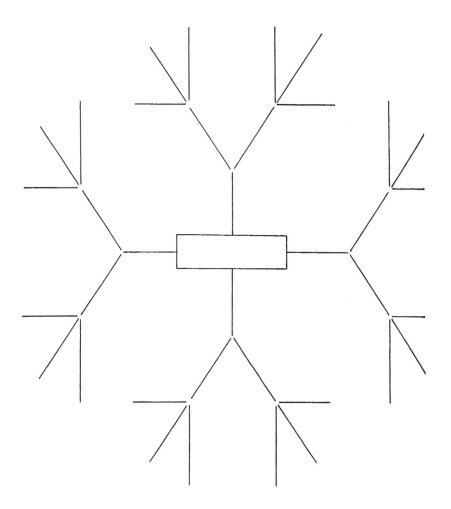

Story Map

Title: _____

Setting:
```
┌─────────────────────────────────┐
│                                 │
│                                 │
└─────────────────────────────────┘
```

Problem:
```
┌─────────────────────────────────┐
│                                 │
│                                 │
└─────────────────────────────────┘
```

Event 1 _____

Event 2 _____

Event 3 _____

Event 4 _____

Event 5 _____

Solution:
```
┌─────────────────────────────────┐
│                                 │
│                                 │
└─────────────────────────────────┘
```

Characters:_____   _____

_____   _____

_____   _____

Main Idea Table

Compare and Contrast Venn Diagram

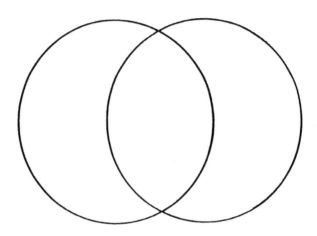

Analogy Model

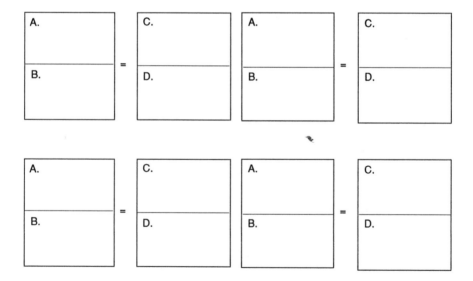

Character Map

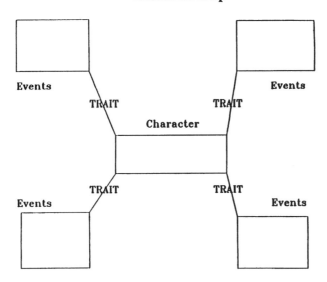

Events

Events

TRAIT   TRAIT

Character

TRAIT   TRAIT

Events

Events

Decision-Making Model

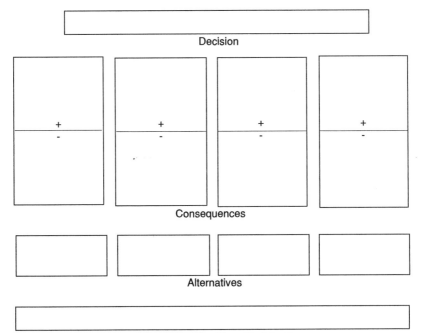

Decision

+

-

+

-

+

-

+

-

Consequences

Alternatives

What is the Need for a Decision?

Extended Story Map

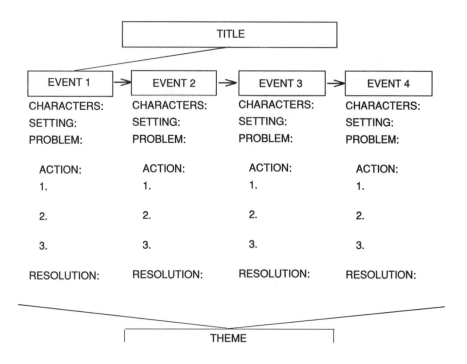

Sequence Chain

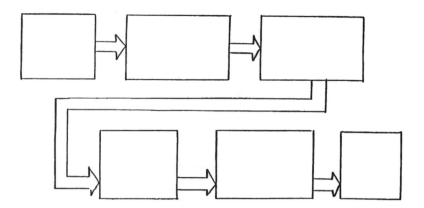

the United States with a Parisian bride, Alexander held a succession of dead-end jobs, but which provided experiences that would be the basis and cloth for Prydain, his invented kingdom. "I was writing out of my own life and experience," comments Lloyd Alexander (*Something about the Author*, Vol. 3, p. 9). "But....I learned a writer could know and love a fantasy world as much as his real one."

And so the Wales countryside of his memory became the kingdom of Prydain, and the adventures shared by Taran and his fellow wanderers were those that had their foundation in Welsh mythology known as *Mabinogion.* Thus the five books of the *Chronicles of Prydain* emerged—a brilliant tale of adventure, magic, the struggle between good and evil, and the ultimate triumph of the human spirit.

"If Wales gave me a glimpse of Prydain," writes Alexander, " I think Prydain gave me a glimpse of what every writer must do: to say, each in his own way, what is deepest in his heart. If writers learn more from their books than do readers, perhaps I may have begun to learn." (*SATA*, 3).

Linell Smith published an in-depth interview with Lloyd Alexander (*The Evening Sun*, October 15, 1984), in which the author offered some insights both into his writing and into his own personality.

> For some reason, I looked on the child's book as an art form, the same way the sonnet is a form....It seemed to me that whatever it was I had in mind to say—and I didn't know what it was—it required the form of a child's book....
>
> Some people can use external stimuli, and they're very lucky because they're never short of ideas. Whereas I have to work from the inside out. I work from what the poet Delmore Schwartz called a 'taste in the head' because you can't define it although you know what it is....Gradually the process is to rationalize the non-rational....
>
> I don't really think I have a style. As far as I'm concerned, style is being as simple as I can. It serves the subject. But there's a certain tonality which is different depending on the nature of the book....
>
> I'm not writing for kids as kids. I'm not trying to teach kids where they are now. I'm trying to teach them where they're going to be. And that's a little different.

Unit Objectives

In this unit, students will be able to:

- define and describe the nature and qualities of a hero, and the nature of destiny.

- recognize and describe forces that corrupt: power, greed, envy, and pride.
- use graphic organizers to represent abstract or implicit information in more concrete form.
- use graphic organizers to depict the relationships between characters in a fantasy novel.
- identify metaphor and other figurative language used in a fantasy novel.
- practice imaginative and creative thinking skills on a dual level: reading for plot, and reading for an appreciation of symbolism.

Teaching Strategies

1. The teacher:	**The students:**
introduces the book as a story about a young man who wants to be a knight and a hero.	
leads brainstorming discussion about the qualities of heroism as students perceive them.	participate in defining qualities of heroism.
asks students for examples of heroism in today's world.	contribute examples, such as recent war in the Middle East, life-saving efforts of police, fire fighters, etc.
lists examples and qualities of heroism on chalkboard or overhead projector and asks students to copy list into reading journals.	copy lists from chalkboard or overhead projector.
asks students to refer to their lists as they read *The Black Cauldron* for similarities between the characters in a fantasy and their realistic assessments.	

---

2. The teacher:	**The students:**
refers to Lloyd Alexander's biographical information to familiarize students with the author's creation of an imaginary kingdom, Prydain.	take notes in reading journals.

2. The teacher:	**The students:** *(cont.)*
reads aloud a passage from the "Author's Notes" that precede Chapter 1: "Although an imaginary world, Prydain is essentially not too different from the real one, where humor and heartbreak, joy and sadness are closely interwoven. The choices and decisions that face a frequently baffled Assistant Pig Keeper are no easier than the ones we ourselves must make. Even in a fantasy realm, growing up is accomplished not without cost."	listen to passage read aloud.
explains that this quote will be used frequently throughout the discussion of *The Black Cauldron.*	note the location of the passage in some significant way (by starring, bracketing or other means).

3. The teacher:	**The students:**
introduces the Welsh pronunciations of character and place names used in *The Black Cauldron.*	
presents the list of characters, either in a printed list or written on the overhead or chalkboard, and asks students to copy the list of characters in a single column in their reading journals. The list should include the following: Taran, Caeri, Dallben, Prydain, Avren, Ellidyr of Pen-Llarcau, Orddu, Eilonwy, Gurgi, Gwydion, Fflam, Doli, Smoit, Adaon, Taliesin, Morgant, Cantrev, Arawn, Fflewddur, Annuvin, Idris, Melynlas, Melyngar, Islimach, Ystrad, Lluagor, Eiddileg, Gwystyl, Orwen, Orgoch, Gwythaint.	copy list according to directions.
guides students in deciding on a consistent pronunciation of each	take turns pronouncing names of characters and

3. The teacher:	The students: *(cont.)*
name. For example, ch=hh *crochan* pronounced *cro han;* dd=th *Orddu* pronounced *Orthu;* and ll=hl *Llyr* pronounced *Hleer.)*	places, using group decision for pronunciation.
4. The teacher:	**The students:**
explains that since there are so many characters introduced in the first chapter, it will be read aloud.	follow the text of Chapter 1 as the teacher reads it aloud.

The Black Cauldron

The Story

In this second book of the *Chronicles of Prydain* series, Taran, the Assistant Pig Keeper of Caer Dallben, is frustrated because he feels that he is able to lead a more exciting life. He decides to venture forth in a quest to overcome evil and attain manhood, but though he begs to attend the council and be part of the action, Taran is assigned to the group headed by Adaon, a peacemaker and philosopher.

The plot revolves on the efforts of three groups of warriors and kings to locate and destroy the Black Cauldron of King Arawn, an evil and sinister antagonist. This black cauldron is used to create robot-like creatures known as "the Cauldron Born," who having once died, are restored to comprise the armies of the evil King Arawn. Taran's determination and the help of his loyal friends overcome obstacles and dangers, and Taran emerges as a maturing hero.

Discussion Questions and Activities (Chapter 1)

1. Who are the main characters introduced in this chapter?
2. Using the information about the character given in this chapter, develop a "Cast of Characters" similar to a list of performers in a play.
3. Select from Chapter 1 a character you find especially interesting. Describe this character in your journal, both physically and psychologically. Try to include both objective information from the chapter, and subjective thoughts generated from your reading.

4. How can the reader determine possible conflicts between and among characters described in Chapter 1? Name some distinguishing characteristics of each character and suggest how there might be a possible conflict with another character.

5. How does dialogue influence or reveal characteristics of the protagonists and antagonists in this chapter?

6. Who would you predict will be major characters in the book, based on information in this chapter?

7. In your reading journal, draw a diagram of the Council Table as you imagine it looks from the description given in Chapter 1.

8. In the first chapter, the knights come together to discuss a "new threat." What is this new danger? Record your answer in your journal.

9. What is the defense strategy the group devises to protect themselves from danger? Record your answer in your journal.

Discussion Questions and Activities (Chapter 2)

1. Prepare a chart in your journal showing the three bands, the leader of each band, and the mission of each band. Compare and contrast by using graphic organizers such as a web or a Venn diagram.

2. Using dialogue from Chapter 2, write a script showing how each character reacts to his or her assigned role. Present the dramatization to other groups and have them evaluate the performance.

3. In *The Black Cauldron,* Eilonwy is the only major female character. Read the section of the chapter that describes her helping Taran with his sword, and then predict what her future role in the story will be. Use evidence from the chapter to support your view. Write your opinion as a persuasive essay in your journal.

Discussion Questions and Activities (Chapter 3)

1. Recalling the literary terms you have learned, record in your journal instances of figurative language used by the various characters in the book. What kind of pattern do you see emerging?

2. In Chapter 3, the character of Adaon is developed. Taran discovers many sides to Adaon's personality. How does the author let us know that Adaon is a peacemaker? (p. 33, Adaon's song) Or a prophet? (p. 30, Adaon's dreams) Or a philosopher who thinks deeply about life? (p. 31,"there is greater power in a field well-plowed"; p. 32, "the more we find to love, the more we add to the measure of our hearts")

3. Conflict is developed in Chapter 3 between several characters. Describe the conflict between Taran and Ellidyr, between Gwydion and King Morgant.

4. What event shows the reader some of the dimensions of Ellidyr's personality? (Ellidyr's strength in rescuing Taran and the horse, Melynlas; Ellidyr's anger and pride; his aloofness)

5. There are many examples of figurative speech in this chapter. Give an example of a simile. (p. 33, "he recalled Adoan's dream and felt a shadow like the flutter of a dark wing"; p. 40, "the warriors of King Morgant's train moved like shadows") Give an example of personification (p. 42, "Morgant's sword was broken and weeping blood")

6. Use a graphic organizer of your choice to describe, compare, and contrast the Cauldron Born with the Huntsmen of Annuvin. (A web is a good choice for each of Arawn's warriors; a Venn diagram may be used for the comparison and contrast.)

7. How does Gwydion find out about the movements of the enemy? (He has Doli make himself invisible and gather information.)

8. Why does Gwydion caution his followers *not* to kill the Huntsmen of Annuvin, even though they are mortal? (Arawn has given them the power to gain more strength whenever one of their number is killed.)

9. Which of the two groups, the Cauldron Born or the Annuvin Huntsmen, do you think should be more feared? Give reasons for your answer from the text.

10. Make a "Wanted: Dead or Alive" poster that could be used in public places. Imagine what the Caudron Born and Huntsmen of Annuvin look like, and draw a portrait of them for the poster. The completed posters may be judged on such criteria as fierceness and accuracy to the author's description.

11. How does Lloyd Alexander indicate Taran's future role? (By using Adaon to predict, or foreshadow, events envisioned in his dreams.)

12. How do you think the relationship between Taran and Ellidyr will develop? What clues do you find in the chapter to help you predict their future interactions?

Discussion Questions and Activities (Chapter 4)

1. Each of the four characters—Eilonwy, Gurgi, Fflewdur, and Doli—have a special possession or power. List the character and the special possessions in a series of four squares across the top of a sheet of paper in your reading journal. This chart will be the basis for recording cause

and effect through the story, showing how each special possession aided the band in their quest to seek and destroy the Black Cauldron. (Eilonwy has a "bauble" of light; Gurgi has a magic wallet that never runs out of food; Fflewddur has a harp of truthfulness; and Doli has the power to make himself invisible.) From the events in Chapter 4, two of these special possessions have been used. Where should the reader record this information on the chart? (Gurgi uses food; Doli has used invisibility to spy on the enemy.)

2. There is another confrontation between Taran and Ellidyr in Chapter 4. What has happened to provoke this confrontation? (Eilonwy's appearance) How does Eilonwy react to the confrontation? (She is flattered at Taran's defense of her.)

Discussion Questions and Activities (Chapter 5)

1. In Chapter 5, there is an exciting description of the battle between the Huntsmen of Annuvin and Adaon's band. How does the author convey a sense of speed, violence, and heroism?

2. In describing the encounter, does the author give the reader a sense that Adaon's band will escape the Huntsmen? Find evidence in the text for your answer.

3. Assume the character of Taran and write a journal entry replying to Ellidyr's contemptuous response to Taran, who has just thanked him for saving his life. (p. 60, "It is a small debt. You value it [life] more than I do.")

4. The author does not elaborate on the crimson brand that each Huntsman has embedded in his forehead. Design a brand that you think Arawn, the Evil King, would place on his warriors as an identifying symbol. Draw the brand you have designed in your reading journal.

5. Find examples of figurative language in this chapter and record them in your reading journal. (p. 54,"the sun had begun to unravel in scarlet threads"; p. 56, "[Gurgi] ....furious as a hornet")

6. Why does Doli become so angry? How does he explain the presence of Fair Folk in the forest?

7. Why do you think that Adaon makes his band move on through the forest instead of letting them camp for the night?

8. What additional character traits can now be added to the graphic organizer comparing and contrasting Ellidyr and Taran?

Discussion Questions and Activities (Chapter 6)

1. Although Doli and Gwystyl are both Fair Folk, they are very different in looks and personality. Use a graphic organizer to compare and contrast the two.
2. The author uses many different words and phrases to describe Gwystyl's melancholy disposition. Find and list some of the descriptive words in preparing a web about Gwystyl.
3. The chamber or way station that Gwystyl was in charge of is carefullly described in this chapter. Choose a way to visually represent this chamber—a diorama, a mural, or a collage—and display the finished product as part of a Black Cauldron Gallery of Art.
4. The idea of a way station or safe haven has been used both in literature and in factual history. Research the Underground Railroad used by escaping slaves before and during the Civil War, and share your findings with the group. What key words could you use to locate more information about the uses of way stations in history and literature?
5. Why did Gwystyl have to give shelter to Adaon's band even though he was reluctant to do so?

Discussion Questions and Activities (Chapter 7)

1. In this chapter, Eilonwy seems to assume a leadership role. Why do you think the author has her reinforce Gwydion's instructions instead of Adaon, the appointed leader?
2. Orddu, Orwen, and Orgoch are not identified or described in the chapter. In your journal, write a prediction of what or who these creatures might be. You will use this character description later to see whether your prediction is correct.
3. Again, Fflewddur exaggerates or uses hyperbole to describe his exploits, and a harp string breaks. What does Fflewddur claim?
4. Why do you think Adaon refuses to give a command to his followers? What do you think he means when he says (p. 83), "this choice cannot be mine. I have said nothing for or against your plan; the decision is greater than I dare make."
5. Prepare a panel discussion, taking the roles of Taran, Eilonwy, Ellidyr, and Adaon, and debate the two possible courses of action that could be taken. Be true to the character in presenting arguments.

Discussion Questions and Activities (Chapter 8)

1. In Chapter 8, the conflict between Taran and Ellidyr reaches a climax. What events in this chapter show this? (Taran removing stone from Islimach's hoof; Ellidyr's disappearance during his watch time)

2. Why do you think Adaon decides to tell the group about the brooch he wears? Give reasons why Adaon selects Taran to inherit his horse and possessions of healing herbs and brooch if harm comes to him in battle?

3. Lloyd Alexander involves the reader in the excitement of battle. Find phrases that are particularly action-oriented, and write them in your journal.

4. Adaon shows his philosophical nature when he says to Taran (p. 92): "Is there not glory enough in living the days given to us? You should know there is adventure in simply being among those we love and the things we love, and beauty, too." Explain Adaon's remarks in an essay, using concrete examples from your own life and the lives of your friends and family.

5. Assume that you are a reporter for CNN or another news network. Describe the battle between the Huntsmen and Adaon's band. Use video equipment that is available to you either at home or at school to record your commentary.

6. Why do you think that Adaon insisted that a confrontation take place when he already knew that the Huntsmen were strengthened by the death of a single member?

Discussion Questions and Activities (Chapter 9)

1. Chapter 9 is one of ideas and serious thoughts. Do you think that Adaon, who had recounted his dream of a "fair place," knew that he was going to die in battle? Why or why not?

2. If Adaon had the gift of prophesy and healing, why do you think he died? Write a journal entry in the form of an obituary notice. Look in your local papers to see how an obituary is written. You may include information you know about Adaon from earlier chapters in *The Black Cauldron*, and use a character trait graphic organizer to channel your information.

3. A cause and effect graphic organizer is a helpful tool at this point in the book. Use a sequence chain graphic organizer to explain the action in Chapter 9.

4. When Adaon gives Taran the brooch he wears, and entrusts it to his safekeeping, incredible things begin to happen. How would you explain Taran's sudden ability to predict future happenings?

5. Look for evidence in the chapter that shows that Taran is changing in character. List these clues in a character map graphic organizer.
6. Immediately following Adaon's death, Taran has a troubling dream. What were some of the things that Taran saw in his dream? Do you think that this dream sequence will be the basis for further conflict in the book? Why or why not?

Discussion Questions and Activities (Chapter 10)

1. Alexander builds suspense by describing the Marshes of Morva as a place of mysterious and uncomfortable elements. What are some of the ways he describes the marshes? Find and record these descriptive passages in your journal.
2. How does Fflewddur explain Taran's ability to predict rain? (p. 111, arthritis, rheumatism, old wounds) Locate a weather map showing the path of a rainstorm. Share your findings with a group, describing the meteorological facts involved in weather forecasting.
3. Gurgi adds some new rhymed and paired words to his vocabulary. What are some of these pairs and how do they have an effect upon the setting? (p.111, "slippings and drippings"; p. 113, "dashings and crashings")
4. What does Fflewddur say the bardic symbol on Adaon's clasp means? (p. 112, "knowledge, truth and love") Draw your interpretation of the bardic symbol from the description given in the chapter. (p. 112, "three lines, like an arrowhead")
5. As a reader looking for symbolic meanings, what can you predict from Taran's dream about Ellidyr? Write a journal entry interpreting Taran's dream.
6. Alexander uses figurative language in this chapter to create a mood. Find an example of personification that gives a vivid mental picture of the marshes. (p. 115, "ropes of fog"; p. 117, "black bog")
7. How did Taran's earlier dream of wolves save his life in the marshes?
8. Bogs, marshes, and quicksand all have geological properties that cause them to act as "sucking" areas. Research bogs to find out about these properties and what causes them. The library media center may have a number of books and materials in the "500s," or Natural Science section.

Discussion Questions and Activities (Chapter 11)

1. Three new characters are introduced in Chapter 11. Who are they? What do they look like? What kind of personalities do they have?

2. The symbolic number "three" appears often in legend, folk tales, and fantasy. Brainstorm "famous 3s" in literature and name the story in which they appear. This can also be a good "Jeopardy Game" category. (Mrs. Who, Whatzit, Which in *Wrinkle in Time;* three witches in *Macbeth;* three dogs in Andersen's *Tinder Box;* three bears, three pigs, and three billy goats)

3. The three enchantresses have a lively dialogue in this chapter. Select three readers and a narrator to perform a reader's theater of these pages of dialogue in the chapter.

4. As an art activity, design and make masks to represent Orddu, Orwen, and Orgoch.

5. Why do you think Alexander creates additional complications by giving the three enchantresses the ability to change into each other? Do you think this will cause difficulties? Why or why not?

6. Eilonwy continues to use similes in her conversation. Find examples in this chapter, and add them to your characterization map.

7. The witches use affectionate terms in talking to Taran and his friends. Begin a list of these endearing terms in your journal.

8. Do you think the wanderers are in real trouble in this new setting? Why or why not?

Discussion Questions and Activities (Chapter 12)

1. In Chapter 12, Orddu, Orwen, and Orgoch explain that they had found Dallben the wizard and Taran's master in the marsh. What happened to cause them to send Dallben away? (Spilled potion of wisdom, tasted it, and became as knowledgeable as they were)

2. When Dallben left, the three enchantresses offered him a sword, a harp, or the Book of Three. Which did he choose? Why do you think he made that choice? In a journal entry, defend or challenge his choice, and give reasons for the decision you would have made.

3. What do you think the three objects symbolized? Explain your decision in a short journal entry.

4. Why do you think the three enchantresses were so vague about the whereabouts of the Black Crochan (Cauldron)?

Discussion Questions and Activities (Chapter 13)

1. Who finds the cauldron? Do you think the author made a good decision in having this character locate the cauldron? Why or why not?

2. Select a reader to read the description of the cauldron (p.144) aloud. As the reader presents the selection, sketch the cauldron in your journal, using the passage being read for details.
3. How does Lloyd Alexander use figurative language (personification) to describe the cauldron. List several examples in your reading journal. (p. 144, 149)
4. What explanation can you suggest for the change in appearance in the three enchantresses?
5. The author does not describe the change except to let the reader know they were "beautiful." Using the information in earlier chapters, draw a picture of the three hags. Next to each figure, draw a visual interpretation of each of the three beautiful women spinning.
6. What happens when Taran and his friends try to steal the cauldron?

Discussion Questions and Activities (Chapter 14)

1. In Chapter 14, the emphasis is on exchange. The three enchantresses offer to trade the cauldron for something Taran or his friends prize as much as the cauldron. What do the friends offer? What reasons do the hags give for declining their offers?
2. Prepare a page similar to a mail-order catalog. Draw the object each of the band is offering, and write a persuasive argument for selecting it.
3. Do you think that the objects the three enchantresses request—the North Wind, the South Wind, and a perfect summer afternoon—are in keeping with their personalities? Why or why not?

Discussion Questions and Activities (Chapter 15)

1. How does Taran show a developing maturity of character in this chapter? Read Taran's dialogue (pp. 162-163) for signs of this character growth. Then record additional traits on your character trait graphic organizer.
2. What is the only way the cauldron can be destroyed, according to Orddu?
3. Orddu tells Taran and his friends that "whoever gives up his life to Crochan must give it willingly, knowing full well what he does." Predict who you think will perform this task, based on all of the characters in the book. Give reasons for your choice.
4. What does the band decide to do with the cauldron? Do you think they made a wise decision? Why or why not?
5. This exchange of thoughts is the turning point of the plot; the rising action has reached a climax. Use a story map to show the progress, or rising action so far. The story map will be extended and concluded as the book progresses.

Discussion Questions and Activities (Chapter 16)

1. In this chapter, Taran shows his maturity and character growth by beginning to make sound and practical decisions without the help of Adaon's brooch. Find examples of these decisions, and list them in your reading journal. (p.172, making a sling for the cauldron of vines and branches; crossing the river)
2. Eilonwy shows her character growth through her supportive and positive responses to their dilemma. What are some of the arguments she gives Taran for continuing their journey with the heavy cauldron?
3. Eilonwy continues to express herself in similes (p. 175). Find the example on the page, and explain the analogy.
4. When Fflewddur is hurt, he engages in a dialogue with Eilonwy and Taran that is at "cross-purposes." Fflewddur is talking about the harm done to his harp, while Taran and Eilonwy are assuring him that they can cure his broken arm. Why do you think the author introduces this humorous detail in such a suspenseful chapter? (To relieve tension)
5. "The cauldron crouched like a glowering beast of prey." This example of a simile differs from earlier metaphors when the cauldron was described in terms like "its leering, gaping mouth taunted him, and the cauldron dragged at his strength." Do you think the author had a purpose in comparing the cauldron to a beast now rather than a person? Why or why not?
6. When you read the last sentence in the chapter, who do you predict will be the shadowy figure? Give reasons for your prediction.

Discussion Questions and Activities (Chapter 17)

1. How does Ellidyr explain his presence? When he boasts of his encounters with the Huntsmen of Annuvin and the gwythaints, how do Taran and his companions react?
2. What reasons does Ellidyr give for deserting the band when Eilonwy accuses him of sneaking away?
3. Why do you think Taran refuses to respond to Ellidyr's taunt, "Why do you not climb into it [the cauldron] yourself?...Or are you a coward at heart?" Give reasons for your answer from the story.
4. What conditions does Ellidyr set for helping Taran and his companions remove the cauldron from the river?
5. The conflict between Taran and Ellidyr reaches its height during this confrontation. There is conflict of values, ideas, honor, truth. Take Ellidyr's question (p. 189), "What is the honor of a pig-boy...compared

to the honor of a prince?" and write an essay about the virtue of honor, its importance, and how you personally consider its meaning.

6. What happens when the cauldron is dragged from the river? What do you think causes Ellidyr's distrust of Taran?

7. This chapter is an effective example of Alexander's cliffhanger approach. Writers use this technique to build suspense and motivate readers. Brainstorm examples of television shows that also use this cliffhanger technique. ("Star Trek") Films use this technique in suggesting sequels. (*Indiana Jones* and *Star Wars*) Can you think of computer games that use the cliffhanger technique? Share your findings from the media with the group.

Discussion Questions and Activities (Chapter 18)

1. Eilonwy tells Taran (pp. 199-200), "you're not a pig-boy; you're an Assistant Pig-Keeper!....One is proud, the other isn't. Since you have a choice, take the proud one!" What do you think Eilonwy is really trying to tell Taran? Do you think her admiration for Taran is evidenced in this chapter? Why or why not?

2. What are the feelings of the group when King Morgant appears? Why does Taran feel uneasy?

3. When King Morgant accuses Taran of ignoring Gwydion's instructions, Taran responds defensively. What do you think would have happened if Taran had been obedient to Gwydion's original orders?

4. Eilonwy breaks the oath the group had sworn to Ellidyr by telling King Morgant what has happened. How does Morgant react to the news?

5. What is the first clue that Taran gets that King Morgant is not the true knight he had supposed him to be? (Ellidyr beaten and tied up)

Discussion Questions and Activities (Chapter 19)

1. Five characters have taken possession of the Black Cauldron: King Arawn, the three hags acting as one, Taran, Ellidyr, and Morgant. Use a graphic organizer to compare their motives. When the comparison is complete, decide on which character had the highest motives, and write a brief journal entry giving reasons for your choice.

2. King Morgant challenges Taran with the question (p.211): "Will you be first among my warriors—or first among my Cauldron Born?" What is the meaning of this question? Do you think that Morgant's reasons for tempting Taran to join him rather than inviting Ellidyr are good ones? Why or why not? Use knowledge of Taran's character, written on your character trait graphic organizer, to predict Taran's future decision.

3. Throughout the book, references are made to the presence of a "black beast" in Ellidyr's personality. Do you think that Adaon's prophecy that Ellidyr would be swallowed by this black beast will come true? In what way?

4. The medieval warriors and knights judged a person's character in terms of battle materials. When King Morgant describes Taran as having "good mettle," and being a "rare metal" that is "ready to be tempered," to what is he referring? Research knights and the Middle Ages by consulting reference books in the History (900) section of the library media center. While you are locating information, include Morgant's reference and promise to Taran to make him his "liege lord."

5. Eilonwy continues to be the most practical member of the group when she comments (p. 214): "It's hard to think about where to run as long as your hands and feet are tied up." How does this statement encourage the band?

6. Ellidyr apologizes to Taran for his actions at the end of the chapter. How does Taran accept Ellidyr's statement that he stole the cauldron "out of pride, not evil." Have Ellidyr's past actions given Taran much of a basis for forgiveness? Explain in a journal entry what course of action you feel Taran might have taken at this point.

Discussion Questions and Activities (Chapter 20)

1. In this final chapter, which is the resolution of the story, the author brings all of the original characters full circle. This literary technique lets the reader have a feeling of satisfaction and completion. Do you think Alexander's resolution is a satisfying one? Why or why not? (Remember that *The Black Cauldron* is Book 2 in a series of five adventures, and that the unit will include all of them.)

2. Read and recall the deaths of Ellidyr, the Crochan, Morgant, and Islimach. Try to recreate the descriptions of these violent deaths in a diorama or collage.

3. Who do you think paid the highest price in the pursuit of the Black Cauldron? Give evidence for your choice from events in the book.

4. Gwydion tells Taran (p. 228), "You chose to be a hero not through enchantment but through your own manhood. And since you have chosen, for good or ill, you must take the risks of a man. You may win or you may lose. Time will decide." What do you think Gwydion means by this statement? What do you think time will decide for Taran?

5. Gwydion, the knight that Taran so admires, played no part in the recovery of the Black Cauldron, and in fact, did not participate in the action at all. Why do you think the author chose to keep this heroic figure in the

background? If this were the only book you read in the series, would you have the same great admiration for Lord Gwydion that Taran has? Why or why not?

Additional Activities for The Black Cauldron

1. In your journal, develop an outline of the story using only the end-of-the-chapter anticipatory previews. By using the author's cliffhangers, you will create a summary of the book. When the summary is completed, compare it with your work on your on-going story map graphic organizer. Are they similar?

2. In literary arts, words often have a *contextual* meaning as well as a *dictionary* definition. Using the following list of words from *The Black Cauldron,* create a comparison chart with three columns: the word, the Prydain meaning (context), and the dictionary meaning. Some of the words exist *only* in Prydain.

oracular	conical	sedge
scullery	liege	grimace
insolence	realm	quest
bard	cajoling	fathom
scythe	untethered	waypost
contrev	shards	wattle-and-daub
caer	enchantress	fledgling
raiment	destiny	gwythaint
implacable	burdock	gurgi

3. Plan a "Day in Prydain." Use the map of the country, have members of your group assume the roles of characters from Prydain, and speak as that character would—in "Fflewddur-isms," Gurgi rhyming words, or Orddu terms of endearment. Students may suggest costumes of their characters through masks, streamers, or props with which the characters are associated. Celebrate with food, music, or dance appropriate to the Middle Ages.

4. Consider the original discussion on the themes of the book. Now that you have completed the book, use the author's message to answer the questions: What is a hero? How did Taran exemplify one? What is the nature of destiny? How did events affect Taran's destiny? What are the forces that corrupt? How is this message conveyed in *The Black Cauldron*? How can truth and reality balance opposing forces such as good and evil or peace and war. How is this balance portrayed in the book?

UNIT 2: LAURENCE YEP

Biographical Information

One of the few writers to chronicle the Chinese-American experience in children's literature, Laurence Yep has examined his own Chinese anteced-ents and carefully traced the mythology, legend, and fantasy of that culture as it affects a traditional California upbringing.

> Having been raised in a Black ghetto and having commuted to a bilingual school in Chinatown, I did not confront White American culture until high school. Approaching as something of a stranger, I have been fascinated by all its aspects—from its great novels to its chidren's literature. (*Something About the Author*, Vol. 69, pp. 230-34)

Because Yep viewed himself as an amalgam of cultures, and an observer of different ethnic backgrounds, he finds the concept of the alien or an alienated hero a comfortable persona in his writing. Yep wrote and sold his first science fiction short story when he was 18 years old, and seemed destined to make science fiction his milieu. His book, *Sweetwater,* describes the heroic struggles of a young boy to save his doomed city. Tyree, descendent of Earthlings who first colonized the city of Harmony, must deal with aliens called Argans. Out of this conflict came an insight for the author. "It only occurred to me after it (*Sweetwater*) was published that the aliens of the novel, the Argans, are similar in some ways to the Chinese in America. Out of *Sweetwater* grew *Dragonwings,* in which I finally confronted my own Chinese-American identity" (Harper and Row Publicity Brochure, 1978).

When the children's television series *Readers' Cube* was in the design phase, content specialists noted that a young author had received an Honor Book Award from the Newbery Committee for his book, *Dragonwings.* It is the story of a young boy whose father, a Chinese immigrant in San Francisco, had a lifelong fascination with flying and aeronautical engineering. It seemed to the creators of the television series that this book would make an exciting dramatization and on-camera interview with the author that would interest and attract the adolescent readers for whom the series was targeted.

In the studio, Laurence Yep proved to be an articulate and personable guest, and was immediately recognized as an author of integrity and sincerity who greatly appealed to audiences. *Dragonwings* became a popular book in middle school English classes and libraries, partly because the story com-bined traditional values of hard work and inventiveness with a fantasy element based on Chinese culture. In the spring of 1991, a note arrived from Laurence

Yep: "*Dragonwings* has been dramatized once more, and this time the stage at the Kennedy Center in Washington, D.C. will be its performance site." Selected as a performance piece for the series of children's theater presentations, *Dragonwings* continues to fascinate and delight readers and audiences.

One of the highlights surrounding the opening of the Sackler Gallery of Asian Art, part of the Smithsonian complex, was the introduction of a Museum Shop that featured an extensive collection of children's literature based on Asian themes, legends, myths, and modern fiction. The novels of Laurence Yep are an integral part of this collection. Page Salazar, who selected the books and developed the book department of the Sackler Museum Shop, indicates that the popularity of this author of books based on his own Chinese cultural heritage proves that readers appreciate the multicultural aspects and universal qualities of Yep's characters.

Currently, Laurence Yep resides near San Francisco and teaches creative writing at the University of California, Berkeley. Through his novels for young persons, he has introduced Chinese culture, literature, and mythology, and has skillfully blended his characters and plots in a multicultural setting. With great sensitivity, Yep points out that peoples of varying cultures and beliefs can come together in common cause and that traditional ethnic values have a basis in a universal scheme based on respect and appreciation for differences.

Unit Objectives

In this unit, students will be able to:

- use a traditional journal or a word processing program to participate in an independent literary arts experience.
- apply literal, interpretive, and critical thinking skills to a fantasy novel.
- understand the motives of characters and their relationships.
- identify and appreciate figurative language.
- create and build a file of information about several books by a specific author, either in a traditional journal or as part of a software program.

Teaching Strategies	
The teacher:	**The students:**
obtains multiple copies of books by Laurence Yep.	select one of the books.

The teacher:	The students:
meets with the literary arts class to explain the process of the independent reading program and using a journal to record and communicate information about the books.	listen to and follow directions.
explains the parameters of the project: 1. Students may read as many of Laurence Yep's books as they choose in the five-week time period; 2. Students will obtain a list of discussion questions and activities for each book read, and record their responses in their journals; 3. Journals will be collected at intervals for critique and evaluation.	attend the instruction.
is available for conferences and guidance in book selection.	seek out assistance when desired.
prepares and provides discussion questions and activities based on the novels of Laurence Yep.	
collects and examines student journals at intervals. each book is completed.	submit journals for teacher evaluation as
records comments on student responses after evaluation.	read teacher comments for reinforcement of learning.

Sweetwater

The Story

Tyree lives in an unusual world. A flood has engulfed his city, but residents have learned to live only in the upper levels of their homes and other environments. Transportation in this futuristic Venetian city takes place by boat, and there is fear and apprehension everywhere because of two factions: the Silkies and the Argans.

Tyree is a lonely young man who turns to music for companionship. He fashions his own flute and attempts to teach himself to play it. Angry at the sound of his son's music, Tyree's father forbids him to play the flute. In desperation, Tyree turns to Amadeus, the Argan song master, and the two soon form a close friendship.

Discussion Questions and Activities

1. This novel is considered by some critics to be a science fiction adventure more than a fantasy. Compose a persuasive essay expressing your opinions about the literary genre Yep has chosen. Remember to provide evidence from the book, either quotations or references to events in the story, that supports your personal opinion. Your essay should be a minimum of five paragraphs.

2. In *Sweetwater,* Laurence Yep has invented and created imaginative nonhuman creatures, which he describes throughout the story. Sketch at least three of these nonhuman creatures as you think they would look according to Yep's description and characterization. Keep your sketches in your journal.

3. In the book, Tyree makes and plays his own flute. Visit the library media center and use an encyclopedia or other reference material to learn what the instrument looks like, how it is played, and its history. Record your findings in your journal.

4. A special relationship develops beween Tyree and Amadeus, the Argan songmaster. How does Tyree show he respects, yet fears, Amadeus? Compose a brief response and enter it in you journal.

5. Amadeus tells Tyree: "You hold your soul back from the music like you can't forget you're a human playing Argan music. You just have to remember it's the music that counts—not the one who plays it." What message is Laurence Yep, the author, giving to all musicians by having Argan make this statement? Record your response in your journal. You might wish to consult an accomplished or professional musician to gain insight on how musicians view their work.

6. There is a great deal of figurative language in this book. Yep is particularly good at the simile and the metaphor. Find examples in the book and list them in your journal. Include the example of figurative speech, and the page on which the example appears.

7. Compose a paragraph in your journal in which you contrast or point out the differences between Amadeus and Tyree.

8. Predicting is an important part of enjoying and participating in literature. Prepare a list of predictions about the novel *Sweetwater,* that can be given to a student who has not yet read the book. Then ask someone in your group to prepare a list of predictions for you about a book by Laurence Yep that you have not yet read. Record predictions in your journal. You may wish to use some of the predictions given here as idea generators. Predictions should be made after reading only the first chapter of the novel.

Prediction Possibilities

1. Tyree was forbidden to let another Silkie hear him play the flute. Will Tyree disobey his father? Will Tyree's father ever accept his music making?
2. The Argans were astonished at Tyree's ability to play the flute. How do you think the Argans might react to Tyree's playing in the future? Will Tyree continue to feel embarrassed about his playing?
3. Tyree was not permitted to talk about himself, nor would Amadeus talk about himself. Do you think that Amadeus will ever tell Tyree about himself? Will Amadeus and Tyree continue to play music together?

Dragonwings

The Story

Moon Shadow, a young Chinese boy, travels from his home in China to join his father and other male relatives in San Francisco, California. It was customary for Chinese men to live in communities called Companies, and to work and live in a section of the city known as Chinatown. Occasionally, one of the men would accumulate enough money to bring his other family members to America, or to return to China for a brief visit.

Moon Shadow is frightened of this new environment in San Francisco; his father, Windrider, seems distant and absorbed in plans for building kites. After an angry and dangerous confrontation with one of his cousins, Windrider takes Moon Shadow to live in a different section of San Francisco, in a stable belonging to an independent and interesting woman named Miss Whitlaw. Here Moon Shadow meets Robin, and the two gradually become friends, as the Chinese boy learns about the ways of the "Demons," as the Chinese community refers to Caucasians.

When an earthquake occurs, people of the city are drawn together through their mutual losses. Through it all, Windrider continues his engineering studies, and has Moon Shadow write to the Wright Brothers in North Carolina to ask for advice and guidance in building a flying machine.

The climax of the novel comes when Windrider is finally able to launch his man-powered flying machine, and actually becomes airborne for a few minutes. This is a novel that portrays a culture that is not widely known, the Chinese-American world of the early twentieth century.

Discussion Questions and Activities

1. In *Dragonwings,* Laurence Yep describes the impressions that a young boy, Moon Shadow, has when he comes to San Francisco, California. The author expresses Moon Shadow's lack of familiarity with English place names and colloquial expressions by using *italics* to indicate these words or phrases. Many of these phrases reflect the stereotypical, cruel way in which the "demons" or Caucasians, perceived the Tang Peoples. In your journal, comment on some of the events in the story where these stereotypes were very pronounced. Do you feel that the same labeling exists in your locality today?

2. Chapter 3 is titled, "The Dragon Man." How does this title prepare us for the fantasy that follows? Windrider shows Moon Shadow examples of scientific inventions, but his son fears the unknown mystery of the electric light or the radio set. Windrider then tells his son about a fantastic dream or out-of-body experience that he has had. Read the chapter again, and then summarize the events of the story of Windrider and the Dragon King. You may make an outline first, and then fill in details. Your summary should include all of the important parts of Windrider's experience.

3. When Moon Shadow and Windrider moved to Polk Street and Miss Whitlaw's stable, there were many things that were strange and repugnant to the Chinese boy. In Chapter 6, Moon Shadow is introduced to milk, gingerbread, and Robin. Describe his reaction to the possessions that Miss Whitlaw shares: the stereoptical slides, the stained glass window, and the piano. Record this description in your journal.

4. Moon Shadow travels as a go-between from his father to Uncle Bright Star and the other members of the Company. What do we learn about cultures and traditions from this? Prepare a chart showing some of the likenesses and the differences between the "demons" and the Tang peoples and keep the chart in your journal.

5. How did the city react to the earthquake? Compare the earthquake of 1906 with the recent Loma Prieta earthquake that devastated parts of San Francisco in 1989. Research magazines and newspapers that described the quake and the reactions of the people of California. Then write a composition comparing the ways in which ordinary citizens react and respond in times of great emergencies.

6. The climax of the story comes when Black Dog reappears and demands money from Windrider. Black Dog threatens to kill Moon Shadow if Windrider does not give him money. What is the father's decision? How does this affect plans to launch Dragonwings? How does the Chinese community unite with the Americans to insure that the flight will take place? Answer these questions in paragraph form in your journal.

Child of the Owl

The Story

Casey is used to her life with Barney. Together, she and her father have led a nomadic existence up and down the coast of California, picking fruits and vegetables, or simply doing odd jobs. But when Barney's gambling debts land him in the hospital and he is unable to take care of his 12-year-old daughter, Casey is sent to relatives in San Francisco, pompous Uncle Phil and his family. Through Casey's eyes as first-person narrator, the reader is introduced to a upwardly mobile Chinese family. Uncle Phil is an ambitious lawyer, former president of the California Bar Association, and his wife and daughters are striving to live the life they perceive to be an acceptable, assimilated lifestyle. Casey is unimpressed by their pretensions, and following numerous confrontations, she is dispatched to *Paw-Paw*, the Chinese word for grandmother. Here in a cold walk-up flat in San Francisco's Chinatown, she begins a life that is rich in Chinese tradition. Casey hates her school, with its imperious Chinese-language teachers, but grudgingly admits that Paw-Paw is an interesting relative to have. Fantasy is embedded in this novel just as in Yep's *Dragonwings*. In this book, Paw-Paw tells the story of the owls and the "walkers." The fantasy then becomes the symbol for Casey's immersion in her Chinese heritage. When a robbery occurs, Paw-Paw is injured but refuses to disclose who broke into the apartment. At first, Casey is sure it is Gilbert, the Pachinko chauffeur for gamblers and drug dealers, but when the real thief is revealed to be Barney, Casey's father, Casey, though heart-broken, is able to deal with her problems with the support and affection of her Chinatown friends.

Discussion Questions and Activities

1. Select two of the thought questions below. Compose a short essay in which you state your opinions, using evidence from the book to support those opinions.

    (a) In this book, we meet the characters from Casey's point of view, and are given her perception of them. How does Casey feel about her Uncle Phil and his family? How does the author convey Casey's feelings?

    (b) When Casey meets Paw-Paw, her grandmother, what are her reactions?

    (c) Do you think Paw-Paw approved of her son's insistence on adopting American habits and culture?

    (d) What do you think accounts for the great difference between Casey and her cousins, Pam-Pam and Annette?

    (e) Who are the main characters in this book? Who are the minor characters? How would you classify the characters in the fantasy section about the owls and the walkers?

2.   Students at the Chinese school made Casey feel like an outcast, even though she was Chinese, while schools outside of Chinatown had accepted her. This is a paradox. A paradox is a statement that is contrary to common sense, but is perhaps true. Describe in a journal entry how Casey reacts or responds to this paradoxical situation.

3.   Prepare a week of journal entries based on Casey's description of a typical week's schedule at the Chinese school. You may wish to review the narrative on pages 40-43 of *Child of the Owl* where the schedule is described.

4.   All of Casey's letters to her father, Barney, were returned to her because his address was unknown. What do you think Casey put in the letters to her father? Select one event in the story and compose a letter as though Casey had written it. Record the letter in your journal, using appropriate format for a friendly letter.

5.   What circumstances prompted Paw-Paw to tell Casey the story of Jasmine and Peony, the owl sisters? This story is embedded fantasy; that is, the author has the character tell a story that is not an essential part of the action, but which provides an explanation in symbolic terms. How would you suggest that Casey use the events in the fantasy to help her understand her own personality? Record your thoughts in your journal in a personal narrative style.

6.   In the fantasy segment, the concept of sacrifice is stressed. When the family was starving because of the draught, the first son submitted himself to slavery; the second son sliced off parts of his arms and legs to make a nourishing broth for his parents, and when he was totally disfigured, got into the kettle himself; the third son vowed to find his brother and set his two souls free. How could this fantasy be applied to Casey's life? Answer in expository essay form in your journal.

7. Do you think that the idea of a person having two souls is possible? Why or why not? Do you think that the two souls could symbolize Casey's Chinese ancestry and her American upbringing? Why or why not? Record your answer in your journal.

8. Laurence Yep uses setting effectively in this book. The Chinatown section of San Francisco, California, is described in detail, from the tourist souvenir shops to the grocery stores. Paraphrase the author's description of Chinatown by describing your neighborhood or the mall where you shop frequently. Use sharp, descriptive words so that readers can visualize your vignette.

Sea Glass

The Story

Sea Glass is a novel told from a first person point of view. Craig believes that he is fat, uncoordinated, and poor at sports. His low self-esteem is eroded even more when his family moves to the small town of Concepcion, California, where he is one of the few Chinese-American students at his school. Ridiculed by his "Americanized" cousins, Stanley and Sheila, and criticized constantly by his father for his lack of athletic skill, Craig finds solace with Uncle Quail, an elderly friend of the family. Uncle lives in a tiny shack overlooking a cove near the Pacific Ocean. In exploring the sea life of the cove with Uncle Quail, Craig learns many things about himself. His friendship with Kenyon, flamboyant daughter of aging "flower children," also enables him to view his perceived failings in a more realistic way. When Craig finds the courage to communicate with his father in an honest way, he begins to see what Uncle Quail has been teaching him all along: "The true victory is not to remember just the bad things. Someone must also remember the good things about this way of life."

Discussion Questions and Activities

1. *Sea Glass* emphasizes natural science, particularly marine life. Research tide pools and specific species of marine life, such as the sea anemone, the star fish, and other examples, using reference books in the library media center. Prepare a brief instructional module on these examples of marine life that can be used as part of a science program.

2. In this book, Craig's father has given up his dreams and his love of drawing. Sketch examples of marine life you have researched in an art style that you think Craig's father might have used. Label the marine animals and include them in the instructional module you have prepared.

3. *Sea Glass* is filled with artistic descriptions of the sea, the sunset, and the flowers that Mr. Chin is growing. Yep uses color word pictures effectively in these passages. Locate sentences in the book that seem particularly visual, record them in your journal, and then compile a list of exotic words for primary colors. (*Hint:* Think of the box of 64 crayons as an idea generator.)

4. Have you ever felt that you have disappointed someone in their expectations for you? Write a short, personal statement for that person, explaining that your talents and interests lie in another direction from the one that the other person has decided should be your goal.

5. Uncle Quail introduces Craig to the fantasy of the *Dragon Mother*. Find that part of the story and then compose a poem about how the woman nurtured the rock until it hatched. Since the Chinese tradition usually involves a Dragon Father who controls the seas, the storms, and natural occurrences, the perspective of a *Dragon Mother* lends itself to poetic thought. In the novel, the dragon is symbolic of more than one thing. Think about the symbolism and try to express it in your poem. Record the poem in your journal.

The Star Fisher

The Story

Joan Lee feels that her family is completely American. Born in Canton, Ohio, and raised in small-town surroundings, Joan is unprepared for the bigotry and narrow-minded perceptions that some of the people of Clarksburg, West Virginia, harbor. The Chinese-American family has moved to West Virginia to open a laundry. Their landlady, a retired school teacher named Miss Lucy Bradshaw, welcomes the Lee family and offers to teach Mrs. Lee housewife skills. Mrs. Lee, who speaks very little English depends on Joan to translate for her. Resentful and bitter at being the oldest and most responsible daughter, Joan tries to become a popular high school student. Her efforts at friendship are rejected by the school girls, except for Bernice, who is considered "different," too.

Finally, through Mrs. Lee's determination to learn to bake an edible apple pie, the family is accepted by the community as the respectable businesspersons that they are. Joan finds that acceptance can take many forms, and that a pie social at a country church can provide the setting for understanding and welcome. The embedded fantasy of the "star fisher" provides a symbol for Joan's view of herself as an outsider.

Discussion Questions and Activities

1. Yep introduces the fantasy element smoothly and delicately as Joan tells a bedtime story to soothe her little sister, Emily. In your journal, outline the story elements of the fantasy in a story map. Prepare a character trait web depicting the farmer and the beautiful star fisher maiden who was forced to become his wife.
2. Why does Joan feel that she is a star fisher in the life she shares with her Chinese-American family? What characteristics does Joan think she shares with the beautiful star fisher? Compare and contrast the personalities of these two characters: the fantasy bird-woman and the high school student. Record your comparison in your journal.

UNIT 3: THE ELECTRONIC JOURNAL

An optional curriculum for a literary arts independent reading program may be designed using word processing programs. Many schools have computer labs, and students are familiar with their operation and applications. A unit such as the literary analysis of the books of Laurence Yep may be adapted for electronic journal.

Unit Objectives

In this unit, students will be able to:

- use a word processing program to participate in an independent literary arts experience.
- apply literal, interpretive, and critical thinking skills to a fantasy novel.
- understand the motives of characters and their relationships.
- identify and appreciate figurative language
- create and build a file of information about several books by a specific author.

Teaching Strategies

The teacher:

schedules time on the
computer with the
cooperation of the computer
specialist.

meets with the literary arts
class to explain the process
of independent reading using
computer applications for
recording and communicating
information about the books
read.

asks the computer specialist to
review the basics of computer
use, e.g., off/on techniques,
opening a file, closing a file.

explains the parameters of the
project: 1. Students may read as
many of Laurence Yep's books as
they choose in a five-week time
period; 2. Using the selected word
processing program, students will
record information about the book
in an outline format; 3. Students
will receive a data disk that
is exclusively for their own
use as an electronic journal;
4. The teacher then demonstrates
the process, using the outline format.

is available for conferences and
guidance in book selection.

works cooperatively with the
computer specialist to achieve
literary unit objectives.

inputs general questions about
the novels of Laurence Yep, and
opens individual files for each
of the novels with more specific
writing tasks about the books.

The students:

have a basic knowledge
of computer usage, and
know the rudiments of a
word processing program.

listen to directions and
follow them appropri-
ately.

work with the computer
specialist to review
technical skills

attend the instruction
and demonstration.

seek out assistance
when desired.

read and record indi-
vidual opinions and
criticism.

choose the specific file
needed for the literary
arts task.

The teacher:	The students:
collects and examines student data disks at intervals.	submit data disks for teacher evaluation as each book is critiqued on disk.
records comments on student data disks after evaluation.	read teacher comments to reinforce learning.

The electronic journal may be used as a convenient tool for teacher and student communication. One of the program strengths of the California Reading Initiative is the recognition that students need an opportunity to use a wide variety of technology, including computers, word processors, and compact disks.

Discussion questions and activities that accompany the units in this book may be converted to an electronic journal format with a minimum of effort.

STUDENT RESOURCES

Books by Lloyd Alexander

————. *The Chronicles of Prydain.* New York: Holt, Rinehart and Winston.

*The Book of Three.*1966.

The Black Cauldron. 1967.

The Castle of Llyr. 1966.

*Taran Wanderer.*1967.

*The High King.*1968.

————. *The Drackenberg Adventure.* New York: Dutton, 1988.

————.*The First Two Lives of Lukas-Kasha.* New York: Dutton, 1978.

————. *The Foundling and Other Tales of Prydain.* New York: Holt, Rinehart & Winston, 1973.

————. *The Illyrian Adventure.* New York: Dutton, 1986.

————. *The Kestral.* New York: Dutton, 1982.

————. *The Marvelous Misadventures of Sebastian.* New York: Dutton, 1970.

————. *The Truthful Harp.* New York: Holt, Rinehart & Winston, 1967.

————. *Westmark.* New York: Dutton, 1988.

————. *Coll and His White Pig.* New York: Holt, Rinehart & Winston, 1965.

Books by Laurence Yep

————. *Child of the Owl*. New York: Harper, 1977.
————. *Curse of the Squirrel*. New York: Random House, 1987.
————. *Dragon Cauldron*. New York: HarperCollins, 1991.
————. *Dragon of the Lost Sea*. New York: Harper, 1982.
————. *Dragon Steel*. New York: Harper, 1985.
————. *Dragonwings*. New York: Harper, 1975.
————. *Kind Hearts and Gentle Monsters*. New York: Harper, 1982.
————. *Liar, Liar*. New York: Morrow, 1983.
————. *Lost Garden*. New York: Messner, 1991.
————. *The Mark Twain Murders*. New York: Four Winds, 1982.
————. *Mountain Light*. New York: Harper, 1985.
————. (Reteller). *The Rainbow People*. (Collection of Chinese-American folk tales). Illustrated by David Wiesner. New York: Harper, 1989.
————. *Sea Glass*. New York: Harper, 1979.
————. *The Serpent's Children*. New York: Harper, 1984.
————. *Shadow Lord*. New York: Harper, 1985.
————. *Star Fisher*. New York: Morrow, 1991.
————. *Sweetwater*. New York: Harper, 1973.
————. *Tom Sawyer's Fires*. New York: Morrow, 1984.
————. *Tongues of Jade*. New York: HarperCollins, 1991.

Additional Resources for Chinese-American Literature

Heyer, Marilee. *Weaving of a Dream*. Viking, 1986.
Wyndham, Lee. *Tales the People Tell in China*. Messner, 1971.
Yuzhen, Ding. *The Long Haired Maiden*. China Books, 1987.

PROFESSIONAL RESOURCES

Armbruster, B., and R. Anderson. (1980). *The Effect of Mapping on Free Recall of Expository Text* (Technical Report 160). University of Illinois, Urbana-Champaign. Center for the Study of Reading.
China and Chinese Culture: A Selected Booklist to Promote A Better Understanding, Grades K-8. (1990). Bethesda, MD: Chinese American Librarians Association.
Commire, Anne, ed. (1970). *Something About the Author,* Vol. 3, Detroit: Gale Research, p. 9.
————. (1988). *Something About the Author,* Vol. 52, Detroit: Gale Research.

Georgiou, Constantine. (1969). *Children and Their Literature.* Englewood Cliffs, NJ: Prentice-Hall.

Hearne, Betsy, and Marilyn Kaye, eds. (1981). *Celebrating Children's Books.* New York: Lothrop, Lee and Shepard Books.

Johnson, Edna, ed. (1977). *Anthology of Children's Literature.* 5th ed. Boston: Houghton Mifflin.

Jones, B.F., M. Amiran, and M. Katims. (1985). "Teaching Cognitive Strategies and Text Structures within Language Arts Programs." In J.W. Segal, S.F. Chipman, and R. Glaser, eds., *Thinking and Learning Skills, Vol. 1: Relating Instruction to Research.* Hillsdale, NJ: Lawrence Erlbaum Associates.

LeGuin, Ursula K. (1979). *The Language of the Night.* New York: Putnam.

Paulin, Mary Ann. (1985). *Creative Uses of Children's Literature.* Hamden, CT: Library Professional Publications.

Smith, Linell. (1984). "Lloyd Alexander's Way with Words and Children." Baltimore: *The Evening Sun,* October 15, 1984.

Sutherland, Zena. (1986). *Children and Books.* 7th ed. Glenview, IL: Scott-Foresman.

Tunnell, Michael O. (1980). *The Prydain Companion: A Reference Guide to Lloyd Alexander's Prydain Chronicles.* Westwood, CT: Greenwood Press.

Tunnell, Michael O., and James S. Jacobs. (1990). "Fantasy at Its Best: Alexander's Chronicles of Prydain." *Children's Literature in Education* (December): pp. 229-36.

Williams, Frank E. (1970). *Classroom Ideas for Encouraging Thinking and Feeling.* 2d ed. Buffalo, NY.

6

Trilogies and Series:
A Literary Family Reunion

INTRODUCTION

"I thought she was talking about a *soap opera*," Amelyia's mother confided after a parent-teacher meeting. "You know how teen-agers get into those things. But it wasn't at all. Amelyia was talking about the Tillermans! Imagine, a *book* family," she concluded, looking to me for confirmation.

I nodded. "Literary arts does strange things to readers," I admitted ruefully.

When students reach middle school, or grades six through eight, emotions are an integral part of each school day. Channeling the overflow is a daily task, so it's a great experience to be able to live vicariously through the emotional ups and downs of literary characters, sniffling, smiling, erupting with a "Yes!" at particularly climactic moments, as familiar characters face yet another dilemma with fortitude and valor, and even, occasionally, with humor.

Authors of books for young persons seem to have discovered this loyal following of readers, and library media specialists and teachers are grateful to writers for their talents in leading their characters through plots that are complex, in settings that are symbols of either success or failure, to climaxes that are satisfying and rewarding but still afford the anticipation of another book. Such writers are to be praised and emulated. Cynthia Voigt, Ursula LeGuin, John Christopher, and others have captured the hearts and imaginations of adolescent readers. These authors use intricate and sometimes convoluted plots to involve readers in the exciting events of their characters' lives.

This chapter approaches literary arts through a study of these talented and popular authors. And since imitation is considered a sincere form of flattery, this chapter introduces writing fiction with young persons as an opportunity to use the best that they have read to stimulate the best efforts that they may bring to writing. This literary arts component offers a model that integrates composition and literary analysis within the context of the trilogy or series of novels. Opportunities to develop critical thinking skills, enhance knowledge of literary elements, participate in creative activities, and analyze text structure are provided, with writing assignments based on the novels under consideration.

Four goals are emphasized:

- applying literary elements to the student writing experience
- using literature as a model to enhance writing
- utilizing the elements of story structure as a natural part of student writing
- utilizing writing to summarize and clarify material read and discussed.

In an author approach to literature, students are invited to consider each author's work within the following framework:

1. *Organization:* analyzing trilogies or series novels which deal with various forms of social patterns.
2. *Change:* recognizing the types of change that are reflected in the novel: personal, relationship, group, social, civilization.
3. *Continuity:* considering the trilogy or series as a reflection of universal truths: notions of truth, honor, beauty, justice, and dignity.
4. *Diversity:* appreciating human differences, particularly those stemming from cultural diversity.
5. *Limitation:* analyzing how external and internal forces limit the nature of human choice, and recognizing the extent to which human beings are limited in physical, emotional, or intellectual ways.
6. *Interaction:* considering how the novels reflect the nature of human interaction and relationship patterns, and deciding what causes positive or negative interactions. Readers are asked to reflect on how human interaction varies from culture to culture, age to age, and person to person.

Students who have been involved in a literary arts program, following the developmental patterns suggested in this book, should be prepared to participate in goal setting, time management, higher-level thinking skills, and seminar discussion and analysis of the author's work.

CREATIVE WRITING IN A MODIFIED WHOLE-LANGUAGE PROGRAM

There are many connections between the two processes of reading and writing, some simple and easily visible, others complex and highly theoretical. According to Jay McTighe of the Maryland State Department of Education:

> Able readers use writing to help them process what they read....These visible ways that reading and writing complement each other are deepened by research that suggests that they are also complementary processes of meaning-making....Reading and writing both tap into "schemata"; cognitive structures or scripts for organizing information hierarchically into a meaningful whole.

Teachers and library media specialists who want to move toward a greater integration of reading, writing, and thinking may want to begin by surveying what is available for students in the school setting. Studies confirm that writers imitate the reading to which they are introduced. Surrounding student writers with well-written models of many genres and styles will enlarge the resources at their disposal when they write. Teachers or library media specialists who call attention to the choices authors make as they write also help students identify with authors as role models.

In a modified whole-language program, students are placed into the writer's role and are encouraged to "read like a writer." Allowing young writers to access many books with literary merit, and illustrating how the styles and strategies implicit in these books can be generalized to new tasks, are two contributions teachers can make to establish an integrated reading-writing-thinking environment.

Writing is a complex skill and learning to write well requires frequent practice. Throughout the chapters of this book, activities are suggested that involve journal-keeping, recording personal responses to an author's work, paraphrasing an author's style, and extending the forms of writing to include essays, letters, and poetry. Frequent writing builds familiarity and comfort with writing, contributing to fluency in generating and revising ideas. It also increases knowledge of the expectations for written products, encouraging students to make better decisions about how to approach new writing tasks.

What better "consultants" in writing are available to a school-based literary arts teacher or library media specialist than the authors of exciting and well-written novels? While popular authors provide models for imitating figurative language, characterization, plot development, and other literary devices, the teacher has many opportunities to directly teach strategies for writing well. Generating ideas, methods for revising, and approaches to editing are best taught as part of the ongoing literary arts courses.

Teachers who encourage their students to share their writing and to give and receive responses to works in progress help their students learn how to support each other as writers. McTighe (1990) calls this support a "culture of writing," in which students are challenged to think more deeply about their work, to clarify their ideas, and to value writing.

With a supportive, trusting atmosphere, students can begin to write expressively as a way to make immediate, long-lasting connections with fine literature.

UNIT OBJECTIVES

In this unit, students will be able to:

- use critical thinking skills in analyzing a series of novels by the same author.
- apply knowledge of literary elements in analyzing the text structure of a series of novels.
- use literature as a model to enhance writing.
- extend and develop vocabulary through extensive reading.

Teaching Strategies

The teacher:	The students:
explains the process of diagraming the plot of a novel using graphic organizers.	review existing skills in using graphic organizers.
gives a time line for reading the trilogy or series of books, with milestones for discussion periods and writing assignments.	record a calendar of milestone dates in their reading journals.
provides time for silent reading, writing exercises, and directed teaching activities.	work independently or in small groups to complete assignments.
works cooperatively with the library media specialist to teach writing skills as indicated in writing calendar.	work with both teacher and library media specialist to write, illustrate, and bind an original story.

UNIT 1: URSULA LeGUIN

Biographical Information

Ursula LeGuin writes fantasy and science fiction with literary precision for young persons. Her elegant style is much admired and imitated; her characters are unique and complex, and her geographically specific settings in a fantastic world are imaginative.

Born in Berkeley, California, LeGuin grew up the daughter of an anthropologist and a writer. She has stated (*Something About the Author*, Volume 52, pp. 107-12):

> I have been writing ever since I was six, mostly fantasies and science fiction. As a science fiction writer I always get asked, "Where do you get those weird ideas from?" As a fantasy writer I always get asked, "Don't you ever want to write about the REAL world?" All I can answer is that I do write about the real world, and I get all my weird ideas from it too. It is just that reality is much stranger than many people want to admit. After all, the real world is not made up only of the actual. If it were, it would stop right now. It is also made up of the possible and the probable; they are part of it now and always have been.
>
> It doesn't seem probable that one's grandfather was once an egg the size of a pinhead; that leaves eat light; that whales sing in choruses deep under the sea; that when you look at a distant star you are seeing the past; yet all these things are actual—are real. I could never invent anything so improbable, so unexpected. Indeed, I can't invent anything; none of us writers can. We can only take what we know and put it together in a different way. And that is the essential process of life itself, expressed in terms of the mind.
>
> Imagination is one of humanity's greatest tools. It can be badly used, just as an axe can. A writer can lie, or refuse to admit facts he doesn't like, just as a scientist can. But skillfully and honestly used, imagination is our best means of understanding reality, and the chief tool of both the scientist and the artist. What it produces may be theories about the origin of the universe, or stories about hobbits. That's the beauty of it. The human mind is as various, and as improbable, as the universe man is part of.

A Wizard of Earthsea

The Story

Young Duny is discovered to have certain powers of spell-weaving and magic tricks when he saves his village from destruction by creating a thick mist that envelopes the town and its people. Because of this talent, he is sent to study with an old wizard, the Mage Ogion. Impatient to learn more of the sorcerer's spells, Duny (now renamed Ged) delves into the wizard's secret book of Runes and conjures a black, shadowy mass of evil. When Ogion returns to find this evil presence, he sends Ged to the sorcerer's training school at Roke so that Ged can learn to master his great powers.

At Roke, Ged meets Jasper, another student and the two become adversaries. When Jasper challenges Ged to perform an illusion, Ged summons a spirit from the past to prove that he can, but in so doing, Ged unleashes a terrible and powerful black mass. The mass attacks Ged and almost kills him. However, Ged is saved and after a long recuperation, the hideously scarred young man sets out on a quest to find and destroy the evil force he has let loose in the world.

In the course of his travels, Ged encounters a dragon that has victimized islanders, temptations of the Court of the Terrenon, the attempted slavery to the Power of the Stone, and other fearsome adventures. The climax of the story comes as Ged, reunited with his old friend and fellow-wizard Vetch, sails beyond Lastland into the uncharted seas to the coast of death's kingdom. There in a final mythic battle, Ged faces the Dark Shadow, is victorious, and is restored to wholeness of body and spirit. So ends Book I of the *Earthsea* trilogy.

Discussion Questions and Activities*

1. What are some types of power that people seek today? What means do they use to try to get that power? Do you think there is a hierarchy of power? Explain your opinion in a brief persuasive essay.

2. The main character throughout the *Earthsea* books is Ged. According to the author, who is Ged? How did he acquire his first powers? How did he first demonstrate his powers? Who was his first teacher? Describe his trip to Roke.

3. In your journal, list as many physical and character traits of Ged as you can.

4. Describe the setting of Gont in a brief journal entry. Draw or sketch what you imagine Gont to look like. Follow the author's description as closely as possible.

5. Arrange the major events leading up to Ged's decision to go to Roke in six sequential sentences. When you have listed these events in your journal, write a short entry on whether these events led logically to Ged's decision.

---

*These questions have been adapted from the Literary Arts Curriculum Guide, p.6-10, published by Prince George's County Public Schools, Maryland, 1988, and used with permission.

6. If you could write yourself into the story, what role would you select for yourself? Choose a section of the book and rewrite it, starring, or featuring yourself.
7. Do you feel that the first two chapters provide an adequate foundation for the rest of the novel? Why or why not?

Visual Responses

1. Draw a picture of the shadow Ged saw crouching beside the closed door, using only your imagination and whatever description LeGuin has provided.
2. Look at the map of Earthsea. Trace Ged's journey from Gont to Roke. Mark each location mentioned in Chapter Two during this trip.
3. Construct a diorama or other visualization that depicts a scene from the novel.
4. Research psychological aspects of the relationship between Jasper and Ged. Examine their changing attitudes, from Jasper's servantlike initial encounter with Ged, through Ged's original distrust. Recalling the developing attitudes of Jasper's mocking, Ged's embarrassment, and finally the jealousy and scoffing demonstrated by Jasper and the burning hatred Ged feels for his fellow-prentice, write a psychological case study of how such intense adversarial emotions may lead to catastrophe.
5. One of Ged's teachers tells him: "Magic consists of this...the true naming of a place." Names play a pivotal part in this book. Protecting one's true name was critical to the characters in *A Wizard of Earthsea*. Do you think that response to different names contributes to the multiple personalities LeGuin portrays? (Duny, Ged, Lord Sparrowhawk) Why or why not?
6. Explore the literary history of dragons, and the importance of this mythical creature in different cultures. In Laurence Yep's books, the character of "Father Dragon" is described in great detail; the Dragon of Pendor, as characterized by Ursula LeGuin, has a Northern European cast. Select references to dragons in multicultural literature and prepare a chart of likenesses and differences. In doing research, be sure to include bibliographic references to sources.
7. Ursula LeGuin writes in the style of epic poetry, with inverted sentences, long narrative paragraphs, and rich figurative language. Select several passages that show this literary style. Then practice the writing technique of paraphrasing, that is, writing a selection imitating the structure of an existing literary work. Choose something that has happened recently, e.g., a sports event, and write it in an epic style. Your writing will be evaluated and used as part of a *Trilogy News* publication.

The Tombs of Atuan

The Story

This novel begins as five-year-old Tenar leaves her parents' loving and protective home to be taken to the tombs of Atuan in order to become the high priestess to the ancient Powers of the Earth. She has been selected because her birth time coincided perfectly with the death of the former High Priestess, and so she is believed to be the reborn spirit of a succession of priestesses through the ages.

Raised and trained by a group of powerful women, guarded by eunuchs in a world without men, Tenar, now renamed Arha, has very little knowledge of human feelings or emotions. She exists in an environment of cold darkness, struggling to perform the rituals expected of her, but finding deep inner resources of human emotions that both puzzle and confuse her. The opening chapters of the book are the story of Arha as she is trained by Kossil and Thar, two aging and jealous priestesses. Gradually, Arha loses all sense of light and beauty as she becomes the powerful mistress of labyrinths and underground caverns in which the Treasures of Atuan are stored. Men are forbidden entry to this Kingdom of Darkness, but one person defies this restriction. Arha accidentally comes upon this man in one of the dark passages and enraged by his presence, promises to avenge the violation of the Tombs of the Nameless Ones.

The person who has found his way to the Tombs of Atuan is Ged, the wizard, searching for the missing half of the amulet of Erreth-Akbe. Although Arha realizes that her role is to destroy this man, she begins to have doubts about the powers of the Nameless Ones, who have not destroyed the wizard instantly. Instead of having Ged killed, she leads him through the labyrinth to the Painted Room where he is given just enough water to keep him alive. Arha tells no one of Ged's presence except her faithful eunuch servant, Manan. However, Kossil discovers the deception and insists that Arha have the prisoner killed.

Enlisting the help of Manan, Arha tricks Kossil into believing that she had ordered Ged killed, and is, in turn, persuaded by Ged to try to escape the underground Tombs and return to the Inner Lands with him. When the missing half of the Amulet of Erreth-Akbe is found in the treasure hall, the two young people decide to try to escape. Arha realizes that the mythical powers of the Nameless Ones are merely shadowy recollections of the priestesses who worship memories, and flees with Ged.

An earthquake envelopes the Tombs of Atuan, and only Ged's power as sorcerer protects them from being buried in the rubble. Safe on the outside, Arha, now restored to her Earth-name of Tenar, finds that she really has no identity, she is neither a child of Earth nor Underworld. But with patience and love, Ged leads Tenar back to the reality of a beautiful world. Although Tenar insists that she must be left on an uninhabited island to atone for her wrongs, Ged patiently explains that she has done no evil, and takes her instead to his old master, the Mage Ogion where she can learn the lessons of life. With the ring of Erreth-Akbe on her wrist, she sails into the harbor of Havnor. This ends Book Two of the *Earthsea* trilogy.

Discussion Questions

1. The setting for this book is reminiscent of mythological stories about Persephone and Pluto, which are also set in the underworld. Prepare a contrast-compare graphic organizer citing relationships and differences in the two stories.

2. Just as Ursula LeGuin has drawn on mythology and legend to invent her plot for *The Tombs of Atuan,* current filmmakers have used LeGuin's high fantasy to create exciting films. Recall films such as *Star Wars,* and see how these epic films reflect settings and events in LeGuin's books. Write a short evaluation of the effectiveness of a film as compared to the memories generated by a novel.

3. Create a scene between Kossil and Arha that might have been added to the novel. LeGuin suggests that Kossil might have escaped to the Temple of the Godking. What might have happened if the two had confronted each other after the earthquake? Write the scene in script form to be presented as a reader's theater.

The Farthest Shore

The Story

Ged has been the Archmage of Roke for some time when a messenger arrives bearing the news that a strange malady has fallen on his father's kingdom. Wizardry and sorcery has all but vanished in the country, and the people are afflicted by a strange combination of boredom, despair, and loss of self-esteem. Arren, the young son of the prince of Enlade has come to beg the Archmage and his wise council of wizards to come to their assistance.

The Archmage decides that he must leave Roke to try to assess the strange attitudes throughout the Inner Lands, and he takes Arren as his companion in travel. Arren has developed an intense affection for Ged and begs to be his trusted prentice, assuring the Archmage that he will be loyal through any trials they may face together. Arren is skilled at sailing, and so the two set out in the Archmage's old vessel, the *Longfar*. Their first stop is the garish and greedy port of Hort Town, where merchants pander to visiting sea travelers, and a ghetto of huge proportions exists just outside the prosperous city gates. Here in this ghetto lie the drug addicts of the city, enslaved by the hazia plant. This group includes the town wizard, who has given up all of his knowledge of sorcery in order to maintain a certain level of unconsciousness to the human misery of his city. Arren is attacked and kidnapped by thieves in Hort Town, but Ged rescues him and the two continue their journey. Everywhere they go they find the same condition; anxiety, stress, and despair have paralyzed whole communities, all hope and optimism have disappeared. It is, as Arren observes, a "life without joy."

Most of the book is devoted to the interactions between Ged and his young companion, Arren, and takes place during a long, slow sea voyage to the "farthest shore," in search of the villain who is controlling the spirits of the people.

After Ged is almost mortally wounded by the spears of the people of Oebehol, he is saved by the children of the open sea, or raft-people. At the Long Dance of Midsummer's Eve, the Archmage is visited by the fearsome dragon, Orm Embar, who informs Ged that dragons have lost their voices and ability to communicate. He begs Ged to come at once to the outmost reaches of the sea to help the dragons that remain and to put an end to their enslavement by the evil power that now controls both man and beast.

Finally, Ged unleashes the Mage wind and he and Arren speed over the seas to the faraway island of Selidor, where they find the dragon, Orm Embar, dying on the rocks of the island. In the final encounter of their quest, a battle between the evil forces exerted by the wizard, Cob, and the powers of the Archmage, Cob tempts Ged, offering him immortality in exchange for a partnership of evil. In the struggle that ensues, Ged is able, through the sheer force of his will and mighty powers, to close the door to Evil, and restore balance to the World once more.

Arren and Ged return to Roke, and the Archmage announces that Arren will take his place as King of Havnor and become the earthly ruler. "When you come to your throne in Havnor, my lord and dear companion, rule long and well," he tells Arren. Then the Archmage departs on the wings of Kalessin, the Dragon of Pendor, to take up a life of meditation and contemplation in the forests of his beloved mountain home on Gont.

This departure closes Book Three of the trilogy of *Earthsea*.

Note: Ursula LeGuin has written a fourth book about Earthsea, titled *Tehanu*. In this book, Tenar returns to the cast of characters and a character mentioned only once in Book Three as the "White Lady" is developed.

Discussion Questions

1. *The Farthest Shore* may be considered an allegory for the different approaches to life. Consider some of the groups that Ged and Arren encountered in their quest—the greedy merchants of Hort Town, the drug-addicted Hazia groups, the Raft-People—and brainstorm ways in which LeGuin's created cultures reflect current, reality-based ones. Report your summary as a panel discussion.

2. How does LeGuin explain the effects of the plant, hazia? Do you think it might be important to have her explanation reflect current scientific thinking about substance abuse? Why or why not?

3. The crafts persons of Lorbanery earned their living in the silk trade. Why do you think LeGuin chose this particular textile industry? What reasons are given for the despair of the workers? Can you suggest current economic problems that are similar to the ones that the people of Lorbanery faced? Why do you think the people of Lorbanery have become madmen?

4. Only the Raft-People, the Children of the Open Sea, seem serene and unaffected by the anxiety and despair that affects land-bound peoples. What reasons might you suggest that would cause them to remain calm in the face of such despair? How do the Raft-People preserve their culture? Can you think of current instances in which people seek to maintain their culture in a water-based lifestyle?

5. Dragons once again play a significant role in the novel. Find descriptions of the dragons on Selidor, and also the description of Kalessin, and design a Museum of Dragons, with models or murals depicting the scenes in which dragons figured.

6. Write an essay interpreting the trilogy as a single piece of literature. Consider each novel and its characters and setting, and compare the plots of each as they contribute to a unified whole. This interpretive essay should be in the style of a personal literary criticism, using literary elements as a basis for the criticism.

UNIT 2: CYNTHIA VOIGT

Biographical Information

> *Writing is a task which I approach with an eager heart...because you never quite know what will happen, even with material you have been working with for years.*—Cynthia Voigt

There is slush on the parking lot at the Juvenile Sales in Annapolis, residue of a heavy, wet post-Christmas snow. We meet at the entrance; her tall, intense son holds the door for us. "We just got a call that this place got in a shipment of transformers—a little late, but still absolutely necessary for him!" It is Cynthia Voigt, mother, doing mother stuff with a handsome young son who could have been James-at-ten.

It's a beautiful autumn afternoon on the campus at Key School. I am doing a guest shot for my good friend who is librarian in the lower school. We sit at small tables in a room with a working fireplace and visit afterward. Outside, a group of high school students walk together. They are talking in animated tones with their mentor. It is Cynthia Voigt, teacher, enjoying lively literary discussion with her students, evoking Windy and Stewart of New Haven, or Tom and Jerry of Annapolis.

It's a crowded hotel ballroom at a literary luncheon. I have been invited to introduce the honored guest and principal speaker. Glancing at my notes to make sure I have included mention of all of her awards, especially the Newbery Award, I am aware that this author is also scanning *her* notes. It is Cynthia Voigt, author, confirming her own research with typical thoroughness.

Residents of Annapolis miss her since she moved. In a town noted for its proliferation of artists, writers, and poets, Cynthia Voigt was a neighbor and friend.

Cynthia Voigt was born in Boston, Massachusetts, but became a Marylander when she and her husband moved to Annapolis. When she began to write, she worked in a basement room of her house, and then moved to a study her husband created by enclosing a back porch. The Voigt family liked to spend their summers on the Eastern Shore of Maryland on Philpots Island, just off Matapeake, where they enjoyed boating, crabbing, and swimming, and Voigt absorbed the traditions and lifestyle of a Maryland shorewoman.

About the characters in her books, *Homecoming, Dicey's Song,* and other books about the Tillerman family, Cynthia Voigt says (*Read the Authors,* Interview with Maryland Instructional Television, 1984):

> Dicey takes the challenge of shepherding everyone down Route 1 from Bridgeport to Crisfield because she has to. It's a real, recognizable dilemma, not some burst of fantasy. Kids can identify with that and immediately see the implications in their own lives.

Cynthia Voigt expresses her feelings about her characters that are developed through multiple books in an interview with Hazel Rochman (*Booklist,* April 15, 1989):

I work with outlines and I had this thing blocked out in outline for *Homecoming* and then somehow the character of Gram sprang into my mind, full-blown, so the book became twice as long. Then I knew I had to write *Dicey's Song* and that completes the mother's story. And Jeff came into the second book, and I knew I had to write his story next....I think there's a danger with a series that you take your own characters for granted and don't do as well by them, and I don't want that to happen.

Homecoming

The Story

This book is the story of an odyssey—a journey begun in desperation and completed with family bonding. When Liza Tillerman tells her four children to stay in the car, listen to Dicey, the oldest sibling, and enters a shopping mall, the reader is immediately alerted to the problem. The children are being abandoned. Dicey senses this too, and her manner of coping with the awesome responsibility of keeping her brothers and sister alive and together until they can locate some members of their family is the plot of *Homecoming*.

Dicey knows of only one living relative, an elderly aunt called Aunt Cilla who sends an annual Christmas card. This relative lives in Bridgeport, Connecticut, but Dicey, James, Maybeth and Sammy are in a small town in northeast Connecticut. Dicey realizes that they must abandon the car on the parking lot to avoid being found by police and remanded to foster homes, and so she leads them away on foot, with only a few dollars, and a bag of peanut butter sandwiches . Dicey has a map, however, and is excellent at directions. Part I of the book deals with their progress, slow and painful, toward Bridgeport. The group hides in abandoned houses, lives on stale doughnuts, fruit, and milk, spends time in state parks, but Dicey manages to keep them together, fed and clean, and safe from detection. With the help of two students in New Haven, Dicey and her siblings reach Aunt Cilla's home, only to discover that their aunt has died, and the only survivor is timid Cousin Eunice, a devout Catholic who looks upon this descent of children as a duty to be performed as a true Christian. Dicey decides that they will have to stay and be duly grateful for Eunice's charity, but finds it extremely difficult. She takes on odd jobs in town, washing windows and accumulating funds in a shoebox.

Dicey learns that she has a grandmother in Crisfield, Maryland. Abigail Tillerman is Dicey's maternal grandmother. Because Liza had run away from home and had her children out of wedlock, her mother has refused all contact with her. Dicey decides to make a quick, solitary trip to Maryland to see what kind of a grandmother she has. Her intention is to return and get her brothers and sister if Abigail seems welcoming. But her siblings recognize signs of departure, and demand to go, too.

Part II deals with the Tillermans' trip to Crisfield, by bus and by foot. They are befriended by Will Hawkins, owner of a small circus that tours the small country towns on Maryland's Eastern Shore. Will takes the children to their grandmother, who is rigid and unwelcoming. Dicey decides that if they simply stay and begin to repair the rundown buildings and farm where her Grandmother has isolated herself, Abigail will simply assimilate them into her life. Confrontations between Dicey and her flinty grandmother give readers an opportunity to learn more about Mrs. Tillerman's background.

Book One of the Tillerman saga concludes with the children registered in school, Dicey working hard to rebuild a beloved sailboat, and grandchildren and grandmother living together, coping guardedly with their individual and family needs.

Discussion Questions and Activities

1. Cynthia Voigt tells readers that she is accustomed to working with outlines in designing her books. In your journal, prepare two outlines: one is to be a chronological outline of major events in the book; the second outline is to be a geographical outline of the Tillerman children's travels from the opening of the book. Refer to the text to maintain accuracy.
2. Prepare a genealogy table for the Tillerman family. Use only the family members mentioned in *Homecoming*. As you read other books in the Tillerman saga, you will be able to add characters and family members to your genealogical chart.
3. Write an essay on literary limitations as expressed in the book, *Homecoming*. In your essay, analyze how external and internal forces limit the nature of human choice in Dicey Tillerman. Consider also the extent to which the characters in this book are limited in physical, emotional, and intellectual ways.
4. In *Homecoming,* very little is known of Dicey's mother, Liza. She does not appear as a character with dialogue anywhere in the book, yet her personality permeates the book. Why do you think Cynthia Voigt chose this method of characterization? In a journal entry, express your opinions on the way the character of Liza is viewed by her children, her mother, and by other relatives.

Dicey's Song

The Story

In the second book of the Tillerman Family cycle, Dicey gets a well-deserved respite from care-giving as Abigail Tillerman, the children's grandmother takes on the responsibilities for her daughter Liza's sons and daughters. On a rundown farm in Crisfield, Maryland, Dicey, James, Maybeth, and Sammy settle into a routine of school, chores, and rural life. "Gram" is a very private person, unwilling to share information about the Tillermans with her recently discovered grandchildren.

But Dicey senses that her grandmother has begun to develop a special affection for Sammy, the youngest, because of his resemblance to Abigail's son Bullet. Maybeth, with a learning problem that makes it difficult for her to retain reading and math skills, is protectively nurtured by Gram. When Mr. Lingerle, the school music teacher, offers to give Maybeth private piano lessons, the family accepts his offer as a fine opportunity to help Maybeth develop her musical talents. James, the earnest student, adjusts well to his new environment, taking on a paper route to help out and making friends quickly. Dicey, in the eighth grade of junior high school, finds a job in a small grocery store in Crisfield, and finds a friend in Jeff, whose guitar-playing and singing attract Dicey. The story is a narrative of transition, as the Tillerman children learn how to be a family with traditional celebrations and values, and Gram begins to trust her emotions and legally adopts the four children.

Several new characters are introduced in this book: Mr. Lingerle, the fat and lonely music teacher, who is grateful to be invited to share meals and family events with the Tillermans; Mina Smiths, daughter of a minister and a classmate of Dicey's, a bright, sensitive girl who yearns for a meaningful career; Jeff, a quiet and somewhat secretive young man who enjoys sharing music and ideas with Dicey and her family; Millie, a butcher and illiterate proprietor of the grocery story in which Dicey works after school.

Voigt interweaves these new characters' lives and personalities with the Tillerman family in a subtle plot development with an authentic setting on Maryland's Eastern Shore. The traumatic climax of the story is foreshadowed by letters arriving from a Boston hospital. Gradually the reader learns that Liza Tillerman, who had deserted her four children in a mall parking lot, has become a patient in a Boston mental hospital, and there is little hope for her recovery. When Gram announces to Dicey that they are to fly to Boston, but offers no additional details about the trip, Dicey surmises that the sudden decision must have been precipitated by bad news about her mother. Gram is silent and preoccupied during the flight, but Dicey is aware that her grandmother is having enormous internal conflict trying to resolve her deliberate estrangement from her daughter with the growing love she feels for her grandchildren.

After Liza's death, Dicey and her grandmother share a solemn time together, deciding on cremation as a means to guarantee that Liza will be returning home to Crisfield. This second book in the cycle concludes with Gram bringing photograph albums down from the previously off-limits attic, and beginning to introduce her four grandchildren to their extended family of Tillerman antecedents.

Discussion Questions and Activities

1. Setting plays a prominent part in this book about the Tillerman family. How does Cynthia Voigt use the setting of the Chesapeake Bay area as a function of the plot?
2. In *Dicey's Song,* the characters of Dicey, Maybelle, James, and Sammy acquire individuality that was not as prominent in their characterization in *Homecoming.* Select one of the following situations and write a character study: (a) Jeff describing Dicey; (b) Mina Smiths describing Dicey: (c) Mr. Lingerle describing Maybelle; (d) Abigail (Gram) Tillerman dscribing Sammy or James.
3. How does Cynthia Voigt deal with the literary element of change in *Dicey's Song*? Consider personal, social, relationship, and group change in analyzing three characters that appear in this novel.
4. Which characters can be added to the genealogical chart prepared earlier? How can minor characters in *Dicey's Song* be charted? Use a web, or other graphic organizer, to visualize these relationships.
5. How many levels of conflict are present in this novel? Descibe the conflict that exists between Gram and the townspersons; between Dicey and Mr. Chappelle; between Dicey's feelings toward her dying mother, and her growing affection toward her grandmother?
6. Gram is a complex character in this book. Consider several of the causes for her estrangement from members of her family, and write a diary or journal entry as Gram might have expressed her private thoughts in a personal narrative.
7. Cynthia Voigt has been a teacher, yet her treatment of characters who portray teachers in her novels is somewhat unsympathetic. What do you think might be her reasons for this ambivalence? Select one or two scenes in which teachers appear and prepare a short video dramatization of the episode. Then follow the dramatization with a panel discussion of how the teacher could have handled each situation differently.

8. Organize a small seminar discussion with a group of classmates to discuss the nature of interactions, considering how Voigt's books reflect the nature of human interaction and relationship patterns, and deciding what causes positive or negative interactions.

A Solitary Blue

The Story

Book Three in the Tillerman cycle of novels belongs to Jeff Greene. It is a sort of "prequel," a word coined from television to denote background events. In this case, the story deals with the lonely and silent childhood of Jefferson Greene, before he and his father settled in Crisfield, Maryland, and long before Jeff and Dicey met and became friends.

The son of an intellectually reclusive professor and a pseudo-environmental activist, Jeff learns early in life to be very quiet, both at home and in school. When Jeff is in the second grade at the University School, he comes home one afternoon to find a note from his mother telling him that she is going away "to save all the other little children." Jeff reacts to this news with stoic acceptance; after all, it is *he* who must shield his father from any change. Change might upset the Professor and cause him to leave too, Jeff reasons.

Jeff is so careful to maintain equilibrium in the family that he becomes seriously ill with bronchial pneumonia before his father has even been aware of him being mildly ill. Brother Thomas, a colleague of Professor Greene, intervenes and gently guides father and son into a more caring relationship.

Two summers spent in Charleston, South Carolina, with his maternal great-grandmother convince Jeff that his mother, Melody, is a shallow, lying person who uses people to her own advantage. This revelation comes slowly but achingly clear. Jeff retreats once more into loneliness and isolation, and finds solace in an old rowboat he has bought for 15 dollars.

Back in Baltimore once again, failing in school and suffering clinical depression, Jeff finally gets help from Brother Thomas and an understanding psychiatrist. Jeff and his father decide to leave the little house that is symbolically cluttered with sad and lonely memories and settle somewhere else. The "somewhere else" ultimately becomes Crisfield, Maryland, where they purchase land outside of town on the edge of a marsh. Jeff finds peace here, watching the blue herons, attending the town high school, and concentrating on his guitar and his musical abilities.

But Melody continues to intrude on Jeff's life; she appears in Crisfield and forces a confrontation between them that leaves Jeff sad and hurt, and feeling isolated once again. When an attorney arrives from Charleston to tell

Jeff that he is heir to his great-grandmother's estate, Jeff realizes that Melody's schemes and lies have nothing to do with a mother-son relationship, but everything to do with her own survival.

Jeff is finally free to establish friendships and to help not only Brother Thomas, who is experiencing a spiritual crisis, but also the Tillermans and his father. As the book ends, Jeff gives Melody the diamond ring his great-grandmother has willed him. He knows she will use it to support herself and Max, probably in an illegal drug operation in Colombia, South America. But it is all right. Jeff knows that he and his father have a mutual respect that is more valuable than possessions.

Discussion Questions and Activities

1. How does Cynthia Voigt use literary elements to introduce the character of Jeff Greene? Readers have already met this character in *Dicey's Song.* Is there consistency in the personality of Jeff in both of these books? How does Voigt show growth in Jeff's character from early childhood through his teen years? What are some of the events that have shaped Jeff's life?

2. Prepare an oral presentation explaining Cynthia Voigt's use of the literary element of point of view. You may want to use a Venn compare and contrast graphic organizer to compare the points of view of Jeff and Dicey in a scene viewed from each other's perspective; the scene in which Jeff first comes to the grocery store to try to make friends with Dicey,(*A Solitary Blue,* p. 180) and the same scene viewed from Dicey's perspective (*Dicey's Song,* p. 130). Another example of this technique appears in the scene in which Jeff surprises Dicey working on her boat (*Dicey's Song,* p. 142) told from Dicey's point of view, and from Jeff's perspective (*A Solitary Blue,* p. 182-83) in which Jeff is stung by a perception of further rejection. This activity becomes a powerful one when performed as a dialogue between two players.

3. What is the relationship that exists between Jeff and his father, the intellectually reclusive professor? What role does Brother Thomas play in Jeff's life?

4. Compare the characterization of Melody (Jeff's mother) and Liza (Dicey's mother). Why do you think Voigt chooses the absentee mother as the negative force in family life?

5. In both *Homecoming* and *A Solitary Blue,* young persons assume the maturity of a nurturing adult figure. There is a spartan awareness that life is filled with dangers that need to be avoided rather than addressed. Both

Dicey and Jeff are led by circumstances into the role of child-as-parent. How would you, as reader, empathize with the situations in which Jeff and Dicey find themselves? What would you offer them as support?

6. How does Cynthia Voigt use objects as a means of visual imagery? Discuss the symbol of the clutter and confusion of Jeff's house in Baltimore and how it relates to the symbolic clutter of sad and lonely memories.

The Runner

The Story

In this novel about the Tillermans of Crisfield, Maryland, two characters briefly alluded to in *Homecoming* and *Dicey's Song* become principal characters: Bullet and his father, the senior Tillerman. The story opens in anger, and Bullet's character is immediately established: brash, rebellious, and impetuous.

Bullet is a champion high school cross-country runner. He is also a silent loner, who runs for the pure enjoyment of it and cares little for competition. His is a complex character, brooding on the futility of his life with a father who is authoritarian and a mother frightened into silence. Bullet's sister, Liza, has left home and so has his older brother John, victims of his father's bullying. And Bullet plans to leave high school as soon as he is 18 and enter the army.

There are no happy events in this novel. It is stark in its description of racism and bigotry in a small Maryland shore town; the story is told in seething anger in the silent thoughts of Bullet. Only a friendship with Patrice, a French immigrant who is a waterman and Bullet's employer, helps Bullet come to terms with his internal anger. And the character of Mr. Walker, a student teacher, is drawn with compassionate strokes as he tries to reach Bullet through poetry. The book fast-forwards to 1969, when Abigail is informed of Bullet's death in Vietnam.

Discussion Questions and Activities

1. This book is another "prequel" in the Tillerman saga. That is, a book in which the major character is carefully and fully defined in a time period prior to the arrival in Crisfield of Dicey and her siblings. How does Cynthia Voigt use this device, and yet avoid confusion in time and place? Could a reader choose books from the Tillerman saga in any but a sequential order? Why or why not?

2. Answer a critic who has described *The Runner* as a book "with no happy events...stark in its description of racism and bigotry in a small Maryland shore town." Give reasons why you agree or disagree with this evaluation of the plot.
3. The narrative is told from the point of view of Bullet, the youngest member of the Tillerman family. Describe his relationship with his parents as Bullet perceives it. Do you think this is a general viewpoint of young persons? Cite reasons for your opinion.
4. Bullet has two good friends—Tamer Shipp, a track teammate, and Mr. Walker, a student teacher, who tries to reach Bullet through poetry. Prepare a talk describing how both physical and mental abilities can bring about bonding friendships. Use examples from contemporary sports and literary figures to illustrate your points.
5. Cynthia Voigt frequently uses individual traits of her characters to express deeper feelings. For example, Gram's loafers or bare feet as described in *Dicey's Song* are symbols for the resentment and animosity she experienced at being required by her husband to wear high-heeled shoes for dinner each night. Cite other examples in which objects aptly convey two levels of meaning.

Come a Stranger

The Story

Mina Smiths was a natural dancer, and so it was inevitable that she would be selected to attend an exclusive Connecticut summer program as the token black student. During the first summer, when Mina was only in fifth grade, it was a memorable experience, working with wealthy white dance students to present an original dance composition based on *The Lion, the Witch, and the Wardrobe*. But during the second summer, Mina has lost her natural gracefulness in adolescent gawkiness. She is sent home to Crisfield, Maryland, embarrassed and bitter. During the summer, she meets the "summer minister," Tamer Shipp, and develops an immediate crush on him. Tamer has returned to Crisfield with his wife and three children because it was his boyhood home; he had been on the track team with Bullet Tillerman and still missed his old friend. Pieces of the Tillerman family puzzle are neatly fitted together as this novel builds to an emotional climax.

Mina finds that she is a very competent tennis player, and she also begins to realize that she can do something very special to help Tamer Shipp bring closure to his grief over the death of his friend Bullet. She arranges a meeting at her father's church and introduces Tamer to Abigail Tillerman. Gram's reserve is shattered at finally meeting someone who has known her son well, and Mina is able to see that by bringing Reverend Shipp and Mrs. Tillerman together, she has done a mature and generous thing.

The novel ends with Jeff Greene's graduation from high school, and introduces yet another character, Dexter Halloway, son of a physics professor who is a friend of Jeff's father. The reader is left with a feeling of appropriate relationships in place: Dicey and Jeff, Mina and Dexter, and all the other cast members of this panoramic series in the Tillerman chronicle.

Discussion Questions and Activities

1. Cynthia Voigt concentrates on the Smiths family of Crisfield, Maryland, in this novel. Design a family tree showing the genealogy of Reverend Smiths and his family. As the story unfolds, add characters from other books in the Tillerman saga, and show their relationship to the Smiths.

2. Diversity is an important element in *Come a Stranger.* In a journal entry, describe Mina's feelings at (a) being accepted at the ballet summer camp, and (b) her feelings when she is dismissed from the camp the following summer. Try to use the narrator's voice to explain Mina's changes, both physically and psychologically.

3. Mina's family has a strong sense of values, and the reader is told that they are accustomed to working together to achieve positive results. Using the literary element of limitation as a guide, develop an essay analyzing how external and internal forces limit the nature of human choice, and the extent to which human beings are limited in physical, emotional, or intellectual ways.

4. What are some of the ways that Cynthia Voigt uses her stories to convey her own philosophy of creative writing? Consider the scene in which Mr. Chappelle assigns a "character study," and then evaluates both Dicey's and Mina's essays.

5. What is the difference between a personal assessment and an observer's account of a particular person? Find examples in the book that demonstrate these two methods of using point of view as a literary element.

6. In *Come a Stranger* (p. 181), a scene is repeated that occurred initially in *Dicey's Song,* (p. 113). It is the scene in which Mr. Chappelle accuses Dicy of plagiarism in her character study essay. As Mina tells it in *Come a Stranger,* she has perceived Dicey's coolness as racially motivated; from Dicey's point of view in *Dicey's Song,* Mina is the open, popular, funny student who is determined to befriend her, no matter how hard she tries to distance herself. With a group, prepare a panel discussion on the

way we perceive the motivation of others. Use examples from the Tillerman saga books to support your opinions. This panel discussion will be presented to another literary arts class.

7. The characterization of teachers in Voigt's books is expanded in *Come a Stranger*. With members of your group, script a series of monologues in which Mr. Chappelle, the moody and insecure English teacher at Crisfield High School; Mr. Walker, the student teacher; Mrs. Edges, the tennis teacher; Ms. Maddington, the ballet teacher; and Mr. Lingerle, the music teacher, portray their philosophy of teaching. This performance could be presented as part of a school Open House program, linking literature with life situations.

8. How does Mina manage to bring Abigail Tillerman and Tamer Shipp together? What is the reason for this meeting? How does it affect each of the characters?

9. Dexter Halloway is introduced as a new character at the conclusion of *Come a Stranger*. Do you feel this is a contrived event? Why or why not? Explain your thoughts in a journal entry, using Voigt's method of characterization as your starting point.

Sons from Afar

The Story

This is a continuation of the saga of the Tillerman family of Crisfield, Maryland. This book picks up with Dicey away at the University of Maryland; James, a very bright but shy high school student; Sammy, a gifted athlete and charmingly open kid; and Maybeth, still slow intellectually, but musically gifted.

The story revolves around James's curiosity about their father: who he was, where he lived, why he never married the children's mother, but stayed with her through four children. He involves Sammy in his search, and the two brothers begin a hunt that takes them from Cambridge, Maryland, to Annapolis, and finally, to Baltimore, in what are the very rough neighborhoods of Fells Point and Lower Broadway. They find enough missing pieces of the Francis Verriker puzzle to satisfy themselves that they have inherited some of both his irresponsible tendencies and charming personality, but that they are comfortable with Gram in Crisfield. James takes a job in a doctors' office (two women physicians), and thinks about a medical career; Sammy meets a new friend, Robin, and enlists him in the crabbing business with him.

This is the boys' story, and Dicey only appears briefly on a college vacation. Maybeth is a growing character, and the reader is left with the possibilities of a future book about Maybeth and her music teacher, the rotund Mr. Lingerle.

Voigt is wonderful at setting: the Eastern Shore is beautifully depicted, and the reader can actually see the locales. Gram remains a somewhat shadowy but strong character.

Discussion Questions and Activities

1. *Sons from Afar* is told from a male perspective, with James and Sammy as the protagonists. What are some literary elements Voigt uses to indicate the change in voice and point of view? How does the author convey the curiosity that the Tillerman boys feel toward their absent father?
2. James and Sammy plan their trip to Baltimore carefully and secretly. This book has many qualities inherent in the mystery story genre. What are some of these elements? Find evidence in the text that demonstrate the element of foreshadowing. This theme will be discussed with another group of literary arts students.
3. Prepare a TripTic or travel itinerary for James and Sammy. Include all the places they need to go to try to trace the person they suspect to be their missing father.
4. Why do you think it is so important for the Tillerman boys to find Francis Verriker? Consider your response in the light of the literary element of interaction, reflecting on how the novel reflects the nature of human interaction and relationship patterns, and decide what causes positive or negative interactions.
5. In the Tillerman saga, Cynthia Voigt reflects on how human interaction varies from culture to culture, age to age, and person to person. Select several characters from *Sons from Afar,* and write an expository essay expressing how the characters you selected demonstrate this variety of interaction.

STUDENT RESOURCES

Books by Cynthia Voigt

Voight, Cynthia. *Building Blocks*. New York: Atheneum, 1983.
———. *Callender Papers*. New York: Atheneum, 1984.
———. *Izzy, Willy Nilly*. New York: Atheneum, 1986.

———. *Jackaroos.* New York: Atheneum, 1985.
———.*Tell Me If the Lovers are Losers.* New York: Atheneum, 1982.
The Tillerman Saga. New York: Atheneum.
> *Homecoming.* 1981.
> *Dicey's Song.* 1983.
> *A Solitary Blue.*1983.
> *The Runner.* 1985.
> *Come a Stranger.* 1986.
> *Sons From Afar.* 1989.
> *Seventeen Against the Dealer.*1989.

Books by Ursula LeGuin

Le Guin, Ursula K. *The Farthest Shore.* New York: Bantam Spectra, 1989. First published by Atheneum, 1972.
———. *Tehanu: The Last Book of Earthsea.* New York: Bantam Spectra, 1991. First published by Atheneum, 1990.
———. *The Tombs of Atuan.* New York: Bantam Spectra, 1989. First published by Atheneum, 1970.
———. *A Wizard of Earthsea.* New York: Bantam Spectra, 1989. First published by Parnassus Press, 1968.

PROFESSIONAL RESOURCES

Cogell, Elizabeth Cummins. *Ursula K. LeGuin.* G.K. Hall, 1983.
DeBolt, Joseph W., ed. *Ursula K. LeGuin: Voyager to Inner Lands and to Outer Space.* Kennikat, 1979.
McTighe, Jay and Barbara Reeves. (1990). *Better Thinking and Learning.* Maryland State Department of Education, Division of Instruction.
Rochman, Hazel. (1989). "The Booklist Interview: Cynthia Voight." *Booklist*, April 15, 1989. Chicago: American Library Association.
Voight, Cynthia. (1984). "Read the Authors." Maryland State Department of Education, Division of Instructional Television.

Shakespeare, His World and Ours

INTRODUCTION

When the Shakespeare Theater at the Folger decided to mount a summer production of *Merry Wives of Windsor* in an outdoor amphitheater in downtown Washington, D.C., the skeptics could be heard all the way to Stratford-upon-Avon. Outdoor Shakespeare? In the city? Shakespeare is a suburb thing! And even if the tickets *are* free, and there's a great cast, who's going to go downtown to *get* the free tickets?

The brilliant theatrical mind of director Michael Kahn knew the answers to his critic's questions, and when the play opened at the Carter Barron Amphitheater, it played to packed houses nightly. The sultry and steamy Washington dusk reverberated with laughter and applause—William Shakespeare knew his audiences in Elizabethan times, and because of his genius and knowledge of human nature, the multicultural audience gathered in an outdoor amphitheater in the summer of 1991 were enjoying his comedic sense as thoroughly as the groundlings and aristocrats of sixteenth-century London.

One of the most striking aspects in the success of this outdoor production was the way in which it attracted young persons. Kids hung around during the day, watching rehearsals, running errands, helping when they were invited to perform some task, and then, these same kids returned in the evening, with their families and friends, to savor the professional performance of a Shakespearean comedy.

Was this because of a love of literature? Hardly. The metropolitan Washington achievement test scores were abyssmal. It is more likely that this keen interest in the performing arts, and Shakespeare in particular, stems from a love of action, a vicarious involvement in comedic moves, and the sheer pleasure of watching a pompous old windbag get his come-uppance from a couple of bright and with-it women.

Another example, this time in the "burbs." A traveling Shakespeare company rolls into a regional park. It is not a cart on great wooden wheels. It is an 18-wheeler tractor trailer, and it carries scenery, costumes, props, and a complete set-up for a project known as "Shakespeare on Wheels." This college-based acting company has been performing for several years, and the plays are eagerly anticipated by audiences (who live in communities that all sound like the names of world-class bourbon whiskey).

Residents have dragged lawn chairs, coolers, blankets, strollers, babies, and grandchildren to the grassy area selected for the performance. Teens enjoy boom boxes and pizza while they wait for the Shakespeare company to set up. Seniors sip iced tea and discuss their finances. The choice of performance is usually a comedy, *Midsummer Night's Dream* or *As You Like It*, and when performed beside a lake, with tall, shady trees and the seasonal sounds of crickets combined with the light show of fireflies at dusk, the Shakespearean mystique clicks in, and an audience of upwardly mobile and happily sedentary persons find themselves magically and suddenly in a 1991 version of the Forest of Arden.

During the winter, the Shakespeare Theater at the Folger plays to capacity audiences, and only the space limitations of the replicated Globe Theater prevent many other theater lovers from attending performances. However, there is another force at work here. The Folger Education Department has an outreach program to the schools in the metropolitan and suburban areas near Washington, D.C., and a touring company called "Bill's Buddies" travels to these schools to perform scenes from Shakespeare, demonstrate sword play, sing a few Elizabethan songs, and comment on the life and times of the Bard. This program has been so successful that there is always a waiting list to book the group. In the spring, there is a student festival held at the Shakespeare Theater at the Folger, and students from both elementary and secondary schools compete and perform scenes from Shakespeare in a two-week long celebration that climaxes with an enthusiastic celebration of Shakespeare's birthday. The student performances are bounded only by the students' imaginations. With the basic guidelines—the words must be faithful to the original Shakespeare—there have been performances ranging from *Julius Caesar* selections played in "power suits" as a corporate, hostile takeover of a business, through *Taming of the Shrew* done as a beach party at Malibu!

What is responsible for such a lively and literary interest in the works of an Elizabethan playwright, poet, and author? Perhaps the answer is simply that William Shakespeare is the consummate writer, who used his knowledge of human nature to produce an emotional bonding that spans the centuries.

This chapter provides a curriculum for implementing a study and enjoyment of the works of William Shakespeare in a kindergarten through eighth grade continuum.

A MODEL FOR A SCHOOLWIDE THEME PROJECT BASED ON SHAKESPEARE

A schoolwide commitment to introduce the works of William Shakespeare to students in grades kindergarten through eight is the goal of this project. Arts, Enrichment, and Academic teams of faculty members from many departments join together in a program of instruction integrating Shakespearean experiences into the curriculum. The celebration of Shakespeare and his work is a festival of music, drama, dance, media production, and creative writing.

This curriculum resource model is designed as an instructional package for use by classroom teachers and resource personnel in a single-school setting. All departments incorporate a Shakespearean motif into the curriculum and participate in developing and presenting activities appropriate to the grade level of the student and the content of the established course of study.

The curriculum guide is organized to provide opportunities for a school to have a renewed emphasis on literature, and a strong cultural foundation for reading and writing instruction. In addition to these primary goals, this model provides a unifying theme for instruction in art, music, social studies, science, mathematics, and physical education.

Teachers, or teams of teachers, may select from a variety of activities, directed teaching, and performance modes. Since skills emphasized within the theme include goal-setting, time management, research, and the higher-level thinking skills, the model may be used cross-grades. Through an emphasis on Shakespeare, students discover how his keen observation of human nature reflects the philosophical universals—truth, honor, beauty, justice, and dignity—and how his depiction of the human condition in all its cultural diversity reflects multicultural perspectives, particularly the complexity of differences and similarities among racial, ethnic, gender, and age groups.

UNIT 1: WILL, THE PILGRIMS, AND THE INDIANS—A KINDERGARTEN-PRIMARY SOCIAL STUDIES EXPERIENCE

Background Information

One of the reasons for William's Shakespeare's universal appeal to all ages is his ability to project an enjoyment of the rudimentary pleasures of life. Foods and eating are evident throughout his plays, from the overindulgence of Falstaff to the elaborate wedding feast of Katherine and Petruccio, and the holiday fare of Twelfth Night.

The groundlings who filled the pit of the Globe Theater were especially entertained by the gastronomical excesses of the comic figures in Shakespeare's plays. Wisely, the playwright recognized that his Elizabethan audience could relate to his invented or historical characters through organic elements. Food represented social events, opportunities to share fellowship, time for dancing and singing and general merry making.

The global and universal ritual of food is an interesting study. While Pocahontas and her family were preparing the Great Feast of the Green Corn, a thanksgiving celebration acknowledging a bountiful harvest, held on the banks of the Werowicomico River, Elizabethan families may have been celebrating a wedding with sumptious refreshments accompanied by great quantities of ale on the banks of the Thames.

And though American Indian feasts had a decidedly religious and spiritual focus, Elizabethan revels celebrated physical pleasure. There were exotic additions to the traditional English cuisine as a result of the formation of the East India Company, and British palates were treated to rare spices, fruits, and sugary confections made with chocolate.

American Indian food staples, on the other hand, consisted mainly of natural health foods—corn, fish, deer, and oysters. These foods were acceptable to the solemn Puritans who settled Plymouth. These colonists had eschewed the food orgies of the Elizabethan fairs in their quest for a simple agricultural, political, and spiritual life.

Unit Objectives

The unit will enable students to:

* recognize foods eaten during Elizabethan times.
* relate Shakespeare's time in London with colonial times in America.

- compare the dress of Elizabethan persons with the dress of Native Americans.
- prepare a simple meal using food typical of the American colonial and English Elizabethan periods.
- describe English social customs of the period, and contrast them with Native American lifestyles.
- recite lines from Shakespearean plays or poems that relate to food.

Teaching Strategies

1. The teacher:

introduces the unit by explaining that while the Pilgrims and Indians were sitting down to a feast in New England many of the recipes that the Pilgrims used came from their family cookbooks which they had put together in England.

describes some of the foods that Shakespeare's friends and families probably enjoyed eating, and asks students if they can describe some of the foods that the Pilgrims and Indians ate at the first Thanksgiving dinner.

begins a chart of foods of the Elizabethan period, with space to compare and contrast colonial American foods. (See the Food Comparison Chart that follows.)

The students:

listen and contribute to the discussion when appropriate.

listen to description of foods, and suggest foods that were eaten by Pilgrims and Indians, based on their knowledge.

participate in developing chart of foods.

Food Comparison Chart

Food	Shakespeare	Pilgrims
Chicken	Yes	Yes
Herbs	Yes	Yes
Gingerbread	Yes	Yes
Apples	Yes	Yes
Corn	No	Yes
Fish	Yes	Yes
Salad	Yes	No

1. The teacher:	**The students:** (*cont.*)
reads *The First Thanksgiving Feast* and leads a discussion of it.	listen to the story, participate in discussion of the pictures, recall as many foods eaten at the feast as they are able.
shares recipes from Renaissance menus.	listen to descriptions of Faire food.
explains that they will cook foods from both feasts and eat the food at a class party. (See "Recipes for an Elizabethan Feast," below.)	agree to participate.

2.The teacher:	**The students:**
explains that one of the reasons people remember the works of William Shakespeare is because he wrote lines about all kinds of things.	listen and comment where appropriate.
writes three quotations from Shakespeare that relate to food or parties, and helps students read the quotations:	read quotations aloud.

"Here comes more company!" *As You Like It, Act IV, Sc. 3;*

"I hope you'll come to supper." *Henry IV, Part II, Act II, Sc. 1;*

"But sup them well, and look after them. Tomorrow I intend to hunt again." *The Taming of the Shrew, Introduction, Sc. 1*

leads discussion about quotations and suggests that even though the words are from Shakespeare's plays, they could be used by the Pilgrims, the Indians, or even themselves on an invitation to a party.	interpret quotations to their experience and background knowledge.
suggests that students choose one of the quotations for the cover of an invitation to their Shakespeare/Pilgrim/ Indian feast and distributes paper and other materials to prepare invitations.	choose a favorite quotation and make an invitation.

RECIPES FOR AN ELIZABETHAN FEAST

These recipes have been selected from authentic recipes of the times and adapted for use by student cooks.

Salads

Into a glass bowl, put 2/3 as many slices of sweet oranges as you do of sweet onions. Add leaves of fresh mint, basil, or borage. Add the blossoms of boarage or nasturtiums. Sprinkle very lightly with fennel seeds and strew with light oil and vinegar.

Into a bowl, put fine fresh and crisp romaine lettuce. Add snippings of escarole, and fresh dill and/or fennel. To this add thinly sliced purple onion rings, sliced hard-cooked eggs, and diced celery and cooked beets. Strew with oil and vinegar. Add salt and cracked pepper to taste and just a hint of sugar.

Main Courses

Herb Roasted Chicken

Cook 8 boneless chicken breasts in 2 tablespoons butter until brown on both sides. Place chicken in shallow ovenproof dish. Sprinkle herbs (1 teaspoon each of chervil, dill, thyme, and parsley), and add 1 cup of chicken broth. Bake for 1 hour at 325° F, basting frequently.

Cod Fish Casserole

Cover 2 pounds of cod fillet with cold water, heat to boiling, then reduce heat and simmer very slowly for about 6 minutes or until fork cuts through. Then remove from water immediately and drain. In the meantime, boil 2 large peeled potatoes. When done, cut into small cubes. Peel and chop 2 large onions. Then prepare the following sauce: 6 cups milk, 6 tablespoons butter, 4 tablespoons flour, 1 teaspoon salt, 1/2 teaspoon pepper, 10 drops Worcestershire sauce, 1 tablespoon chopped parsley.

Put the butter in a saucepan and heat until light golden color. Add flour and stir rapidly. When mixture starts to thicken, add milk and stir constantly. Add salt, pepper, and Worcestershire sauce and cook until sauce starts to bubble. Then add all of the onions and cook slowly for about 3 minutes. Remove from heat and add potatoes and fish. Top with parsley sprinkled over the top.

Breads

Cranberry Bread

Sift 2 cups flour, 1 cup sugar, 1-1/2 teaspoons baking powder, 1/2 teaspoon baking soda, and one teaspoon salt into a large bowl. Cut in 1/4 cup margarine until mixture is crumbly. Add 1 egg, 1 teaspoon orange peel, 3/4 cups orange juice. Stir just until mixture is evenly moist. Fold in 1-1/2 cups raisins, and 1-1/2 cups fresh cranberries, chopped. Spoon into a greased 9 x 5 x 3-inch loaf pan. Bake about 1 hour at 350° F. Remove from pan and cool on a wire rack.

Indian Corn Bread

Combine 1 cup corn meal, 1/4 cup sugar, 1 teaspoon salt, 1 cup sifted flour, and 3 teaspoons baking powder. Add 1 egg, 1 cup milk, 1/2 cup melted margarine, 1 small can creamed corn, and one cup cottage cheese. Pour batter into a greased 9 x 13-inch baking pan. Bake at 425° F for about 40 minutes.

Desserts

Stratford-upon-Avon Fair Cake

Blend well together 1/2 cup butter, 1/4 cup honey, and 2 eggs. Add a bit of salt, 1 teaspoon ground cinnamon, a bit of nutmeg and clove, and 2 teaspoons of powdered ground ginger. Add 2 teaspoons baking powder, 2 cups sifted flour, and enough milk to make a thick batter. Fold in 2 cups chopped walnuts and 2 cups raisins. Pour into well-greased baking pans and bake at 350 to 375° F for about 25 minutes. Serve in thin slices with cream cheese.

Yalmpton Baked Apples

Core apples, but do not peel. Mix together equal amounts of brown sugar and butter. Add a healthy shake each of cinnamon and powdered ginger, and a few currants. Pack this mixture into the cored apples. Wrap each apple in a piece of rich pastry and seal well. Set all the apples in a baking pan, paint with beaten egg and sprinkle lightly with sugar and cinnamon. Bake at 350° F until the apples are soft when pierced with a skewer. These tarts should be served with whipped cream.

UNIT 2: THE FLOWERS ARE SWEET—A PRIMARY SCIENCE EXPERIENCE

Background Information

William Shakespeare had the ability to describe flowers, weeds, and herbs with great freshness and a sense of reality; he describes the country and outdoor life that he loved so much through the characters and lines of his plays and poetry. When Shakespeare tells us where to find the honeysuckle (woodbine) in *Midsummer Night's Dream* (II.i), we feel that he had a specific spot in mind.

> I know a bank where the wild thyme blows,
> Where oxlips and the nodding violet grows,
> Quite overcanopied with luscious woodbine,
> With sweet musk roses and with eglantine.

And, in *The Winter's Tale* (IV.iv), Shakespeare shares the feelings of heat and stillness of a summer day:

> Here's flowers for you,
> Hot lavender, mints, savory, marjoram;
> The marigold that goes to bed wi' the sun
> And with him rises weeping. These are flowers
> Of middle summer.

Ellen Eyler recounts in her book, *Early English Gardens and Garden Books,* that orchards, herb gardens, and kitchen gardens had always furnished food for people, but it was not until the sixteenth century, in Shakespeare's time, that flower gardening became a popular art. Until then, only the monks and aristocrats had flower gardens. With the development of gardening as an art form, there followed a great demand for books on the subject. The authors of these books saw gardening as a part of life and wrote enthusiastically about flowers and the look of the garden.

At the same time that flower gardening was being popularized, scientists were beginning to categorize plants according to the botanical classifications of the time and to give suggestions as to how herbs could be used for medicines and other purposes.

So it is very natural to find so many references to flowers in Shakespeare's works, and he used these references both in the aesthetic sense and in accord with the medical beliefs of the day. It is easy to imagine Shakespeare on his way to Stratford-upon-Avon to court Ann Hathaway. He must have seen lots of wild flowers along the banks of the river Avon. He describes the tall purple and yellow iris, the violet, the daisy, the daffodil, and the buttercup, as well as crowflowers or ragged robbin, and the antecedent of the pansy, known as Johnny-jump-up or hearts'-ease. The naturalness and ease with which the Bard of Avon integrates his references to flowers is one of the factors that preserves his works with such visual integrity.

Shakespeare mentions the rose at least 70 times in his plays and sonnets, comparing the national flower of England to human lips and cheeks, and uses roses to suggest a blush of shame or anger. There is a wonderful historical story about the red and the white rose in *Richard II*.

In England, the cowslip was the children's favorite flower. Each year in April children would go out with baskets to pick the blossoms in the fields and hedges and come home to make "cowslip-balls" or "tossies." Tying the flowers together tightly at the top of the stalk in big bunches, they then cut away most of the stalk and used the bright yellow bundles for springtime games.

Not only did Shakespeare allude to flowers as marks of character and beauty, he used them in a wonderfully humorous way. In *Midsummer Night's Dream*, Thisbe describes herself (according to Bottom's script!) with "lily lips, This cherry nose, These yellow cowslip cheeks...." A list of quotations about flowers and herbs used by Shakespeare in his plays and poems appears at the end of the chapter.

Depending on the policies of the school system, the teacher may wish to explore the beliefs of Elizabethans concerning the use of herbs and flowers as potions, charms, and ingredients for magic spells. (For example, Puck used pansy nectar in *Midsummer Night's Dream* to cause Titania to fall in love with the very next person she saw).

Unit Objectives

In this unit, students will be able to:

- recognize a variety of flowers described in Shakespeare's poems and plays.
- explain the poetic meaning of a variety of flowers.
- describe the uses of a variety of herbs for medicine.
- make a garland or wreath using real, dried, paper, or silk flowers.
- recite lines representative of specific flowers as part of a performance.
- illustrate selected lines from Shakespeare describing flowers or herbs.

Teaching Strategies

1. The teacher:

shares a collection of books or prints showing garden and wild flowers that grew in England in Shakespeare's time.

The students:

look at pictures and listen to descriptions of flowers.

leads discussion on whether students have seen such flowers in their own gardens or on trips.

contribute to discussion when appropriate.

explains that Shakespeare liked to use flowers as images to illustrate his ideas about people—what they looked like, their characters, and their actions.

suggests that students volunteer to share their thoughts of what kinds of flowers they thought they might be. "If you were a flower, what kind would you probably be?"

take turns describing kind of flower they might be: cheerful like a yellow buttercup; friendly like a daisy, etc.

distributes art materials and asks students to draw and color a picture of themselves as a flower that expresses their personalities.

draw and color their interpretations of what flower they might be.

collects drawings and explains that these pictures will be used later as part of a special video project about Shakespeare's use of flowers.

---

2. The teacher:

asks students if they know what flower is special to their birth months and explains that Shakespeare used birth month flowers in his plays and poems as special presents to the characters.

The students:

take turns contributing answers.

uses a bunch of real daisies as motivation for birth month flower for April, Shakespeare's own birth month.

2. The teacher:	**The students:** (*cont.*)
gives each student a card with a picture of the flower that is the student's birth month flower. (See "Shakespearean References to Flowers" and "Birth Month Flowers," below.)	record a Shakespearean quotation on the card. (Grades 2-3 perform this task. See end of chapter for suggested quotations.)
	Make a calendar with a picture of each birth month flower on the month, and list birthdays in appropriate month.

3. The teacher:	**The students:**
displays a variety of over-the-counter remedies students can recognize, such as vitamins, cough syrup, antacids, and aspirin.	
asks students if they can tell what these medicines do, and how they help people.	respond according to their knowledge and experience.
shows students a collection of herbs in jars, bottles, and vases, and asks if students recognize any of them.	respond according to their knowledge and experience.
explains that in Shakespeare's time, every house had a garden, and that in the garden, the family grew herbs that they believed would help cure illnesses and asks why families did this in Elizabethan England, and also in colonial times here.	
leads guided discussion.	contribute ideas leading to concensus that there were few doctors and no technology in those times.
displays a chart showing pictures of herbs, and what these herbs were supposed to do for people.	

Herb Use Chart

Herb	Use
Savory	Used for bee stings.
Garden Clary	Helped weak backs.
Sage	Cured headaches, when mixed with fat and cornmeal.
Pennyroyal	Cured upset stomach, asthma, and relaxed tense muscles.
Wild Daisy	To heal cuts, mixed with animal fat.
Rose Leaves	Good for almost all illnesses. Good source of vitamins.
Marigolds	Used for ointment for the skin. Used in lotion for sprains.
Rosemary and Rue	Used in small bunches to prevent plague.

3. The teacher:

invites parents in health care professions to speak to students about current uses of herbs for medicinal purposes.

leads in-school field trip to office of school nurse or health aide to find out about first aide and household remedies for minor home or school health emergencies.

suggests that group set up a Shakespearean market place, with a florist shop and a drug store.

The students: (*cont.*)

participate in program.

participate in program.

use a variety of art materials and real flowers and herbs to organize products for their market-place. They sell to one another.

4. The teacher:	The students:
returns drawings previously done by students in which they represented themselves as flowers.	
explains that they will make a video scrapbook, classifying the flowers, and sharing lines that Shakespeare wrote about their specific flowers.	learn quotation about their specific flower.
plans with technical aides or the library media specialist for video-taping student production.	
rehearses with students, directs production.	participate in video project as directed.
Suggests an audience for the program and guides preparation of invitations.	contribute suggestions and make invitations and distribute them to families or other classes.
assists in presenting completed videotape production.	share completed video-tape with families and others.

SHAKESPEAREAN REFERENCES TO FLOWERS

Carnations (Gillyvor)
> Sir, the year growing ancient,
> Not yet on summer's death, nor on the birth
> Of trembling winter, the fairest flowers o' the season
> Are our carnations, and streak'd gillyvors.
> —*The Winter's Tale, Act IV, Sc. iv*

Daisy (Lady-Smock, Cuckoo-Bud)
> When daisies pied and violets blue,
> And lady-smocks all silver-white,
> And cuckoo-buds of yellow hue
> Do paint the meadows with delight.
> —*Love's Labour's Lost , Act V, Sc. ii*

There with fantastic garlands did she come,
Of crowflowers, nettles, daisies.
—*Hamlet, Act IV, Sc. vii*

Cowslips (Primula, Primrose)
The cowslips tall her pensioners be;
In their gold coats spots you see;
Those be rubies, fairy favours,
In their freckles live their savours;
I must go seek some dewdrops here,
And hang a pearl in every cowslip' ear.
—*Midsummer Night's Dream, Act II, Sc. i*

Violet
... I think the king is but a man, as I am;
the violet smells to him as it doth to me.
—*Henry V, Act IV, Sc. i*

Harebell (Wild Hyacinth)
...thou shalt not lack
The flower that's like thy face, pale primrose, nor
The azured harebell, like thy veins.
—*Cymbeline, Act IV, Sc.ii*

Pansy (Hearts'-ease, Johnny-jump-up, Viola)
...and there is pansies, that's for thoughts.
—*Hamlet, Act IV, Sc.v*

Rose
So sweet a kiss the golden sun gives not
To those fresh morning drops upon the rose.
—*Love's Labour's Lost, Act IV, Sc.iii*

Woodbine (Honeysuckle)
Sleep thou, and I will wind thee in my arms.
So doth the woodbine the sweet honeysuckle
Gently entwist,
—*Midsummer Night's Dream, Act IV, Sc. i*

Marigolds (Mary-buds)
The marigold, that goes to bed wi' the sun,
And with him rises weeping.
—*The Winter's Tale, Act IV, Sc.iii*

Daffodil

When daffodils begin to peer,
With heigh! the doxy, over the dale,
Why, then comes in the sweet o' the year.
—*The Winter's Tale, Act IV, Sc.ii*

...daffodils,
That come before the swallow dares, and take
The winds of March with beauty.
—*The Winter's Tale, Act IV, Sc.iii*

Lily

To gild refined gold, to paint the lily.
—*King John, Act IV, Sc.ii*

Like the lily, that once was mistress of the field and flourish'd,
I'll hang my head and perish.
—*Henry VIII, Act III, Sc.i*

BIRTH MONTH FLOWERS

January: Carnation	*July:* Morning Glory/Larkspur
February: Gentian Violet	*August:* Gaillardia/Gladiolus
March: Crocus	*September:* Aster
April: Sweet Pea	*October:* Amaryllis/Calendula
May: Lily of the Valley	*November:* Chrysanthemum
June: Rose	*December:* Narcissus

UNIT 3: SHAKESPEARE'S ANIMALS—A PRIMARY SCIENCE EXPERIENCE

Background Information

In Shakespeare's time, there were no formal zoological parks. Wealthy landowners could allow strange and exotic animals like peacocks to roam freely over lawns and gardens. Herds of deer ranged through the woodlands of a large estate, and there are historical references to wild animals like monkeys or lemurs as exotics brought back as souvenirs by members of the East India Company.

There was a lively interest in natural history in the sixteenth century as a result of exploration and travel, and even though most of the general populace had never glimpsed any of these rare birds or animals, imaginative descriptions from sailors and explorers fired Elizabethan curiosity.

Shakespeare incorporated references to these animals and birds in several of his plays. "This ravenous tiger" is cited in *Titus Andronicus,* and in *Richard II* there is a reference to "A lion and a king of beasts." Crocodiles, dragons, rhinos, and sea monsters all find their way into various Shakespearean plays.

Mythical beasts also enjoyed great popular appeal during Shakespeare's time. The griffin and the unicorn were part of the royal coat of arms, and tales of various sea monsters brought home by adventurous seamen extended the mysteries of natural science.

Unit Objectives

In this unit, students will be able to:

- recognize animals mentioned in Shakespearean plays and poems from specific lines.
- illustrate lines from Shakespeare's plays and poems with animal pictures from magazines or hand-drawn sketches.

Teaching Strategies

1. The teacher:	**The students:**
begins unit by asking students about their zoo experiences: When did they go? What did they see? Which are their favorite animals? How did they know what animals they were seeing? How did they find out more information about the animals?	
explains that although there were no formal zoos in Shakespeare's time, very rich persons could keep strange and exotic animals in parks around their estates and castles.	
tells students that there was a great interest in natural history in the sixteenth and seventeenth centuries during	

---

1. The teacher:	The students: (*cont.*)
Shakespeare's lifetime, and that this interest was based on firsthand observation, as well as on the reports of explorers and travelers to faraway lands.	
shows a large world map or globe, and asks students to find where they live, and where Shakespeare lived in England.	respond appropriately.
explains that Shakespeare never left England, but that he saw and heard about many strange animals from friends and persons who had traveled to distant places.	
shows pictures of selected animals, with Shakespearean references printed clearly on cards or posters.	study pictures, identify animals, and participate in guided reading of the quotations.

Format for Cards or Posters on Shakespearean Animals

Animal	Quotation	Source
Squirrel	"Bushy, what news?"	*Richard II*
Camel	"Nature hath framed strange fellows in her time."	*Merchant of Venice*
Tiger	"This ravenous tiger"	*Titus Andronicus*
Lion	"A lion and a king of beasts"	*Richard II*
Crocodile	"What manner o' thing is your crocodile?"	*Antony and Cleopatra*
	"Eat a crocodile."	*Hamlet*
Rhinoceros	"The arm'd rhinoceros"	*Macbeth*
Dragon	"Come not between the dragon and his wrath"	*King Lear*
Zebra	"Hence with thy stripes, be gone"	*Antony and Cleopatra*
Deer	"Set the deer's horns upon his head, for a branch of victory."	*As You Like It*
Cat	"A harmless necessary cat"	*The Merchant of Venice*

Dog	"Dogs, easily won to fawn on any man"	*Richard II*
Beaver	"I am the veriest varlet that ever chewed with a tooth"	*Henry IV, Part 1*
Monkey	"God help thee, poor monkey!"	*Macbeth*
Hen	"How now, Dame the hen!"	*Henry IV, Part 1*
Rooster	"The country cocks do crow, the clocks do toll"	*Henry V*
Whale	"The imperious sea breeds monsters"	*Othello*

2. The teacher:	**The students:**
takes students to the library media center or has books available in the classroom.	
asks students to select a favorite animal from the preceding list, or an animal they would like to learn about, and divides group into committees or individual researchers.	respond by selecting favorite animal and following directions for grouping.
assists students in locating information	show instructor what information about their selected animals they have located, and record information on chart paper. (Kindergarten, first-grade level)
assists students in locating information about their selected animals, and asks students to record their information on data sheets.	Locate and record information.
tells students to include the source of their information, such as the encyclopedia or a book from the general collection.	record simple bibliographic entry.

2. The teacher:	The students: (*cont.*)
invites students to draw their animals to accompany the information they have found and distributes art materials.	draw and color animal pictures.
collects student work and binds the "Student Book of Shakespeare's Zoo."	participate as appropriate.

UNIT 4: WILL, YOU WRITE WELL—A PRIMARY CREATIVE WRITING EXPERIENCE

Background Information

Elizabethans were sensitve to beauty and grace in many forms of literature. Lyric poetry, essays, poetic drama, and narrative poetry were popular and appropriate literary forms. Music was closely related to creative writing, and many poems became lyrics for popular Elizabethan ballads. Songs incorporated into Shakespeare's plays became welcome interludes in a long play.

Elizbethan England was an exciting place to live, and because the country was independent and relatively wealthy, more people had more time to indulge their interest in music, literature, and the theater.

Literary forms and styles were developed during the sixteenth century. The Spenserian stanza (a nine-line rhyme pattern), pastoral lyric poetry idealizing country life, and sonnet sequences were invented and refined at this time. Elizabethan poet Sir Philip Sidney (1554-86) is considered to be the inventor of the sonnet, and this form was warmly embraced by Shakespeare in the familiar and beautiful sonnet sequences he composed. Poetic drama, masques featuring elaborate pageantry, and historic drama flourished.

This robust development of original and creative writing reached its climax in Shakespeare's achievements in poetry and literary forms of historical and romantic drama.

There were two major groups of writers in Shakespeare's time; those who wrote as a means of supporting themselves (Shakespeare, Marlowe, and Jonson), and those who wrote for their own pleasure (the so-called court poets like Wyatt, Surrey, Sidney, and Raleigh.) It is interesting to note that of the two groups of writers, general and widespread popularity continues for those playwrights and dramatists who brought home a weekly paycheck.

Unit Objectives

In this unit, the student will be able to:
- use graphic organizers to classify Shakespearean characters for a story
- compose a four-line poem based on a Shakespearean quotation.
- create an original greeting card using a Shakespearean quotation.

Activities

The teacher uses the selected quotations from Shakespeare given below to design a series of writing activities.

Selected Quotations

"The weakest kind of fruit,
Drops earliest to the ground."
　　　——*Merchant of Venice, Act IV, Sc. i*

"....is the jay more precious than the lark
Because his feathers are more beautiful?"
　　　——*Taming of the Shrew, Act IV, Sc. iii*

"Great floods have flown
From simple sources."
　　　——*All's Well That Ends Well, Act II, Sc. i*

"All the water in the ocean
Can never turn the swan's black legs to white."
　　　——*Titus Andronicus, Act IV, Sc. ii*

"O! It is excellent
To have a giant's strength, but it is tyrannous
To use it like a giant."
　　　——*Measure for Measure, Act II, Sc. ii*

"That which we call a rose
By any other name would smell as sweet."
　　　——*Romeo and Juliet, Act II, Sc.ii*

---

1. The teacher:	**The students:**
explains that now that students have examined some Shakespearean passages, they can design a greeting card	listen and review paragraphs.

1. The teacher:	**The students:** (*cont.*)
that may be appropriate for birthday, get-well, or friendship greetings.	
leads discussion about which quotation is most appropriate for a friendship card; e.g., *"A rose by any other name...."*	participate in discussion and make decisions on the kind of card they will design.
shows how the quotation may be placed on the cover of the card with an illustration, and how the appropriate message of greeting appears inside the folder.	examine samples of greeting cards provided.
distributes heavy paper and art supplies.	
demonstrates how to fold the card and arrange the placement of text and illustration.	follow directions, and design a greeting card.

2. The teacher:	**The students:**
asks students if they can recite a poem from memory.	participate by reciting a short poem.
explains that Shakespeare wrote his plays in poetry forms, but not all of the lines rhyme.	listen to explanation.
tells students that they will listen to some of Shakespeare's poetry that *does* rhyme.	
plays selected Shakespearean songs on a cassette player or record player, and asks students to listen for the rhyming words at the end of lines.	listen to recordings.
asks students to recall rhyming words they heard in the songs.	recall some rhymes.
suggests that students can write a poem of four lines just like	choose a theme for a poem.

2. The teacher:	The students: *(cont.)*
Shakespeare did, using an experience from their own lives, or a poem about a friend.	
assists students with rhyming lines and edits their poems.	write a four-line poem.

UNIT 5: SHAKESPEARE AND THE NEW WORLD—AN INTERMEDIATE SOCIAL STUDIES EXPERIENCE

Background Information

In 1607, Virginia was colonized. In London, Shakespeare produced three historical dramas: *Antony and Cleopatra, Coriolanus,* and *Timon of Athens.*

Overseas expansion had become enormously important to the English. Shakespeare used the "public relations" reports about the New World as an inspiration for his play, *The Tempest,* in which he used his poetic imagination and genius to describe the innate glamour of adventure and to appeal to the genuine English love of the sea and seafaring exploits. Thomas Hariot had chronicled the colony of Virginia in his *Briefe and True Report of the New Found Land of Virginia* in 1588, and John White had produced maps and beautifully detailed watercolors of American flowers and animals. White's illustrations of Native American ways and people provided a foundation for anthropologists and historians, which are the basis of our information about our Native American forbearers.

Unit Objectives

In this unit, students will be able to:

- develop a time line or chronology that shows the relationships between Elizabethan culture and customs and colonial exploration.
- demonstrate ability to compare and contrast, categorize and web events about people, government, and cultural qualities of the Elizabethan period, both in colonial and English environments.
- explain why early Virginia colonies (such as the lost colony of Roanoke) failed, and later colonies (Jamestown and Williamsburg) flourished.
- describe the exploration of the New World as it involved English settlers (Sir Walter Raleigh, Captain James Smith).

Teaching Strategies

1. The teacher:

uses resources as listed to infuse
Shakespearean and Elizabethan
elements into the prescribed social
studies units.

The students:

integrate knowledge of
Shakespeare and his
time with social studies
units through reading
and written assignments.

initiates a discussion of
exploration of the New World
with the following quote from *The
Taming of the Shrew:*

HORTENSIO:...And tell me now, sweet
friend, what happy gale
blows you to Padua here from
old Verona?

PETRUCHIO: Such wind as
scatters young men through
 the world. To seek their fortunes
farther than at home. Where small
experience grows.

leads discussion of motivation for
exploration and discovery.

participate in discussion.

2. The teacher:

introduces the concept of
"Shakespearean Minutes,"
 in which students present
information about memorable
events and historic moments in
Renaissance England.

The students:

take notes, question,
and show interest and
involvement in the
project described.

groups students in a cooperative
learning environment.

participate as parts
of group.

distributes resource material and
encourages groups to select
specific incidents or characters
from Elizabethan times to feature in
a "Shakespearean Minute" video spot.

read together and
decide on the content
for their video "Minute."

2. The teacher:	The students: (*cont.*)
provides time for production of "Shakespearean Minutes" and plans with media specialist for use of equipment and production facilities.	script and develop their video production.
approves scripts and supervises production of video programs.	produce video "Minute" for telecast.
schedules video "Shakespearean Minutes" for telecast during Shakespeare Theme Month.	perform as scheduled.

UNIT 6: SCIENCE AND SHAKESPEARE—AN INTERMEDIATE SCIENCE EXPERIENCE

Background Information

Modern science is generally considered to have developed in the seventeenth century, but in the Elizabethan Age (1558-1603), there were the beginnings of the new experimental method of investigation, and a mechanical, mathematical picture of the universe. Both of these concepts remain the foundation of science as it is practiced today. The most significant scientific advances during Shakespeare's time came in the field of astronomy. This unit suggests activities appropriate both to the science curriculum of grades 4 through 6 and to the Shakespeare Theme Month.

Unit Objectives

In this unit, students will be able to:

- make a scale model of the earth and moon system.
- use a scale model to explore shadows, moon phases, and eclipses.
- predict the behavior of different size bodies that are allowed to drop freely.
- prepare a biography of scientists who were contemporaries of Shakespeare, emphasizing the scientific contributions they made.
- recognize lines from Shakespeare's plays that show his awareness of science.

Teaching Strategies	
The teacher:	**The students:**
introduces the life of Galileo and explains that this "father of modern physics" was a contemporary of William Shakespeare.	
teaches the units of study prescribed by the science curriculum in grades 4-6 that relate to the solar system and astronomy, or plants and animals.	follows the instructions appropriately.

Suggested Activities for Science Units

1. Students can make tin can planetariums, with holes punched in the bottoms of cans to represent stars of various constellations. When a flashlight is shined into the can, the "constellations" are projected onto the wall or ceiling of a darkened room.
2. Two hands-on laboratory experiences can consist of providing students with an assortment of simple lenses. They may experiment with the lenses and even design a simple telescope. A second observation experience could be done with simple pendulums. Discussion might include the relationship between the period of a pendulum and the weight of the bob or the relationship between the period of the pendulum and its length. Students can work in a cooperative learning setting, predicting the behavior of differently sized bodies that are allowed to drop freely, and report findings to the total group.
3. A group of students may research lines from Shakespeare's plays that indicate his awareness of science. For example, in the prologue to *Romeo and Juliet,* there is a reference to "star-cross'd lovers." Star-cross'd means "opposed (crossed) by the stars," which were believed to be in charge of human fate. Even though Galileo and Copernicus were making important discoveries in astronomy, it was still popularly believed by Renaissance writers that the celestial order directly affected the affairs of the world.

UNIT 7: SHAKESPEARE, NOTABLE AND QUOTABLE—AN INTERMEDIATE READING-LANGUAGE ARTS EXPERIENCE

Background Information

William Shakespeare wrote at least 36 plays, 154 sonnets, and 4 longer poems. From this enormous body of work have come speeches, soliloquies, poetic musings, advice, and historical background. Much of his work has found its way into our daily life and conversations, though if one pointed out to students that some of Shakespeare's lines were actually a part of their conversation, the response would be shock and disbelief. In this unit, short epigraphs from familiar plays are analyzed. Critical and creative thinking skills are used, and the Dimensions of Thinking Model designed by the Association for Supervision and Curriculum Development provides the framework.

Unit Objectives

In this unit, students will be able to:

- employ core thinking skills in analyzing a short speech or segment of selected Shakespearean plays.
- predict from the epigraph what could occur next in the play.
- infer from the epigraph what kind of character is speaking the lines.
- paraphrase the epigraph as it could appear in a contemporary setting
- compose an essay about the epigraph.

Teaching Strategies	
The teacher:	**The students:**
selects a variety of short speeches from Shakespeare's plays and prepares a notebook of these speeches to be given to students.	recognize that this notebook will be a textbook-journal for a reading-language arts unit.
(See "Selected Shakespearean Epigraphs," below, and"Core Thinking Skills," Chapter 3.)	
groups students in a cooperative learning environment (four or five students per group).	join an assigned group.

The teacher:	The students:
asks students to select a speech using decision-making skills to arrive at group concensus.	practice decision-making skills and decide on a speech.
makes sure that there are no duplications of selection.	
explains the assignment according to the unit objectives.	
reviews the core thinking skills.	

SELECTED SHAKESPEAREAN EPIGRAPHS

JAQUES:
> All the world's a stage,
> And all the men and women merely players;
> They have their exits and their entrances,
> And one man in his time plays many parts,
> His acts being seven ages.
> —*As You Like It, Act II, Sc. vii*

MIRANDA:
> O wonder!
> How many goodly creatures are there here!
> How beauteous mankind is! O brave new world
> That has such people in't!
> —*The Tempest, Act 5, Sc. i*

MARCUS ANTONIUS:
> Friends, Romans, countrymen, lend me your ears!
> I come to bury Caesar, not to praise him.
> The evil that men do lives after them,
> The good is oft interred with their bones;
> So let it be with Caesar.
> —*Julius Caesar, Act III, Sc. ii*

POLONIUS:
> Neither a borrower nor a lender be,
> For loan oft loses both itself and friend,
> And borrowing dulls the edge of husbandry.
> —*Hamlet, Act 1, Sc. iii*

KING HENRY:
> Once more unto the breach, dear friends, once more:
> Or close the wall up with our English dead.
> In peace there's nothing so becomes a man
> As modest stillness and humility;

But when the blast of war blows in our ears,
Then imitate the action of the tiger...
—*Henry V, Act 3, Sc. i*

PORTIA:

The quality of mercy is not strain'd,
It droppeth as the gentle rain from heaven
Upon the place beneath. It is twice blest;
It blesseth him that gives and him that takes.
—*The Merchant of Venice, Act IV, Sc. i*

BALTHASAR:

Sigh no more, ladies, sigh no more,
Men were deceivers ever,
One foot in sea, and one on shore,
To one thing constant never.
Then sigh not so, but let them go,
And be you blithe and bonny,
Converting all your sounds of woe
Into hey nonny nonny.
—*Much Ado About Nothing, Act II, Sc.iii*

IAGO:

Good name in man and woman, dear my lord,
Is the immediate jewel of their souls.
Who steals my purse steals trash; 'tis something, nothing;
'Twas mine, 'tis his, and has been slave to thousands,
But he that filches from me my good name
Robs me of that which not enriches him,
And makes me poor indeed.
—*Othello, Act III, Sc. iii*

DUKE, SENIOR:

Sweet are the uses of adversity,
Which, like the toad, ugly and venomous,
Wears yet a precious jewel in his head;
And this our life, exempt from public haunt,
Finds tongues in trees, books in the running brooks,
Sermons in stones, and good in every thing.
—*As You Like It, Act II, Sc. i*

BRUTUS:

There is a tide in the affairs of men
Which, taken at the flood, leads on to fortune;
Omitted, all the voyage of their life
Is bound in shallows and in miseries.
On such a full sea are we now afloat,
And we must take the current when it serves,
Or lose our ventures.
—*Julius Caesar, Act IV, Sc. iii*

POLONIUS:
> This above all: to thine own self be true,
> And it must follow, as the night the day,
> Thou canst not then be false to any man.
> —*Hamlet, Act I, Sc. iii*

MACBETH:
> Tomorrow, and tomorrow and tomorrow,
> Creeps in this petty pace from day to day,
> To the last syllable of recorded time;
> And all our yesterdays have lighted fools
> The way to dusty death. Out, out, brief candle!
> Life's but a walking shadow, a poor player,
> That struts and frets his hour upon the stage,
> And then is heard no more. It is a tale
> Told by an idiot, full of sound and fury,
> Signifying nothing.
> —*Macbeth, Act V, Sc. v*

UNIT 8: THEME OF LOVE IN *MIDSUMMER NIGHT'S DREAM*—A MIDDLE SCHOOL READING-ENGLISH EXPERIENCE

Background Information

In this unit, students will read the original text of *Midsummer Night's Dream,* or an adapted version. The theme of love as it is presented in the play will be the main focus for the study. *Midsummer Night's Dream* is a comedy, one of the early works of Shakespeare. There are multiple plot lines, shifting from magic to reality and from imagination to truth. Shakespeare handles all of these elements as a master playwright. In this enchanting tale of love gone wrong in a mysterious forest, of quarrels among imaginary forest folk, of misdirected spells, readers will find a very mature commentary on the nature of human love. This quality keeps the play fresh, and its reading an experience to be remembered. Student projects done in a cooperative learning setting enrich and extend the reading of the play.

Unit Objectives

In this unit, students will be able to:

* read the original text, or an adapted version of Shakespeare's *Midsummer Night's Dream* with teacher guidance.

- answer specific questions about the plots, characters, and settings of the play.
- use higher level thinking skills in a discussion of elements of the play.
- participate in cooperative learning activities relevant to the play.

Teaching Strategies	
The teacher:	**The students:**
introduces *Midsummer Night's Dream*, and explains that the play will be read with an emphasis on how Shakespeare uses the theme of love.	
describes the main characters, and the kinds of love each exhibits: Theseus and Hippolyta (mature love); Oberon and Titania (bickering married love); Demetrius, Hermia, Lysander, Helena (infatuations that become true love); Titania and Bottom (ridiculous and deluded love); and Pyramus and Thisbe (parodied mythological symbols of love).	take notes as appropriate.
distributes summary of play and asks students to read it silently.	read the summaries of each act as written in "The Story" summary, below, duplicated for students.
summarizes characters' interactions in the play.	take notes.
discusses and assigns the projects, Groups 1-8.	
schedules class time or assignment time for reading *Midsummer Night's Dream*.	read the play or adaption as assigned.

The Story

Hermia, a young Athenian girl, elopes into the forest with her true love, Lysander, in defiance of her father and Duke Theseus, who have commanded her to marry Demetrius. Demetrius pursues the fleeing couple, while his spurned lover, Helena, trails after him. On the same midsummer's evening, the weaver, Bottom ,and a group of fellow craftsmen meet in the forest to rehearse the play they hope to perform at the wedding of Duke Theseus to the Amazon Queen, Hippolyta. Meanwhile, in the forest, the fairy king and queen, Oberon and Titania, quarrel bitterly. By the time the four lovers and the rehearsing "mechanicals" arrive, this supernatural discord and the efforts of Oberon's prankish servant, Puck, have filled the forest with magic and mischief enough to turn the mortals' world upside down for one enchanted Midsummer's Eve.

Teaching Strategies

The teacher:	The students:
groups students randomly for a cooperative learning experience, and assigns research projects based on the Shakespeare play.	work with assigned group.
Group 1: Students research the celebration of Midsummer Night in Shakespeare's time. What kind of magic was supposed to take place? Did this festival have special significance to lovers?	work to complete project.
Group 2: Students research the "mechanicals," or craftsmen whose trades were important in the society of Elizabethan England. What were the tasks of the "joiner, bellows-mender, and tiner," for example.	work to complete project.
Group 3: Students research illustrated editions of *Midsummer Night's Dream* with pictures by Arthur Rackham, Richard Dadd, and others and bring the books to share with class, giving brief explanations of the styles of the artists.	work to complete assignment.
Group 4: Students design and make a Midsummer collage, using magazine and newspaper illustrations in an attempt to create a modern visual approach to *Midsummer Night's Dream.*	work to complete assignment.

The teacher:	The students:
Group 5: Students write and produce an Oprah style video program on the subject of love. Students representing the four sets of lovers in the play appear and present their stories in emotional styles.	work to produce the video.
Group 6: Students develop a Midsummer Night's "Dear Abby" column. Characters in the play write to Dear Abby with their problems (as written in the play.) Abby answers them. This could be a satire or a serious response.	work to complete project.
Group 7: Students research various productions of *Midsummer Night's Dream* throughout its history, documenting the changing styles of presentation.	work to complete project.
Group 8: Students research music inspired by *Midsummer Night's Dream,* and bring recordings of songs, operas, or instrumental music to share with the class.	work to complete project.
leads a series of discussions on questions relating to *Midsummer Night's Dream.* (Teachers should use techniques of questioning that reflect the core thinking skills.)	participate in discussions.

Discussion Questions

Cognitive Level

1. How many stories are interwoven in the play? (Four) Who are the main figures in each of the four plots? (Theseus and Hippolyta, the four lovers, the "mechanicals," Titania and Oberon) What is the "fifth" story? (Pyramus and Thisby)

2. What, at the beginning of the play, sends the lovers into the forest? (Duke Theseus' edict that Hermia must give up Lysander, whom she loves, and wed Demetrius.) How do Demetrius and Helena come to follow them? (Helena, in love with Demetrius, tries to win his favor by telling him of the plan.) Describe the relationship among the lovers at the time they enter the forest. (Demetrius and Lysander love Hermia; Hermia loves Lysander and dislikes Demetrius; Demetrius, who loves Hermia, cannot tolerate Helena; Helena loves Demetrius and is a friend of Hermia.)

3. Why are Titania and Oberon quarreling? (Oberon wants as a page a human boy whom Titania will not give him; also, they are jealous of each other's romances.) What, according to Titania's speech in Act II, Scene 1, is the impact of their quarrel on the rest of the world? (Nature has gone awry; the seasons are reversed, with rain and snow in summer and dire consequences for mortals.)

Analysis Level

1. What are the two "worlds" of the play? (Athens and the forest) Which is the world of reason and which is the world of magic? In which world does the play begin and end? (Athens) Does this mean that Shakespeare is depicting the final triumph of reason?

2. In Act III, Scene 1, Bottom says to Titania, "Reason and love keep little company together nowadays." What instances does this play offer of love and reason keeping company? (Probably only Theseus and Hippolyta) Why do you think Shakespeare has Demetrius' change of heart in Hermia's favor take place before the action of the play begins? (So that Demetrius' love for Helena at the end of the play will be a rediscovery of his true feelings rather than a delusion imposed by magic.)

3. The mechanicals' play, *Pyramus and Thisby,* is acted in front of the three newlywed couples, and Shakespeare's dialogue would seem to indicate that it is not very well received. How does the nonsense of "Pyramus" reflect the main plot of the play? (It presents lovers, separated by parental authority, who fail to survive the dangers of the night into which they have fled, as Hermia and Lysander have fled Athens.) If the performance of "Pyramus" is not well received, how does it affect our perception of the Athenian lovers? (It makes us less sympathetic to them because they are unaware of the parallels with their own situation.)

Integrating Skills Level

1. Read several of Shakespeare's sonnets, for example, numbers 130, 137, 138, and 139, and identify scenes in *Midsummer Night's Dream* in which the lovers sound most like the Petrarchan lovers of the sonnets.
2. Why is *Midsummer Night's Dream* a particularly fitting play in which to study the universal theme of love? (This play consists of the interweaving of many love stories, illustrating various aspects of love as they are treated in drama and comedy: young lovers, cast-off lovers, royal lovers, thwarted lovers, the battle of the sexes.)

UNIT 9: MULTICULTURAL INFUSIONS IN *OTHELLO* AND *ANTONY AND CLEOPATRA*

Background Information

In this unit, students will read selections from two plays that include major characters who are black, Othello and Cleopatra. Through a study of the tragic story of *Othello* and the intense love story that infuses the historical drama, *Antony and Cleopatra,* students will recognize that emotions transcend race or gender, and are universal to all humanity. In *Othello,* rage and jealousy cause the destruction of a noble military and political leader, while in *Antony and Cleopatra,* the conflict of loyalties that Antony feels between Caesar and Cleopatra, and the overwhelming love that he feels for Cleopatra lead to *his* downfall. Emphasis in the unit is on the qualities that contribute to personality, and the outside influences that affect personality.

Teaching strategies for *Antony and Cleopatra* may follow the model for *Midsummer Night's Dream.* By relating the plots and characterizations of *Antony and Cleopatra* to other stories of mismatched lovers, students will gain an understanding of the universal quality of William Shakespeare's work. Emphasis should be placed on the elements of individual greed and selfishness that exists side-by-side with power, and how flawed characters are doomed by the combination.

Unit Objectives

In this unit, students will be able to:

• read the original text, or an adapted version of Shakespeare's *Othello* and *Antony and Cleopatra* with teacher guidance.

* recognize the importance of multicultural relationships in Shakespeare's plays.
* answer specific questions about the plots, characters, and settings of the plays.
* use higher-order thinking skills in discussing the dramatic impact of the plays.
* contrast the historical period of Shakespeare's time with the historical time frame of the two plays.
* participate in cooperative learning activities relevant to the plays.

Main Characters in *Othello*

* *Othello,* a black man of great repute in Venice; of royal Moorish blood; a soldier, famed for military success, known for his nobility, wisdom, experience, and skills.
* *Iago,* a Venetian soldier under Othello's command, described with irony always as "honest" Iago. He has always hated Othello; Othello has not made him his second-in command, and Iago's pride and arrogance lead to a monstrous plot to undermine Othello. Iago knows that jealousy is a powerful emotion, and that the mixed-marriage between Desdemona and Othello is a fertile climate for a scheme that will bring him final satisfaction in his hatred of the Moor.
* *Desdemona,* beautiful daughter of Brabantio of Venice; she has enormous love for Othello, and final loyalty to Othello, her chosen husband.
* *Roderigo*, coup plotter with Iago; he loves Desdemona and this powerful love drives him to villainous treachery.
* *Michael Cassio*, aide to Othello. His innocence and youth cause his death at the plotting hands of Iago.

Othello

Othello, a brave soldier of fortune, is much wiser about battle strategies than human emotions. He is betrayed by the person he considered his most loyal assistant, Iago; goaded to jealousy and rage, and finally to murder.

When Desdemona, the beautiful daughter of an aristocratic Venetian marries Othello, Iago swears to bring the military leader to ruin. Iago's plots, lies, and counterplots form the structure for this tragedy of Greek proportions, as characters move irrevocably to a tragic end.

Othello has been dispatched to Cyprus to conquer the Turks, and it is there that much of the action takes place. Cassio, a young officer is dismissed by Othello for drunken violence (instigated and encouraged by Iago). Pretending good will, Iago then persuades Cassio to go to Desdemona to plead his case for reinstatement into the military forces. Othello finds the young officer in his wife's room, and becomes enraged with jealousy. A handkerchief dropped by Desdemona is retrieved by her treacherous maid Emilia. Emilia gives the handkerchief to Iago, who in turn "plants" it with Cassio.

A climax is reached when Othello, in a jealous rage, threatens to kill his wife, Desdemona, for her alleged unfaithfulness. Iago, in the background, suggests that Othello has lost his mind. Ordered by Othello to await him alone and in bed, Desdemona prays and sings quietly to herself. When Othello arrives in the bedchamber, he smothers his beautiful wife with a pillow. Emilia enters, and Othello tries to justify his act by showing Emilia the handkerchief as proof of Desdemona's infidelity. Stunned, Emilia reveals her husband Iago's guilt. The play ends, with Iago stubbornly refusing to admit his perfidy, and Othello describing himself as "one that loved not wisely, but too well." He then pulls out a dagger, stabs himself, and hisses his dead wife as he dies.

Teaching Strategies

1. The teacher:

introduces *Othello* and explains that the play will be studied with an emphasis on multicultural characters and how universal emotions can control the actions of all persons.

describes the main characters, and the emotions of jealousy and distrust that the characters in the play exhibit. Qualities of strength and loyalty are also described.

distributes *Student Handout One: The Story,* and asks students to read the summary.

distributes the discussion questions that are to be addressed during the reading of the play.

The students:

take notes as appropriate.

read the summaries of each act as written in the handout.

1. The teacher:	**The students:** *(cont.)*
schedules class time or assignment time for reading *Othello*.	read the play or adaptation as assigned.

2. The teacher:	**The students:**
groups students randomly for a cooperative learning experience, and assigns research projects based on *Othello*.	work with assigned group.
Group 1: Students consider the thoughts of various critics of the last act of *Othello*. Some believe that Othello regains his nobility, but others feel that he merely excuses himself in his final moments, and that Desdemona is almost forgotten as he attempts to justify his own actions. Students should reread the scene carefully, and then prepare a debate or panel discussion, presenting their views, pro and con.	use analysis and evaluation skills to arrive at a conclusion concerning Othello's character. select sides of the issue, prepare arguments, and present debate or panel discussion.
Group 2: Students select a scene from the play to paraphrase and present to the group. Particularly appropriate are the scene in which Iago persuades Othello of Desdemona's infidelity (Act III, Sc. iii) and the scene with Desdemona's "willow" song (Act IV, Sc. iii).	select scene, assign roles, write script, and present scenes to other groups.
Group 3: Students research and report on great productions of Othello of the past and present. How have the approaches to the play varied? How has the question of Othello's race and personality been handled? Who are/were some of the great black actors who have portrayed Othello?	work to complete research. prepare position paper to share with other groups.

2. The teacher:	The students: (*cont.*)
Group 4: One of the great ballets based on Othello was set to the music of Henry Purcell and titled, *The Moor's Revenge*. Locate a recording of the music, or a video or film of the ballet, and play or show the ballet to the other groups. (If dance students are part of the class, they may wish to prepare a short interpretive dance set to the Purcell music.)	work on assignment in library media center or make an appointment with music or dance teacher to locate the music or film; might also perform dance interpretation.
Group 5: Students research Elizabethan attitudes toward sex and marriage, and the legal status of women, and prepare a report describing how Shakespeare's plays reflect these customs and laws. For example, an Elizabethan woman was not free to marry the man she loved. Yet, in *Othello,* Desdemona defies her father when she elopes with the Moor. In the report, consider that Desdemona saw her other actions as "divided duty," that is, she exchanged her father for a husband, but it never entered her mind to establish her independence.	work to complete project. present an oral report to other groups.
Group 6: Oprah, or another TV talk show host, would be able to devote an entire program to the "generation gap" problems that exist in *Othello*. Problems between parents and children, especially between fathers and daughters, are often important dramatic elements in Shakespeare. Students design and produce a "talk show" segment in which Desdemona defends her choice of husband, and why she defied her father's wishes. Brabanti can also be part of the talk show group.	design, script, and videotape, either at home or with school equipment, a talk show segment. show the video as part of the theme program.

2. The teacher: **The students:** (*cont.*)

Group 7: Students use the format   research African-American
of a "Ted Koppel" news broadcast,   military heroes and
or "McNeil-Lehrer" report, to design   use findings as part of
and script an in-depth report on   their TV show.
issues of race in the military, using
Othello for content. Students
compare the heroic actions
of General Powell in Desert
Storm, with Othello's bravery
and military skills on Cyprus.

Group 8: Students research artists'   work in library media
depictions of Othello, the Moor,   center or art museums
using catalogs, art books, and   researching and
museum directories. If possible,   preparing an art talk.
prints should be obtained to
establish a portrait gallery, or
scene study of various interpretations of *Othello*. Slides are
sometimes available through
museum shops. Students will   present an art talk to
present an art talk describing   groups or as part of
the artist and the way in which the   theme program.
artist has visuallized scenes or
characters from *Othello*.

Group 9: Students select quota-   work to collect appropriate
tions from Othello that best repre-   quotations.
sent the character speaking.
Students may use books of epigraphs or familiar quotations to
illustrate the characters' personal-
ities. Members of the group take on   present reader's theater
the roles and present the selected   to other groups or as
quotations as a reader's theater.   part of theme program.

Discussion Questions

1. What is the relationship between Iago and Roderigo as revealed in the
    first act? (Roderigo is hopelessly in love with Desdemona, and Iago is
    exploiting this affection to swindle and dominate Roderigo. Why do they
    awaken Brabantio? (To tell him of Desdemona's elopement with Othello,
    and to manipulate him into violent anger at his daughter's alleged
    treachery. What reason, in Scene 1, does Iago give for hating the Moor?
    (Cassio's promotion to a post Iago desired.)

2. What is Othello's reaction to the threat of violence posed by Brabantio and his men? (He makes peace, at least temporarily.) What indication of Othello's character does this scene create? (That he is a natural leader, in control of his temper and emotions and not prone to rash action.) What is his defense, before the Duke's council, against Brabantio's charge of witchcraft? (He recounts, in detail, his courtship of Desdemona.) How does he say he won her? (By telling her the story of his life. He says, "She lov'd me for the dangers I had pass'd/And I lov'd her that she did pity them.") What do we learn of his nature in this scene? (That he is eloquent, persuasive, and sensitive.) What is the outcome of this scene? (The senators advise Brabantio to accept the marriage, and they order Othello to Cyprus.) How does Brabantio deal with his defeat? (He is ungracious and despairing, and warns Othello against Desdemona, saying: "Loo to her, Moor, if thou hast eyes to see;/ She has deceiv'd her father, and may thee.")

3. What, by the close of Act 1, have we learned about Desdemona? (That she loves Othello deeply, that she is sufficiently willful to defy her father, that she can speak up with intelligence and courage before the senate, and that she is brave enough to follow her husband to Cyprus.) Summarize Iago's final Act 1 soliloquy? (He will tell Othello that Cassio is "too familiar" with Desdemona.) Why does he feel his scheme will work? (He says that Othello will believe him because the Moor "is of a free and open nature,/ That thinks men honest that but seem to be so.")

4. How does Iago advance his plot in Act II? (He tells Roderigo that Desdemona now loves Cassio; then, getting Cassio drunk, he arranges a fight between the two which results in Cassio's demotion). What part in Iago's plan does the handkerchief play? (It is the apparent "ocular proof"—the seeing-is-believing, of Desdemona's infidelity.) Why is the handkerchief so meaningful to Othello? (It was his first gift to Desdemona.)

5. How was the handkerchief (the chief piece of "evidence" for Desdemona's infidelity) lost? (Desdemona was comforting Othello, and dropped it accidentally. Iago 's wife, Emilia, then stole it secretly.) How did Othello determine that Desdemona no longer had the strawberry-spotted handkerchief? (He asked her for it, claiming he had a cold.)

6. What was the confusion that led to Othello's belief that Cassio and Desdemona were involved in a love affair? (Emilia hid the handkerchief in Cassio's room; Cassio asked Bianca, a young girlfriend, to copy the design; Iago started a conversation about Bianca with Cassio, but knew Othello would overhear, and think Cassio's remarks were about Desdemona.)

7. What was the result of the overheard conversation? (Blind with jealousy and rage, Othello tells Iago that he wants Desdemona poisoned, but Iago suggests that Othello strangle her instead.)
8. Events rush to a conclusion as Iago arranges the stabbing deaths of Roderigo and Cassio. How does Iago plot this double-murder? (He uses Roderigo's love for Desdemona, and jealousy of Cassio, to precipitate a confrontation over the jewels and gold Roderigo has used to seemingly advance his cause with Desdemona.) What foreshadowing is there leading up to the death of Desdemona? (She asks Emilia to put her wedding sheets on the bed, and to wrap her body in them if she dies; Othello makes her turn out the lamps, and say her prayers, and then accuses her of unfaithfulness with Cassio.)
9. What reveals Iago's evil to his wife, Emilia? (Othello claims that Iago knew about Desdemona's infidelity through the handkerchief. Emilia remembers that Iago had her steal the handkerchief.)
10. At the end of the play, Iago refuses to explain his motives to Othello. How did this affect Othello? (Othello never learned about Iago's savage plot based on jealousy and hatred. He tells his faithful colleagues that he has loved "not wisely but too well," and then stabs himself over Desdemona's lifeless body.)

Main Characters in *Antony and Cleopatra*

- *Mark Antony*, a Roman military leader, one of the triumvirs of the Roman world with Octavius Caesar and Lepidus. He is not portrayed as a great judge of human nature by Shakespeare.
- *Cleopatra*, Queen of Egypt, who is portrayed as capricious, devious, spoiled, and capable of any ruse to keep Mark Antony in Egypt as her lover.
- *Enobarbus*, Antony's friend and military companion.
- *Octavius Caesar,* one of the triumvirs of the Roman world.
- *Octavia*, sister of Octavius, who was married to Antony in order to unite the leading families of Rome.
- *Pompey*, young military leader, a threat to the triumvirs.
- *Lepidus*, the aging third member of the triumvirate.

Antony and Cleopatra

Mark Antony has remained in Egypt following his successful battles, and has fallen in love with Cleopatra, Queen of Egypt. Although his Roman colleagues have begged him to return to Rome to help quell the efforts of Pompey to assume leadership, Antony refuses, preferring a life of ease, feasting, and love-making with Cleopatra.

Cleopatra is a romantic ruler, who will do anything to keep Antony in Egypt. When word arrives that Antony's wife has died in Rome, Cleopatra thinks Antony will never return. But duty is strong, and Antony and Enobarbus return to Rome to assess the situation and decide whether war is inevitable. Cleopatra is distraught and rages and screams whenever a messenger brings news she does not like. To unite the ruling families, Octavius Caesar suggests that Antony marry his sister, Octavia, and he does.

When Cleopatra gets that news, her heart appears to be broken. However, Antony is drawn back to Egypt and to his lover Cleopatra, and the tragedy concludes with the death of both of the lovers.

Teaching Strategies	
The teacher:	**The students:**
introduces *Antony and Cleopatra,* and explains that the play will be read with an emphasis on Shakespeare's characterization of Cleopatra in a multicultural setting.	
describes the main characters in the play. (This is essentially a two-character play, with many lesser characters.)	take notes as appropriate.

Discussion Questions for *Antony and Cleopatra*

1. In this play, Shakespeare explores the "fatal attraction" aspect of love. The playwright portrays *Antony and Cleopatra* as mutually needful. In addition to their romantic relationship, what were some of these needs? (Antony needed Cleopatra's wealth to sustain his military campaigns; she needed a Roman alliance to protect Egypt and her kingdom.)

2. Critics have called *Antony and Cleopatra* Shakespeare's "most cinematic" play. What are some of the film qualities in the play? (pageantry, spectacle, character interaction, the struggle between political realities and individual needs)

3. In the play, readers (and audience) are introduced to Cleopatra through the eyes of Enobarbus, who describes the arrival of Cleopatra in elegant, poetic terms. (Act II, sc. i) What does Shakespeare demand of his audience when he uses narration rather than action to personify a character? (Imagination). Give examples from Enobarbus's speech that help to visualize Cleopatra.

4. Without consulting others, draw a sketch of Cleopatra, simply using the words of Enobarbus in Act II, sc. i. that describe Cleopatra's arrival. Remember to include the barge.

5. Here is a list of some of the contrasts evident in *Antony and Cleopatra*. Choose one set of contrasts, and using evidence from the play, prepare a brief essay to be presented as part of a panel discussion.

Public Politics	vs.	Private Love
Deity	vs.	Romantic Love
Roman World	vs.	Egyptian World
Feminine Viewpoint	vs.	Masculine Viewpoint
Woman of Color	vs.	Caucasian Male
Aspects of Night	vs.	Aspects of Day

   In your essay, consider the following: How do these contrasts provide dramatic energy in the play? Which of the contrasts do you think are most powerful in leading to the climax of the play?

6. In your journal, write a narrative exposition, using lines or scenes from the play to support—or dispute—this writing prompt: "In one sense the political action in the play *Antony and Cleopatra* is a struggle towards empire, in another, it is a bonding of love."

7. If Antony loved Cleopatra so much, why did he consent to marry Octavia? (She was Octavius Ceasar's sister; the marriage would force a political union and save the triumvirate.)

8. Throughout the play, Cleopatra is portrayed as vain, passionate, cowardly, and a liar. How do these negative qualities affect Antony? Give evidence from the play to support your view.

9. In Shakespeare's time, racial intermarriage was almost nonexistent, yet two of his powerful plays are set in this relationship. Why do you think that Shakespeare devoted so much of his work to exploring this theme?

10. Why do you think that *Othello* is classified as a tragedy, while *Antony and Cleopatra* is grouped with the history plays?

RESOURCES FOR UNITS IN CHAPTER 7

General Resources

Armour, Richard. (1957). *Twisted Tales from Shakespeare*. Illustrated by Campbell Grant. New York: McGraw-Hill.

Birch, Beverley. (1988). *Shakespeare's Stories: Comedies*. Illustrated by Carol Tarrant. New York: Peter Bedrick Books.

———. (1988). *Shakespeare's Stories: Histories*. Illustrated by Robina Green. New York: Peter Bedrick Books.

———. (1988). *Shakespeare's Stories: Tragedies* Illustrated by Tony Kerins. New York: Peter Bedrick Books.

Callum, Albert. (1968). *Shake Hands with Shakespeare*. New York: Citation Press.

Chute, Marchette. (1961). *Stories from Shakespeare*. New York: World Publishing.

Davidson, Diane, ed. (1986). *Shakespeare for Young People*. Illustrated by Diane Davidson. Music by Sandy Harrison and Diane Davidson. Fair Oaks, CA: Swan Books.

Grohskopf, Bernice. (1963). *Seeds of Time*. New York: Atheneum.

Fox, Levi. (1987). *The Shakespeare Handbook* . Boston: G.K. Hall.

Hodges, C. Walter. *Shakespeare's Theatre*. (1967). New York: Coward-McCann.

Lamb, Charles, and Mary Lamb (1979). *Tales from Shakespeare*. Washington, DC: Folger Books; The Folger Shakespeare Library.

Shakespeare Performances Through the Ages. (1988). Washington, DC: Folger Shakespeare Library.

Resources for Unit 1

Anderson, Joan. (1984). *The First Thanksgiving Feast*. Photographed by George. Ancona. New York: Clarion Books.

Brown, Elizabeth Myers, ed. (1974). *The Pilgrims and Their Times*. Columbus, OH: Highlights for Children.

Holton-Arms School. (1979). *As You Like It Cookery*. Illustrated by M.W. Miller. Washington, DC: Holton-Arms School.

Kerr, Jessica. (1969). *Shakespeare's Flowers*. Illustrated by Anne Ophelia Dowden. New York: Thomas Y. Crowell Company.

McGovern, Ann. (1969). *...If You Sailed on the Mayflower*. Illustrated by J.B. Handelsman. New York: Scholastic.

Resources for Unit 2

Eyler, Ellen C. (1979). *Early English Gardens and Garden Books.* Washington, DC: Folger Books, The Folger Shakespeare Library.
Felsko, Elsa. (1956). *A Book of Wild Flowers.* Illustrated. New York: Thomas Yoseloff.
Kerr, Jessica. (1969). *Shakespeare's Flowers.* Illustrated by Anne Ophelia Dowden. New York: Thomas Y. Crowell.
McNair, James K. (1978). *The World of Herbs and Spices.* San Francisco: Ortho Books.
Rohde, Eleanour S. (1963). *Shakespeare's Wild Flowers.* London: Medici Society.
Spurgeon, Caroline. (1965). *Shakespeare's Imagery and What it Tells Us.* New York: Cambridge University Press.

Resources for Unit 3

Folger Shakespeare Library. (1977). *A Bevy of Beasts: A Coloring Book of Elizabethan Drawings.* Washington, DC: Folger Shakespeare Library.

Resources for Unit 4

Audio Tape Songs from the Plays of Shakespeare. Vols. 1-3. CDL 5242 New York: Caedmon Records, Inc.
Chambers, H.E., ed. (1984). *A Shakespeare Song Book.* New York: Sterling Publishing.

Resources for Unit 5

Carpenter, Frances. (1961). *Pocahontas and Her World.* New York: Knopf.
Chute, Marchette. (1971). *Shakespeare of London.* New York: E.P. Dutton.
Fox, Levi, ed. (1987). *The Shakespeare Handbook.* Boston: G.K. Hall.
Greenblatt, Stephen J. (1973). *Sir Walter Raleigh: The Renaissance Man and His Roles.* Yale University Press.
Morison, Samuel Eliot. (1974). *The European Discovery of America: The Southern Voyages, A.D. 1492-1616.* New York: Oxford University Press.

Resources for Unit 6

Boas, Marie. (1960). *The Scientific Renaissance, 1450-1630.* New York: Harper and Row.
Land, Barbara. (1963). *The Quest of Johannes Kepler, Astronomer.* Garden City, NY: Doubleday.

Lauber, Patricia. (1959). *The Quest of Galileo.* Garden City, NY: Doubleday.
Marcus, Rebecca B. (1961). *Galileo and Experimental Science.* New York: Franklin Watts.
Pine, Tillie S. and Joseph Levine. (1978). *Scientists and Their Discoveries.* New York: McGraw-Hill.

Resources for Unit 7

Dimensions of Thinking: A Framework for Curriculum and Instruction. (1988). Washington, DC: Association for Supervision and Curriculum Development.
Macrone, Michael. (1990). *Brush Up Your Shakespeare!* New York: Harper & Row, Publishers.
Shakespeare, William. *Complete Works of William Shakespeare.* New York: Doubleday, 1988.
Worsham, Antoinette, and Anita J. Stockton. (1986). *A Model for Teaching Thinking Skills: The Inclusion Process.* Bloomington, IN: Phi Delta Kappa Educational Foundation.

Resources for Unit 8

Birch, Beverley. (1988). *Shakespeare's Stories: Comedies.* Illustrated by Carol Tarrant. New York: Peter Bedrick Books.
Brooks, Harold F. (1979). *A Midsummer Night's Dream.* London: Routledge.
Davidson, Diane, ed. (1986). *A Midsummer Night's Dream for Young People.* Illustrated by Diane Davidson. Fair Oaks, CA: Swan Books.
Fox, Levi, ed. (1987). *The Shakespeare Handbook.* Boston: G.K. Hall.
Garfield, Leon. (1985). *Shakespeare Stories.* New York: Schocken.
Lamb, Charles, and Mary Lamb. (1979). *Tales from Shakespeare.* Washington, DC: The Folger Shakespeare Library.
Schultz, Lois. (1987). *The Bard for Beginners.* Middleton, OH: Globe Three.
Vess, Charles. (1988). *A Midsummer Night's Dream, by William Shakespeare.* Illustrated by Charles Vess. Norfolk, VA: Donning.

Resources for Unit 9

Birch, Beverley. (1988). *Shakespeare's Stories: Histories.* Illustrated by Robina Green. New York: Peter Pedrick Books.
———. (1988). *Shakespeare's Stories: Tragedies.* Illustrated by Tony Kerins. New York: Peter Bedrick Books.
National Endowment for the Humanities. (1987). *Three Shakespeare Themes: Teachers' Guide, Othello.* New York: TelEd, Inc.

Index

by Linda Webster